Java Testing with Spock

Java Testing with Spock

KONSTANTINOS KAPELONIS

MANNING

SHELTER ISLAND

Manning Publications Co.
20 Baldwin Road
PO Box 761
Shelter Island, NY 11964

Development editors:	Susan Conant
	Dan Maharry
Technical development editor:	Keith Conant
Copyeditor:	Sharon Wilkey
Proofreaders:	Melody Dolab
	Toma Mulligan
Technical proofreader:	Francesco Bianchi
Typesetter:	Marija Tudor
Cover designer:	Marija Tudor

ISBN: 9781617292538
Printed in the United States of America
1 2 3 4 5 6 7 8 9 10 – EBM – 21 20 19 18 17 16

To Maria, for enduring my endless writing sessions

brief contents

contents

foreword

I've been fortunate enough to have used Spock for the majority of my career as a JVM developer. It's now an implied and inseparable part of my process for making software. By talking to developers around the world at conferences and on mailing lists and the like, I know I am not alone in this regard.

My journey with Spock started shortly after I was thrust onto the JVM, coming from a Perl and Ruby background. "Big E" Enterprise Java held no allure for me, and I was desperate to find tools that would allow me to maintain the nimble and empowering spirit of the tools that I was used to. In Spock I found a tool that far outshined anything that I had previously come across.

My own formative ideas at the time about testing were elegantly expressed in a superior manner in Spock, by its founder Peter Niederwieser. I then supported Peter in Spock's development and helped spread the word of what testing can, and should, be.

Spock's key tenet is that you don't write tests for yourself; you write them for the future you—or for the future developer who will work with the test next. So this is about more than just readability.

Readability as the primary goal takes you down a road of expressing tests in a contorted "natural" language and using barbaric regular expressions based on token extractions in order to turn it into something executable. Here, I'm referring to the testing tool "Cucumber" and its imitators. Such tools are perfectly fine and justified in certain contexts, but these aren't the contexts I find myself working in, at least not most of the time. The tests that I write are for myself and other software developers; we know how to communicate in code. What's more, we have techniques, tools and traditions for crafting and *evolving* this communication.

Spock gives us the platform we need for writing highly expressive and intention-revealing tests *in code*, and embracing these techniques, tools, and traditions. The efficiency of authoring and evolving tests is just as important as readability, and this doesn't necessarily come for free with "readable" tests.

This book is an important resource for anyone wanting to test better, particularly those coming from a strong Java background (though there's also plenty for long-time Spock aficionados). Using Spock to test a Java codebase is a no-brainer. Spock tests are written in Groovy, which seamlessly interoperates with Java. When used in this context, it can be thought of as a more pragmatic version of Java that offers many conveniences that are particularly appealing at test time. Spock also makes strategic use of its reduced syntax, type-flexibility, and advanced features such as compile time transforms to be more convenient and expressive than what is possible with Java.

Konstantinos has done a great job of clearly articulating the value proposition in using Spock, in particular for Java developers. The book goes beyond a mere exploration of Spock's API and feature set to include general testing practices and real-world application. Even if for some bizarre reason you aren't as thrilled as I am about writing Spock tests by the end of the book, you'll still come out a better tester.

LUKE DALEY
SPOCK FOUNDING CONTRIBUTOR

preface

The first time Spock came onto my programming radar (which is always on, looking for interesting news in the Java ecosystem) I have to admit it didn't get the attention it deserved. I briefly read its web page and originally thought that it was the equivalent of JUnit but for the Groovy programming language instead of Java. Since I mainly write Java code professionally, a Groovy testing framework wasn't of much interest to me at that time. I moved along to the next news item of my RSS reader. Big mistake!

Groovy was already very high up on my list of "things that I needed to evaluate" and I kept researching it. I was especially interested in how it connects to Java and the ways it augments your existing Java code base. I learned that Groovy code compiles to the same bytecode as Java, that it also runs on the JVM, and that adding Groovy to a Java code base is as simple as adding the Groovy jar in the Java classpath.

Then it dawned on me: if Java and Groovy code are so close together, can I use Spock (which is the Groovy testing tool) to test Java code? And could I use JUnit to test Groovy code? Coming from a programming background with big Java codebases, I was of course very interested in the first question.

I searched the internet for answers, and all the articles I found (at the time) only explained how to test Groovy code with Spock, but not Java. So I started experimenting with Spock to find the answer to my question. This led me to discover the expressive syntax of Spock—the ability to use full sentences for method names, its clear structuring of tests, its built-in support for mocks, and all the other goodies that you will discover in this book.

Spock combines such killer features as context-aware error reporting with backward compatibility for existing JUnit tools, making its adoption almost effortless. If you thought that your unit tests were complex and cumbersome, then Spock will help you rediscover the joys of unit testing! Welcome to the world of Spock and accompany us on our journey through this book to learn more about its awesomeness!

acknowledgments

Writing a book is a collective effort. In the world of programming, where technologies come and go at a frenetic pace, it would be unrealistic to expect to write a book without a lot of external help, as this would make the book obsolete the moment it was published.

First, I would like to thank my development editors at Manning, Susan Conant and Dan Maharry. They taught me how to write a book and to develop content that is technically sound but also interesting and entertaining to the reader. They are the two people who spent a lot of time with me, explaining what it takes to write a good book and guiding me from the first draft until the final printed book.

Creating a book entails a lot of tasks other than writing the body of the text. Thankfully, I didn't have to concern myself with most of these tasks because a huge army of Manning personnel was there for me. I owe a lot to Kevin Sullivan, Mary Piergies, Janet Vail, Candace Gillhoolley, Aleksandar Dragosavljevic, Keith Conant, Francesco Bianchi, Sharon Wilkey, Melody Dolab, Toma Mulligan, and Gordan Salinovic for allowing me to focus on writing while they took care of layout, graphics, technical reviewing, proofreading, and marketing.

The following reviewers read the manuscript at various stages of its development and provided invaluable feedback: Adam Wynne, Annyce Davis, Chris Davis, David Pardo, Helen Scott, Laurence Giglio, Mario-Leander Reimer, Michael Bateman, Mikael Dautrey, Paul Grebenc, Robert Kietly, Ronald Tischliar, Steve Rogers, William Wheeler, and Zorodzayi Mukuya. Thanks also to all the MEAP readers who posted comments and corrections in the Author Online forum.

This book is the result of a direct collision of two equally important events. The first was the fact that Zeroturnaround allowed me to write a blog post on Spock back in 2013. I thank them because they gave me complete freedom on what to write about, even though Spock was not directly related to their business. The second event was that Michael Stephens of Manning noticed this Spock article and proposed to make a full book out of it. I thank him because he believed in me, even though I had never written a book before in my life.

I am grateful to my colleagues Ioannis Cherouvim, Alex Papadakis, and Zisis Pontikas for reviewing early drafts of the manuscript. Their comments were crucial as they were my first real readers. And special thanks go to Luke Daley who graciously offered to write the forward to my book.

Last, but not least, I would like to thank Peter Niederwieser for creating Spock in the first place! I believe that Spock has a bright future and that this book will help to strengthen its position in the Java ecosystem.

about this book

The central topic of this book is, of course, the Spock testing framework. A secondary theme is the employment of proven test practices and the ability to test all aspects of a Java application. Even though this book is introductory as far as Spock is concerned, there are certain assumptions I have made while writing it. When I think about my ideal reader, I assume that you are a seasoned Java developer. By seasoned I mean that you know your way around Java code and have mastered the basics: you have written JUnit tests and understand their purpose and use, and you want to learn new things and improve your craft.

If you do not fit this description, then there are several books available both for Java and testing in general that you need to read first. Especially for testing I can recommend *JUnit in Action, Second Edition* by Petar Tahchiev, et al. (Manning 2010), *Effective Unit Testing* by Lasse Koskela (Manning 2013), and *BDD in Action* by John Ferguson Smart (Manning 2014).

You may have also used Mockito or a similar framework for your unit tests. While this knowledge is helpful, it is not strictly required to take full advantage of this book as I do introduce these concepts (mocks/stubs/spies) and explain how Spock implements them.

Finally, I do *not* assume that you know Groovy. This is an important driving factor for the organization of the book—a Spock book for Groovy developers would be very different. I will introduce important Groovy traits as needed, but only those that are relevant to Spock testing.

If you are interested in Groovy (the programming language itself), a good place to start would be *Groovy in Action, Second Edition* by Dierk Koenig, et al. (Manning 2015).

Roadmap

There are eight chapters and two appendixes in this book.

Chapter 1 starts with a description of testing frameworks in general. We look at the objectives of Spock, its major features against the competition both in theory and with code examples. We also look at the relation of Java and Groovy and how you can gradually adopt Spock in an existing Java project.

Chapter 2 is devoted to teaching Groovy to Java developers. Because Spock tests are written in Groovy it is essential to learn the Groovy basics. Groovy is a full programming language on its own, but this chapter only focuses on knowledge needed for Spock tests. We see how compact and concise Groovy code can be (compared to Java) and how Groovy handles assert statements. Finally we look at some common Groovy utilities that may prove useful in unit tests

Chapter 3 is a tour of the major Spock features. We will see the basic structure of Spock unit tests, how Spock revolutionizes the way parameterized tests are handled, and some brief use of mocking/stubbing. A series of almost-real-world examples is used that will hopefully be different from examples you have seen in other tutorials.

Chapter 4 is probably the most important chapter in the book. It contains a detailed explanation of all Spock building blocks and how they can be connected together to create an expressive unit test. We also look at setup and cleanup methods for Spock tests along with some useful annotations that can be used for extra documentation of a unit test.

Chapter 5 explains parameterized tests. One of the great strengths of Spock is its expressive syntax with regard to parameterized tests. Input and output parameters can be described in a tabular format, making the syntax of parameterized tests much more pleasant. Spock also supports custom data readers that can be used for even more control of the parameters passed to a unit test.

Chapter 6 is all about mocking stubbing. Spock comes supercharged with a mocking facility allowing you to examine production code in a completely controlled environment. We start with some basic example of stubs, move on to mocks, and also talk about some advanced cases of mocking. If you have never used mocking before, this chapter also contains a bit of theory on what mocks are and where you should use them.

Chapter 7 examines integration and functional tests with Spock. The running theme here is that you can mostly reuse all your Java techniques and libraries that you already have in your JUnit tests. It is impossible to cover all frameworks, and therefore most examples are centered around the popular Spring library. We will cover functional testing of web pages and REST services in this chapter as well.

Chapter 8 is the final chapter, and it explains some extra features of Spock useful to enterprise applications. You will learn about refactoring large tests, using documentation annotations, and automatically ignoring tests using smart conditions. The chapter closes with a lesson on Spock spies, both in theory and practice.

Finally the appendixes explain how to install Spock and describe Spock extensions and tools.

Code conventions and downloads

The code in the book is presented in a fixed-width font like this to separate it from ordinary text. Code annotations accompany many of the listings, highlighting important concepts. In some cases, numbered bullets link to explanations that follow the listing.

The source code for the examples in the book is available from GitHub at http://github.com/kkapelon/java-testing-with-spock. All listings in the book are inside the Git repository and include extra bonus listings as well as solutions to exercises mentioned in the book. For brevity's sake, the text will at times point you to the full source code in GitHub, as it would have been impractical to include the entire source code in the body of the book. To implement the code, you will only need Java and the Maven build tool. Specific instructions on how to run the code and how to include Spock in your own applications are included in appendix A.

The code is open to anyone who would like to add contributions—if you have a suggestion on how to improve the code, you can open an issue or create a pull request via the web interface of GitHub. We look forward to your suggestions!

Author online

Purchase of *Java Testing with Spock* includes free access to a private web forum run by Manning Publications where you can make comments about the book, ask technical questions, and receive help from the author and from other users. To access the forum and subscribe to it, point your web browser to www.manning.com/books/java-testing-with-spock. This page provides information on how to get on the forum once you are registered, what kind of help is available, and the rules of conduct on the forum.

Manning's commitment to our readers is to provide a venue where a meaningful dialog between individual readers and between readers and the author can take place. It is not a commitment to any specific amount of participation on the part of the author, whose contribution to the AO remains voluntary (and unpaid). We suggest you try asking the author some challenging questions lest his interest stray!

The Author Online forum and the archives of previous discussions will be accessible from the publisher's web site as long as the book is in print.

About the author

Konstantinos Kapelonis is a software engineer with more than 10 years of programming experience ranging from writing bare metal C for the PlayStation 3 to Scheme code that mimics human reasoning. He works daily with Java and has a soft spot for code quality and build pipelines.

about the cover illustration

The figure on the cover of *Java Testing with Spock* is captioned "Habit of an Ambian Arab in 1581." The illustration is taken from Thomas Jefferys' *A Collection of the Dresses of Different Nations, Ancient and Modern* (four volumes), London, published between 1757 and 1772. The title page states that these are hand-colored copperplate engravings, heightened with gum arabic. Thomas Jefferys (1719–1771) was called "Geographer to King George III." He was an English cartographer who was the leading map supplier of his day. He engraved and printed maps for government and other official bodies and produced a wide range of commercial maps and atlases, especially of North America. His work as a map maker sparked an interest in local dress customs of the lands he surveyed and mapped, which are brilliantly displayed in this collection.

Fascination with faraway lands and travel for pleasure were relatively new phenomena in the late 18th century and collections such as this one were popular, introducing both the tourist as well as the armchair traveler to the inhabitants of other countries. The diversity of the drawings in Jefferys' volumes speaks vividly of the uniqueness and individuality of the world's nations some 200 years ago. Dress codes have changed since then and the diversity by region and country, so rich at the time, has faded away. It is now often hard to tell the inhabitant of one continent from another. Perhaps, trying to view it optimistically, we have traded a cultural and visual diversity for a more varied personal life. Or a more varied and interesting intellectual and technical life.

At a time when it is hard to tell one computer book from another, Manning celebrates the inventiveness and initiative of the computer business with book covers based on the rich diversity of regional life of two centuries ago, brought back to life by Jeffreys' pictures.

Part 1

Foundations and brief tour of Spock

Spock is a test framework that uses the Groovy programming language. The first part of the book expands on this by making sure that we (you, the reader, and me, the author) are on the same page.

To make sure that we are on the same page in the most gradual way, I first define a testing framework (and why it's needed) and introduce a subset of the Groovy syntax needed for writing Spock unit tests. I know that you're eager to see Spock tests (and write your own), but some features of Spock will impress you only if you've first learned a bit about the goals of a test framework and the shortcomings of current test frameworks (for example, JUnit).

Don't think, however, that this part of the book is theory only. Even at this early stage, this brief tour of Spock highlights includes full code listings and some out-of-the-ordinary examples.

Chapter 1 is a bird's-eye view of Spock, explaining its position in the Java ecosystem, the roles it plays in the testing process, and a brief comparison with JUnit. Feel free to skip this chapter if you're a seasoned Java developer and have already written a lot of JUnit tests.

Chapter 2 is a crash course in the Groovy programming language for Java developers. I promised that I don't assume any Groovy knowledge on your part, and this chapter keeps that promise. In it, I specifically focus only on Groovy features that are useful to Spock tests. By the end of this chapter, you'll be fully primed for reading and writing the Spock Groovy syntax. If you're interested in learning the whole Groovy package (for writing production code and not just unit tests), you can think of this chapter as a stepping stone to full Groovy nirvana. If you already know your way around Groovy code (and are familiar with closures and expandos), you can safely skip this chapter.

Chapter 3 demonstrates the three major facets of Spock (core testing, parameterized tests, and mocking/stubbing). These are presented via a series of testing scenarios for which the Java production code is already available and you're tasked with the unit tests. All the examples present that same functionality in both Spock and JUnit/Mockito so that you can draw your own conclusions on the readability and clarity of the test code. Chapter 3 acts as a hub for the rest of the book, as you can see which facet of Spock interests you for your own application.

Let's start your Spock journey together!

Introducing the Spock testing framework

This chapter covers

- Introducing Spock
- Bird's-eye view of the testing process
- Using Groovy to test Java
- Understanding Spock's place in the testing world

We live in the computer revolution. We've reached the point where computers are so commonplace that most of us carry a pocket-sized one all the time: a mobile phone. Mobile phones can now perform real-time face recognition, something that used to require a mainframe or computer cluster. At the same time, access to cheap and "always-on" internet services has created a communication layer that surrounds us.

As we enjoy the benefits of computerized services in our daily lives, our expectations are also changing. We expect information to be always available. Errors and unexpected behavior in a favorite software service leave us frustrated. E-commerce is on the rise, and all brands fight for customer loyalty as we turn to the internet for our shopping needs. Once I ordered a single chair from a well-known furniture company, and my credit card was charged three times the amount shown on the product page because of a computer error. Naturally, I never bought anything from that online shop again.

These high expectations of error-free software create even more pressure on developers if the "user" of the software is an organization, another company, or even a government agency. Software errors can result in loss of time/money/brand loyalty and, more important, loss of trust in the software.

If you're a software developer at any level, you know that writing programming code is only half of software creation. Testing the programming code is also essential in order to verify its correctness. Software problems (more commonly known as *bugs*) have a detrimental effect on the reliability of an application. A continuous goal of software development is the detection of bugs before the software is shipped or deployed to production.

A bug/issue that reaches production code can have a profound effect, depending on the type of software. For example, if your software is a mobile application for tracking daily intake of calories, you can sleep easily each night knowing that any issues found by users will only inconvenience them, and in the worst case they'll delete your application from their mobile phones (if they get really angry about the problems). But if, for example, you're writing software that manages hotel reservations, consequences are more serious. Critical issues will result in customer anger, brand damage for the hotel, and probable future financial losses.

On the extreme end of the spectrum, consider the severity of consequences for issues with the following:

- Software that controls hospital equipment
- Software that runs on a nuclear reactor
- Software that tracks enemy ballistic missiles and retaliates with its own defensive missiles (my favorite example)

How will you sleep at night if you're not sure these applications are thoroughly tested before reaching production status?

1.1 What is Spock?

This book is about Spock, a comprehensive testing framework for Java (and Groovy) code that can help you automate the boring, repetitive, and manual process of testing a software application. Spock is comprehensive because it's a union of existing Java testing libraries, as shown in figure 1.1.

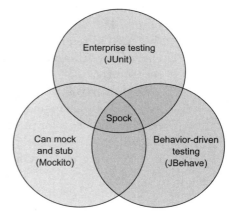

Figure 1.1 Spock among existing Java testing tools

As the figure shows, Spock is a superset of the de facto testing framework for Java: JUnit (http://junit.org/). Spock also comes with built-in capabilities for features that normally require additional libraries. At its core, Spock is a testing framework capable of handling the full lifecycle of a software application.

Spock was initially created in 2008 by Peter Niederwieser, a software engineer with Gradleware.[1] Inspired by existing test tools such as jMock (www.jmock.org) and RSpec (http://rspec.info/), Spock is used by several libraries within the open-source community, including Apache Tapestry (https://github.com/apache/tapestry-5) and MongoDB (https://github.com/mongodb/mongo-java-driver), and by several commercial companies (for instance, Netflix). A second Spock committer is Luke Daley (also with Gradleware), creator of the popular Geb functional testing framework (www.gebish .org) demonstrated in chapter 7. Spock, a new entry in the test framework arena, challenges the undisputed king—JUnit—armed with a bunch of fresh ideas against the legacy techniques of the past. Spock tests are written in Groovy, but they can test either Groovy or Java code.

1.1.1 Mocking and stubbing

The most basic unit tests (called *logic tests* by some) are those that focus on the logic of a single Java class. To test a single class in a controlled environment and isolate it from the other classes it depends on (*collaborators*), Spock comes with built-in support for "faking" external object communication. This capability, known as *mocking and stubbing*, isn't inside vanilla JUnit; you need external libraries—for example, Mockito (https://github.com/mockito/mockito) or jMock (http://www.jmock.org/)—to achieve this isolation of a Java class.

1.1.2 Behavior-driven development

Spock also embraces the paradigm of *behavior-driven development* (BDD), a development process that attempts to unify implementation, testing, and business people inside a software organization, by introducing a central way of documenting requirements and validating software functionality against those requirements, in a clear and repeatable manner. Spock combines these facets into a single convenient package offering a holistic approach to software testing.

1.1.3 Spock's design features

Spock has the following characteristics.

ENTERPRISE-READY

Spock can be easily integrated with the popular build systems, Maven (https:// maven.apache.org/) and Gradle (https://gradle.org/). Spock runs as part of a build

---

[1] The same company behind Gradle, a build system in Groovy (a replacement for Maven).

process and produces reports of automated test runs. Spock can be used to test back-end code, web pages, HTTP services, and more.

COMPREHENSIVE

Spock is a one-stop shop when it comes to testing. It has built-in capabilities for mocking and stubbing (creating fake objects), allowing you to decide on the breadth of the testing context. Spock can test a single class, a code module, or a whole application context with ease. You can perform end-to-end testing with Spock (covered in chapter 7) or isolate one class/method for your testing needs without any external libraries (described in chapter 6).

FAMILIAR/COMPATIBLE

Spock runs on top of the JUnit runner, which already enjoys mature support among tools and development environments. You run your Spock tests in the same way as your JUnit tests. You can even mix the two in the same project and get reports on test failures or code coverage in a similar way to JUnit. Run your tests in parallel or in a serial way; Spock doesn't care because it's fully compatible with existing JUnit tools.

INSPIRED

Spock is relatively new and doesn't carry any legacy burden. It's designed from scratch but at the same time it takes the best features of existing testing libraries (and tries to avoid their disadvantages). For example, Spock embraces the given-when-then structure of JBehave (http://jbehave.org/) but also discards the cumbersome record/replay code of older mocking frameworks.

1.1.4 Spock's coding features

Spock's coding features are as follows.

CONCISE

Spock uses the Groovy syntax, which is already concise and mixes its simplified syntax on top. No more tests that hide the substance with boilerplate code!

READABLE

Spock follows a close-to-English flow of statements that can be readable even by non-technical people (for example, business analysts). Collaboration among analysis, development, and testing people can be greatly simplified with Spock tests. If you always wanted to name your test methods by using full English sentences, now you can!

METICULOUS

When things go wrong, Spock gives as much detail as possible on the inner workings of the code at the time of failure. In some cases, this is more than enough for a developer to understand the problem without resorting to the time-consuming debugging process.

EXTENSIBLE

Spock allows you to write your own extensions to cater to your specific needs. Several of its "core" features are extensions (or started as extensions).

Listing 1.1 provides a sample test in Spock that illustrates several of these key coding features. The example shows a billing system that emails invoices to customers only if they have provided an email address.

> **How to use the code listings**
>
> You can find almost all code listings of this book at https://github.com/kkapelon/java-testing-with-spock. For brevity, the book sometimes points you to the source code (especially for long Java listings). I use the Eclipse integrated development environment (IDE) in my day-to-day work, as shown in the screenshots throughout the book. You can find specific instructions for installing Spock and using it via Maven, Gradle, Eclipse, and IntelliJ in appendix A.

Don't be alarmed by unknown keywords at this point. Even if you know absolutely no Groovy at all, you should be able to understand the scenario in question by the presence of full English sentences. The following chapters explain all details of the syntax. All of chapter 2 is devoted to Groovy and how it differs from Java.

Listing 1.1 Sample Spock test

```
class InvoiceMailingSpec extends spock.lang.Specification{

    def "electronic invoices to active email addresses"() {
        given: "an invoice, a customer, a mail server and a printer"
        PrinterService printerService = Mock(PrinterService)
        EmailService emailService = Mock(EmailService)
        Customer customer = new Customer()
        FinalInvoiceStep finalInvoiceStep = new
                FinalInvoiceStep(printerService, emailService)
        Invoice invoice = new Invoice()

        when: "customer is normal and has an email inbox"
        customer.hasEmail("acme@example.com")
        finalInvoiceStep.handleInvoice(invoice, customer)

        then: "invoice should not be printed. Only an
                    email should be sent"
        0 * printerService.printInvoice(invoice)
        1 * emailService.sendInvoice(invoice,"acme@example.com")
    }
}
```

- The Spock specification can be executed by a JUnit runner.
- Full English sentences describe what the test does.
- Integrated mocking of collaborator classes
- Given-when-then declarative style of BDD
- Verifying interactions of mocked objects

As you can see, the Spock test has a clear given-when-then flow denoted with labels (the BDD style of tests), and each label comes fully documented with an English sentence. Apart from the def keyword and the * symbol in the last two statements, almost all code is Java-like. Note that the spock.lang.Specification class is runnable by JUnit, meaning that this class can act as a JUnit test as far as build tools are concerned. Upcoming chapters cover these and several other features of Spock.

Testing is a highly controversial subject among software developers, and often the discussion focuses on testing tools and the number of tests that are needed in an application. Heated discussions always arise on what needs to be tested in a large application and whether tests help with deadlines. Some developers (hopefully, a minority) even think that all tests are a waste of time, or that their code doesn't need unit tests. If you think that testing is hard, or you believe that you don't have enough time to write tests, this book will show you that Spock uses a concise and self-documenting syntax for writing test cases.

If, on the other hand, you've already embraced sound testing practices in your development process, I'll show you how the Spock paradigm compares to established tools such as JUnit and TestNG (http://testng.org/).

Before getting into the details of using Spock, let's explore why you need a test framework in the first place. After all, you already test your code manually as part of every coding session, when you make sure that what you coded does what you intended.

1.2   The need for a testing framework

The first level of testing comes from you. When you implement a new feature, you make a small code change and then run the application to see whether the required functionality is ready. Compiling and running your code is a daily task that happens many times a day as you progress toward the required functionality.

Some features, such as "add a button here that sorts this table of the report," are trivial enough that they can be implemented and tested in one run. But more-complex features, such as "we need to change the policy of approving/rejecting a loan," will need several changes and runs of the application until the feature is marked as complete.

You can see this manual code-run-verify cycle in figure 1.2.

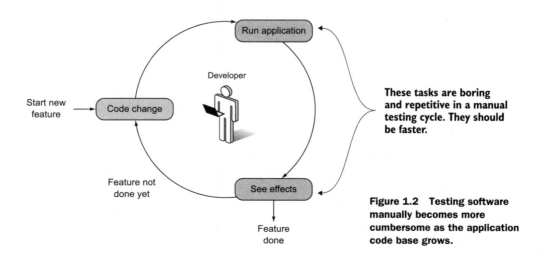

These tasks are boring and repetitive in a manual testing cycle. They should be faster.

Figure 1.2 Testing software manually becomes more cumbersome as the application code base grows.

Manual testing is enough for small software projects. A quick prototype, a side project, or a weekend coding session can be tested manually by a single person. In order for the cycle to work effectively, a single loop must be quick enough for the developer to see the results of the code change. In an ideal case, a single code change should be verified in seconds. If running the whole application and reaching the point where the new feature is found requires several minutes, developer productivity suffers.

Writing software is a creative process that requires getting into the "zone." Having constant interruptions with lengthy intervals between each code change is a guaranteed way to disrupt the developer's thinking about the code structure (not to mention loss of time/money while waiting for the test to finish).

As the programming code grows past a certain point, this manual cycle gets lengthier, with more time spent running and testing the application than writing code. Soon the run-verify time dominates the "developing" time. Another problem is the time it takes to redeploy software with the new changes. Small software projects can be deployed in seconds, but larger code bases (think bank software) may need several minutes for a complete deployment, further slowing the manual testing cycle.

1.2.1 Spock as an enterprise-ready test framework

Spock is marketed as an enterprise-ready test framework, so it's best to explain the need for automated testing in the context of enterprise software—software designed to solve the problems of a large business enterprise. Let's look at an example that reveals why a test framework is essential for large enterprise applications.

Imagine you've been hired as a software developer for a multinational company that sells sports equipment in an online shop. Most processes of the company depend on a monolithic system that handles all daily operations.

You're one of several developers responsible for this central application that has all the characteristics of typical enterprise in-house software:

- The code base is large (more than 200,000 lines of code).
- The development team is 5–20 people.
- No developer knows all code parts of the application.
- The application has already run in production for several years.
- New features are constantly requested by project stakeholders.
- Some code has been written by developers who have left the software department.

The last point is the one that bothers you most. Several areas of the application have nonexistent documentation, and no one to ask for advice.

DEALING WITH NEW REQUIREMENTS IN AN ENTERPRISE APPLICATION

You're told by your boss that because the snow season is approaching, all ski-related materials will get a 25% discount for a limited time period that must also be configurable. The time period might be a day, a week, or any other arbitrary time period.

Your approach is as follows:

1 Implement the feature.
2 Check the functionality by logging manually into the e-shop and verifying that the ski products have the additional discount during checkout.
3 Change the date of the system to simulate a day after the offer has ended.
4 Log in to the e-shop again and verify that the discount no longer applies.

You might be happy with your implementation and send the code change to the production environment, thinking you've covered all possible cases, as shown in figure 1.3.

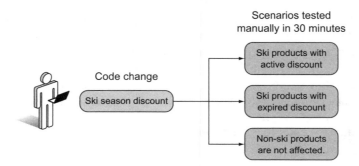

Figure 1.3 **Scenarios tested after a simple code change**

UNDERSTANDING ENTERPRISE COMPLEXITY: OF MODULES AND MEN

The next morning, your boss frantically tells you to revert the change because the company is losing money! He explains that the e-shop has several VIP customers who always get a 10% percent discount on all products. This VIP discount should never be applied with other existing discounts. Because you didn't know that, VIPs are now getting a total discount of 35%, far below the profit margin of the company. You revert the change and note that for any subsequent change, you have to remember to test for VIP customers as well.

This is a direct result of a large code base with several modules affecting more than one user-visible feature, or a single user-visible feature being affected by more than one code module. In a large enterprise project, some modules affect all user-visible features (typical examples are core modules for security and persistence). This asymmetric relationship is illustrated in figure 1.4.

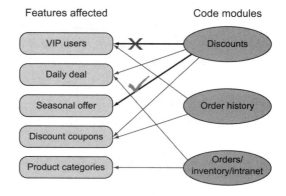

Figure 1.4 **A single change in one place has an unwanted effect in another place.**

With the change reverted, you learn more about the business requirements of discounts. The final discount of a product is affected by the following:

- Types of customers (first time, normal, silver, VIP)
- Three coupon code types (personal, seasonal, special)
- Ad hoc limited-time offers
- Standard seasonal discounts
- Time of products in the warehouse
- 30+ categories of sports equipment of the company

The next time you tamper with the discount code module, you'll have to manually test more than 100 cases of all the possible combinations. Testing all of them manually would require at least four hours of boring, repetitive work, as shown in figure 1.5.

This enterprise example should make it clear that the complexity of software makes the manual testing cycle slow. Adding a new feature becomes a time-consuming process because each code change must be examined for side effects in all other cases.

Another issue similar to module interaction is the human factor: in a big application, communication between domain experts, developers, testers, system administrators, and so on isn't always free of misunderstandings and conflicting requirements. Extensive documentation, clear communication channels, and an open policy regarding information availability can mitigate the problems but can't completely eliminate them.

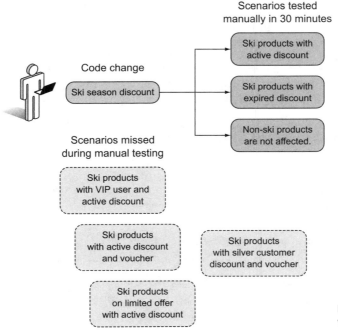

Figure 1.5 Some scenarios were missed by manual testing.

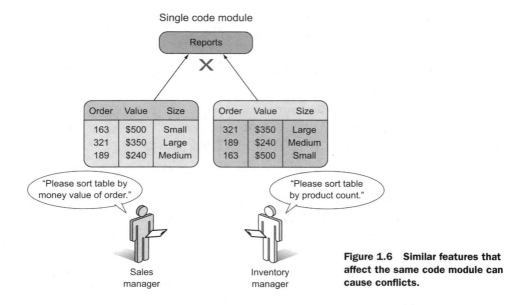

Figure 1.6   Similar features that affect the same code module can cause conflicts.

As an example, a sales manager in the e-shop decides that he wants to see all tables in the back-office application sorted by the value of the order, while at the same time an inventory manager wants to sort the same tables by order size. Two separate developers could be tasked with these cases without knowing that the requirements are conflicting, as shown in figure 1.6.

This enterprise example illustrates firsthand the problems of every large software code base:

- Manually testing every possible combination of data input after a code change is difficult and even impossible in some cases.
- It's hard to predict which parts of the application will be affected by a single code change. Developers are afraid to change existing code, fearing they might break existing functionality.
- Code changes for a new feature can enable previous bugs that have already been fixed to resurface (regressions).
- Understanding all system requirements from the existing code isn't easy. Reading the code provides information only on what happens and not on why it happens.
- Redeploying the application to see the effects of a code change could be a lengthy process on its own and could slow development time even further.

Now you know the major problems faced by a software development team working on a big enterprise project. Next, let's look at various approaches to tackling these problems.

1.2.2   *Common ways to handle enterprise complexity*

All software companies suffer from these problems and deal with them in one of the following three ways or their variations (I've seen them all in real life):

- Developers manually test everything after each code change.
- Big code changes are avoided for fear of unforeseen bugs.
- A layered testing approach is introduced that includes automated testing.

Let's look at each of these solutions in turn.

PERFORMING MINDLESS MANUAL TESTING

In the first case (which is possible with only small- to middle-sized software projects), developers aren't entirely sure what's broken after a code change. Therefore, they manually test all parts of the application after they implement a new feature or fix an issue. This approach wastes a lot of time/money because developers suffer from the repetitive nature of testing (which is a natural candidate for automation).

In addition, as the project grows, testing everything by hand becomes much more difficult. Either the development progress comes to a crawl, as most developers deal with testing instead of adding new features, or (the most common case) developers add features and test only parts of the application that they think might be affected. The result is that bugs enter production code and developers become firefighters; each passing day is a big crisis as the customer discovers missing functionality.

AVOIDING BIG CODE CHANGES

In the second case, the "solution" is to never perform big code changes at all. This paradigm is often embraced by large organizations with big chunks of legacy code (for example, banks). Management realizes that new code changes may introduce bugs that are unacceptable. On the other hand, manual testing of the code is next to impossible because of the depth and breadth of all user scenarios (for example, you can't possibly test all systems of a bank in a logical time frame by hand).

The whole code base is declared sacred. Changing or rewriting code is strictly forbidden by upper management. Developers are allowed to add only small features to the existing infrastructure, without touching the existing code. Local gurus inspect each code change extensively before it enters production status. Code reuse isn't possible. A lot of code duplication is present, because each new feature can't modify existing code. Either you already have what you need to implement your feature, or you're out of luck and need to implement it from scratch.

If you're a developer working in situations that belong to these first two cases (manual testing and the big code base that nobody touches), I feel for you! I've been there myself.

DELEGATING TO AN AUTOMATED TESTING FRAMEWORK

There's a third approach, and that's the one you should strive for. In the third case, an automated test framework is in place that runs after every code change. The framework is tireless, meticulous, and precise. It runs in the background (or on demand) and checks several user features whenever a change takes place. In a well-managed

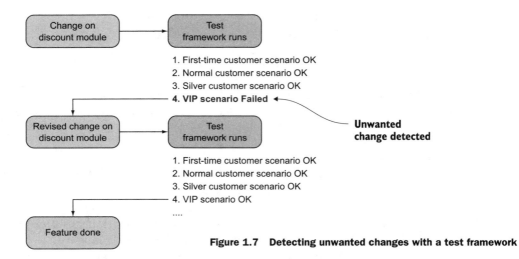

Figure 1.7   Detecting unwanted changes with a test framework

software creation process, the testing framework runs automatically after every developer commit as part of a build pipeline (for example, with the Jenkins build server, available for free at http://jenkins-ci.org/). Results from this automatic run can influence further steps. A common policy is that code modules with failed test results should never be deployed to a production environment.

The test framework acts as an early warning system against unwanted code effects. To illustrate the previous example, if you had a test framework in place, you'd get an automated report after any change, as shown in figure 1.7.

A test framework has the following characteristics.

It reduces

- Feedback time needed to verify the effects of code changes
- Boring, repetitive tasks

It ensures

- Confidence when a new feature is implemented, a bug is fixed, or code is refactored
- The detection of conflicting requirements

It provides

- Documentation for code and an explanation of the reasons behind the current state

Code can be refactored, removed, and updated with ease, because the test framework continuously reports unwanted side effects. Developers are free to devote most of their time to coding new features and fixing existing (known) bugs. Features quickly come into production code, and the customer receives a software package known to be stable and solid for all scenarios supported by the test framework. An initial time investment is required for the testing framework, but after it's in place, the gains outperform the time it takes to write the test scripts. Catching code regressions and severe bugs before they enter the production environment is much cheaper than allowing them to reach the final users.

A test framework also has other benefits not instantly visible with regard to code quality. The process of making programming code testable enforces several constraints on encapsulation and extensibility that can be easily neglected if the code isn't created with tests in mind. Techniques for making your code testable are covered in chapter 8. But the most important benefit of a test framework is the high developer confidence when performing a deep code change.

Let's dig into how Spock, as a testing framework specializing in enterprise applications, can help you refactor code with such confidence.

1.3 Spock: the groovier testing framework

When I first came upon Spock, I thought that it would be the JUnit alternative to the Groovy programming language. After all, once a programming language reaches a critical mass, somebody ports the standard testing model, known as xUnit (https://en.wikipedia.org/wiki/XUnit), to the respective runtime environment. xUnit frameworks already exist for all popular programming languages.

But Spock is not the xUnit of Groovy! It resembles higher-level testing frameworks, such as RSpec and Cucumber (https://github.com/cucumber/cucumber-jvm), that follow the concepts of BDD, instead of the basic setup-stimulate-assert style of xUnit. BDD attempts (among other things) to create a one-to-one mapping between business requirements and unit tests.

1.3.1 Asserts vs. Assertions

If you're familiar with JUnit, one of the first things you'll notice with Spock is the complete lack of assert statements. *Asserts* are used in unit tests in order to verify the test. You define the expected result, and JUnit automatically fails the test if the expected output doesn't match the actual one.

Assert statements are still there if you need them, but the preferred way is to use Spock *assertions* instead, a feature so powerful that it has been backported to Groovy itself. You'll learn more in chapter 2 about Power asserts and how they can help you pinpoint the causes of a failing test.

1.3.2 Agnostic testing of Java and Groovy

Another unique advantage of Spock is the ability to agnostically test both Java and Groovy code, as shown in figure 1.8.

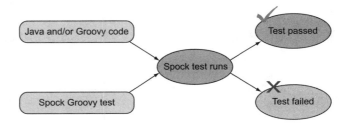

Figure 1.8 Spock can test both Java and Groovy code.

Groovy is a dynamic language that runs in the same Java Virtual Machine (JVM) as Java. Java supporters are proud of the JVM, and some believe that the value of the JVM as a runtime environment is even higher than Java the language. Spock is one example of the power the JVM has to accommodate code from different programming languages.

Spock can test any class that runs on the JVM, regardless of the original source code (Java or Groovy). It's possible with Spock to test either a Java class or a Groovy class in the exact same way. Spock doesn't care about the origin of the class, as long as it's JVM-compatible. You can even verify both Java and Groovy code in the same Spock test if your project is a mix of the two.

1.3.3   *Taking advantage of Groovy tricks in Spock tests*

Finally, you need to know that Groovy is a dynamic language that behaves differently than Java in some important aspects (such as the declaration of variables), as you'll learn in chapter 2. This means that several "tricks" you learn with Spock are in reality a mix of both Groovy and Spock magic, because Spock can extend Groovy syntax in ways that would be difficult with Java (if not impossible). And yes, unlike Java, in Groovy a library/framework can change the syntax of the code as well. Spock is one such library, as you'll learn in chapter 4.

As you become more familiar with Spock and Groovy, the magic behind the curtain will start to appear, and you might even be tempted to use Groovy outside Spock tests as well!

> **AST transformations: changing the structure of the Groovy language**
>
> Several tricks of Groovy magic come from the powerful meta-programming facilities offered during runtime that can change classes and methods in ways impossible with vanilla Java. At the same time, Groovy also supports compile-time macros (*abstract syntax tree*, or AST, transformations in Groovy parlance). If you're familiar with macros in other programming languages, you should be aware of the power they bring to code transformations. By using AST transformations, a programmer can add/change several syntactic features of Groovy code, modifying the syntax in forms that were difficult or impossible in Java.
>
> Spock takes advantage of these compile and runtime code-transformation features offered by Groovy in order to create a pseudo-DSL (domain specific language) specifically for unit tests. All the gory details of Spock syntax are explained in chapter 4.

1.4   *Getting an overview of Spock's main features*

Before starting with the details of Spock code, let's take a bird's-eye view of its major features and how they implement the good qualities of a testing framework, as already explained.

1.4.1 Enterprise testing

A test framework geared toward a big enterprise application has certain requirements in order to handle the complexity and possible configurations that come with enterprise software. Such a test framework must easily adapt to the existing ecosystem of build tools, coverage metrics, quality dashboards, and other automation facilities.

Rather than reinventing the wheel, Spock bases its tests on the existing JUnit runner. The runner is responsible for executing JUnit tests and presenting their results to the console or other tools (for example, the IDE). Spock reuses the JUnit runner to get for free all the mature support of external tools already created by Junit:

- Do you want to see code coverage reports with Spock?
- Do you want to run your tests in parallel?
- Do you want to divide your tests into long running and short running?

The answer to all these questions is "Yes, you do, as you did before with JUnit." More details about these topics are presented in chapter 7.

1.4.2 Data-driven tests

A common target for unit tests is to handle input data for the system in development. It's impossible to know all potential uses for your application in advance, let alone the ways people are going to use and misuse your application.

Usually a number of unit tests are dedicated to possible inputs of the system in a gradual way. The test starts with a known set of allowed or disallowed input, and as bugs are encountered, the test is enriched with more cases. Common examples include a test that checks whether a username is valid or which date formats are accepted in a web service.

These tests suffer from a lot of code duplication if code is handled carelessly. The test is always the same (for example, Is the username valid?), and only the input changes. Whereas JUnit has some facilities for this type of test (parameterized test), Spock takes a different turn, and offers a special DSL that allows you to embed data tables in Groovy source code. Data-driven tests are covered in chapter 5.

1.4.3 Mocking and stubbing

For all its strengths, object-oriented software suffers from an important flaw. The fact that two objects work correctly individually doesn't imply that both objects will also work correctly when connected to each other. The reverse is also true: side effects from an object chain may hide or mask problems that happen in an individual class.

A direct result of these facts is that testing software usually needs to cover two levels at once: the integration level, where tests examine the system as a whole (integration tests), and the class level, where tests examine each individual class (unit tests or logic tests).

To examine the microscopic level of a single class and isolate it from the macroscopic level of the system, a controlled running environment is needed. A developer has to focus on a single class, and the rest of the system is assumed to be "correct." Attempting to test a single class inside the real system is difficult, because for any bugs encountered, it's not immediately clear whether they happen because of the class under test or the environment.

For this reason, a mocking framework is needed that "fakes" the rest of the system and leaves only the class under test to be "real." The class is then tested in isolation because even though it "thinks" that it's inside a real system, in reality all other collaborating classes (collaborators) are simple puppets with preprogrammed input and output.[2]

In the JUnit world, an external library is needed for mocking. Numerous libraries exist, with both strengths and weaknesses—for example, Mockito, jMock, EasyMock (http://easymock.org/) and PowerMock (www.powermock.org/). Spock comes with its own built-in mocking framework, as you'll see in chapter 6. Combined with the power of Groovy meta-programming (as described in chapter 2), Spock is a comprehensive DSL that provides all the puzzle pieces needed for testing.

Now that we've covered the theory and you know the foundations of a solid testing process and how Spock can test classes written in Java, it's time to delve into code!

1.5   A first look at Spock in action

The following examples should whet your appetite, so don't stress over the strange syntax or any unknown keywords. I cover Spock syntax throughout the rest of the book.

1.5.1   A simple test with JUnit

When introducing a new library/language/framework, everybody expects a "hello world" example. This section shows what Spock looks like in a minimal, but fully functional example.

The following listing presents the Java class you'll test. For comparison, a possible JUnit test is first shown, as JUnit is the de facto testing framework for Java, still undisputed after more than a decade.

Listing 1.2 Java class under test and JUnit test

```
public class Adder {                              A trivial class that will be tested
    public int add(int a, int b) {                (a.k.a. class under test)
            return a+b;
    }
}                                                 Test case for the
public class AdderTest {                          class in question
    @Test
    public void simpleTest() {                                          JUnit assert statement
            Adder adder = new Adder();                                  that compares 2 and
            assertEquals("1 + 1 is 2", 2 ,adder.add(1, 1));             the result of add(I,I)
```

Initialization of class under test

---

[2] I always enjoyed this evil aspect of testing—my own puppet theater, where the protagonist can't see behind the scenes.

```
                                    }
                                    @Test
                                    public void orderTest() {
                                            Adder adder = new Adder();
                                            assertEquals("Order does not matter ",5,adder.add(2, 3));
                                            assertEquals("Order does not matter ",5,adder.add(3, 2));
                                    }
                            }
```

Two assert statements that compare 5 with adding 2 and 3

A second scenario for the class under test

You introduce two test methods, one that tests the core functionality of your `Adder` class, and one that tests the order of arguments in your `add` method.

Running this JUnit test in the Eclipse development environment (right-click the .java file and choose Run As > JUnit Test from the menu) gives the results shown in figure 1.9.

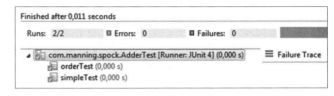

Figure 1.9   Running a JUnit test in Eclipse

1.5.2   A simple test with Spock

The next listing shows the same test in Groovy/Spock. Again, this test examines the correctness of the Java class `Adder` that creates the sum of two numbers.

Listing 1.3   Spock test for the Adder Java class

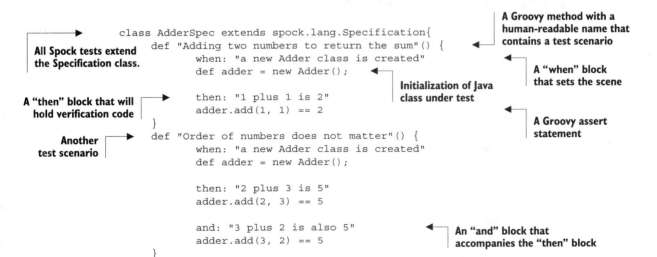

```
class AdderSpec extends spock.lang.Specification{
    def "Adding two numbers to return the sum"() {
        when: "a new Adder class is created"
        def adder = new Adder();

        then: "1 plus 1 is 2"
        adder.add(1, 1) == 2
    }
    def "Order of numbers does not matter"() {
        when: "a new Adder class is created"
        def adder = new Adder();

        then: "2 plus 3 is 5"
        adder.add(2, 3) == 5

        and: "3 plus 2 is also 5"
        adder.add(3, 2) == 5
    }
}
```

All Spock tests extend the Specification class.

A "then" block that will hold verification code

Another test scenario

A Groovy method with a human-readable name that contains a test scenario

A "when" block that sets the scene

Initialization of Java class under test

A Groovy assert statement

An "and" block that accompanies the "then" block

If you've never seen Groovy code before, this Spock segment may seem strange. The code has mixed lines of things you know (for example, the first line with the extends

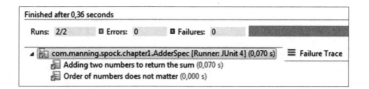

Figure 1.10   Running a Spock test in Eclipse

keyword) and things completely alien to you (for example, the def keyword). Details on Groovy syntax are explained in chapter 2.

On the other hand, if you're already familiar with BDD, you'll already grasp the when/then pattern of feature testing.

The upcoming chapters explain Spock syntax in detail. For example, the def keyword (which stands for *define*) is how you declare things in Groovy without explicitly specifying their type (which is a strict requirement in Java). The Spock blocks (when:, then:, and:) are covered in chapter 4.

How do you run this test? You run it in the same way as a JUnit test! Again, right-click the Groovy class and choose Run As > JUnit Test from the pop-up menu. The result in Eclipse is shown in figure 1.10.

Other than the most descriptive method names, there's little difference between the JUnit and Spock results in this trivial example. Although I use Eclipse here, Spock tests can run on all environments/tools that already support JUnit tests (for example, IntelliJ IDEA).

TAKEAWAYS FROM THESE CODE EXAMPLES

Here's what you need to take away from this code sample:

- The almost English-like flow of the code. You can easily see what's being tested, even if you're a business analyst or don't know Groovy.
- The lack of any assert statements. Spock has a declarative syntax, which explains what you consider correct behavior.
- The fact that Spock tests can be run like JUnit tests.

Let's move on to one of the killer features of Spock (handling failed tests).

1.5.3   *Inspecting failed tests with Spock*

One of the big highlights of Spock code is the lack of assert statements compared to JUnit. In the previous section, you saw what happens when all tests pass and the happy green bar is shown in Eclipse. But how does Spock cope with test failures?

To demonstrate its advantages over JUnit, you'll add another (trivial) Java class that you want to test:

```
public class Multiplier {
    public int multiply(int a, int b)
    {
            return a * b;
    }
}
```

For this class, you'll also write the respective JUnit test, as shown in the following listing. But as an additional twist (for demonstration purposes), you want to test this class not only by itself, but also in relation to the Adder class shown in the previous section.

Listing 1.4 A JUnit test for two Java classes

```java
public class MultiplierTest {
    @Test
    public void simpleMultiplicationTest() {

        Multiplier multi = new Multiplier();
        assertEquals("3 times 7 is 21",21,multi.multiply(3, 7));
    }
    @Test
    public void combinedOperationsTest() {

        Adder adder = new Adder();
        Multiplier multi = new Multiplier();

        assertEquals("4 times (2 plus 3) is 20",
        20,multi.multiply(4, adder.add(2, 3)));
        assertEquals("(2 plus 3) times 4 is also 20",
                    20,multi.multiply(adder.add(2, 3),4));

    }
}
```

A test scenario that will examine two Java classes at the same time

Creation of the first Java class

Creation of the second Java class

Verification of a mathematical result coming from both Java classes

Running this unit test results in a green bar because both tests pass. Now for the equivalent Spock test, shown in the next listing.

Listing 1.5 Spock test for two Java classes

```groovy
class MultiplierSpec extends spock.lang.Specification{
    def "Multiply two numbers and return the result"() {
        when: "a new Multiplier class is created"
        def multi = new Multiplier();

        then: "3 times 7 is 21"
        multi.multiply(3, 7) == 21
    }
    def "Combine both multiplication and addition"() {
        when: "a new Multiplier and Adder classes are created"
        def adder = new Adder();
        def multi = new Multiplier()

        then: "4 times (2 plus 3) is 20"
        multi.multiply(4, adder.add(2, 3)) == 20

        and: "(2 plus 3) times 4 is also 20"
        multi.multiply(adder.add(2, 3),4) == 20
    }
}
```

A test scenario that will examine two Java classes at the same time

Creation of the first Java class

Creation of the second Java class

Verification of a mathematical result coming from both Java classes

Again, running this test will pass with flying colors. You might start to believe that we gain nothing from using Spock instead of JUnit. But wait!

Let's introduce an artificial bug in your code to see how JUnit and Spock deal with failure. To mimic a real-world bug, you'll introduce it in the `Multiplier` class, but only for a special case (see the following listing).

Listing 1.6   Introducing an artificial bug in the Java class under test

A dummy bug that happens only if the first argument is 4

```java
public class Multiplier {
    public int multiply(int a, int b) {
        if(a == 4)  {
            return 5 * b; //multiply an extra time.
        }
        return a *b;
    }
}
```

Now run the JUnit test and see what happens (figure 1.11).

You have a test failure. But do you notice anything strange here? Because the bug you introduced is subtle, JUnit says this to you:

- Addition by itself works fine.
- Multiplication by itself works fine.
- When both of them run together, we have problem.

But where is the problem? Is the bug on the addition code or the multiplication? We can't say just by looking at the test result (OK, OK, the math might give you a hint in this trivial example).

You need to insert a debugger in the unit test to find out what happened. This is an extra step that takes a lot of time because re-creating the same context environment can be a lengthy process.

SPOCK KNOWS ALL THE DETAILS WHEN A TEST FAILS

Spock comes to the rescue! If you run the same bug against Spock, you get the message shown in figure 1.12.

Spock comes with a super-charged error message that not only says you have a failure, but also calculates intermediate results!

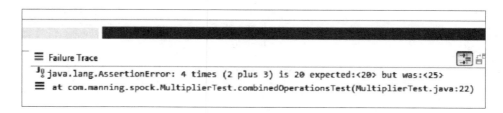

Figure 1.11   Failure of JUnit test in Eclipse

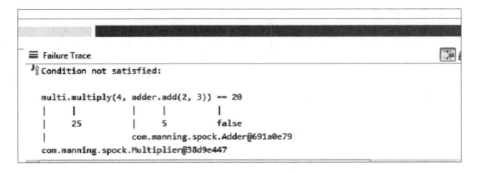

Figure 1.12 **Failure of a Spock test in Eclipse**

As you can see, it's clear from the test that the addition works correctly (2 + 3 is indeed 5) and that the bug is in the multiplication code (4 × 5 doesn't equal 25).

Armed with this knowledge, you can go directly to the `Multiplier` code and find the bug. This is one of the killer features of Spock, and may be enough to entice you to rewrite all your JUnit tests in Spock. But a complete rewrite isn't necessary, as both Spock and JUnit tests can coexist in the same code base, which you'll explore next.

1.6 *Spock's position in the Java ecosystem*

The de facto testing framework in a Java project is JUnit, but *TestNG* is another testing framework for Java that's similar. At one point, TestNG had several extra features that JUnit lacks, resulting in a lot of developers switching over to TestNG (especially for big enterprise projects). But JUnit quickly closed the gap, and TestNG failed to gain a majority in the mindset of Java developers. The throne of JUnit is still undisputed. I've seen junior Java developers who think that JUnit and unit testing are the exact same thing. In reality, JUnit is one of the many ways that unit tests can be implemented.

Unit tests in both JUnit and TestNG are written in Java as well. Traditionally, this has been seen as an advantage by Java developers because they use the same programming language in both production code and testing code. Java is a verbose language (at least by today's standards) with a lot of boilerplate code, several constraints (for example, all code must be part of a class, even static methods), and a heavy syntax requiring everything to be explicitly defined. Newer editions of Java (after version 7) attempt to rectify this issue with mixed success, never reaching the newer "convention-over-configuration" paradigm of other programming languages.

It doesn't have to be this way, though. There's no technical reason to constrain unit tests so that they're in the same programming language as the development code. In fact, production and testing code have completely different requirements. The biggest difference is that testing code runs by definition *before* the application is deployed in production. A good engineer uses the best tool for the job. You can think of Spock as a special domain language created exclusively for testing purposes.

Compilation and running of unit tests is a common task for the developer or the build server inside a software company. Runtime and compile-time errors in unit tests are detected at the same time. Java goes to great lengths to detect several errors during compile time instead of runtime. This effort is wasted in unit tests because these two phases usually run one after the other during the software development lifecycle. The developer still pays the price for the verbosity of Java, even for unit tests. There must be a better way.

Groovy comes to the rescue!

1.6.1 *Making Spock Groovy*

Groovy is a dynamic programming language (similar to Python or Ruby), which means it gives the programmer power to defer several checks until runtime. This might seem like a disadvantage, but this feature is exactly what unit tests should exploit. Groovy also has a much nicer syntax than Java because several programming aspects have carefully selected defaults if you don't explicitly define them (convention over configuration).

As an example, if you omit the visibility modifier of a class in Java, the class is automatically `package private`, which ironically is the least used modifier in Java code. Groovy does the logical thing: if you omit the visibility modifier of a class, the class is assumed to be `public`, which is what you want most times.

The times that I've had to create JUnit tests with `package private` visibility in my programming career: zero! For all these years, I've "paid" the price of declaring all my unit tests (and I guess you have, as well) as `public`, without ever thinking, "There must be a better way!" Groovy has embraced the convention-over-configuration concept, and this paradigm is evident in Spock code as well.

Testing Groovy code with JUnit

The topic of this book is how to test Java code with the Spock framework (which is written in Groovy). The reverse is also possible with JUnit:

- You can write a normal JUnit test in Java, where the class under test is implemented in Groovy.
- You can also write the JUnit test in Groovy to test Groovy or Java code.
- Finally, Groovy supports a `GroovyTestCase` class, which extends the standard `TestCase` from JUnit.

Because this is a book about Spock, I don't cover these combinations. See *Making Java Groovy* by Ken Kousen (Manning, 2013) if you're interested in any of these cases.

With Spock, you can gain the best of both worlds. You can keep the tried-and-true Java code in your core modules, and at the same time, you gain the developer productivity of Groovy in the testing code without sacrificing anything in return. Production code is written with verbose and fail-safe Java code, whereas unit tests are written in the friendlier and lighter Groovy syntax that cuts down on unneeded modifiers and provides a much more compact code footprint. And the best part is that you keep your existing JUnit tests!

1.6.2 *Adding Spock tests to existing projects that have JUnit tests*

Every new technology faces a big obstacle in its path to adoption: resistance to change. Tradition, inertia, and the projected cost of switching to another technology instead of the mature existing solution are always major factors that affect any proposal for improvement when a better solution comes along.

As an example, *Gradle* is a build system, also written in Groovy, which is in many ways more flexible than the de facto build system of Java (Maven). Using two build systems in a big enterprise project is unrealistic. Gradle has to face the entrenched Maven supporters and convince them that the switch offers compelling advantages.

Spock doesn't suffer from this problem. You can integrate Spock today in your Java project without rewriting or removing a single line of code or configuration. This is a huge win for Spock because it allows a gradual adoption; both old JUnit tests and newer Spock tests can coexist peacefully. It's perfectly possible to implement a gradual Spock adoption strategy in your organization by implementing new tests in Spock during a trial period without losing anything if you decide to keep implementing JUnit tests as well.

The standard Maven directory structure is flexible in accommodating multiple programming languages. Groovy source code is usually placed in the src/test/groovy folder so that the Groovy compiler plugin can find it. All your Spock tests can go into this directory without affecting your existing JUnit tests located in src/test/java (or other directories), as shown in figure 1.13.

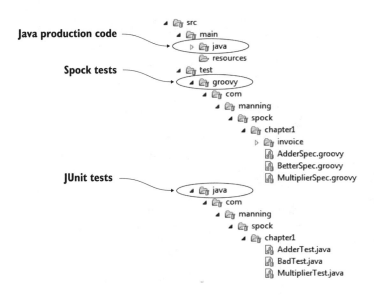

Figure 1.13 Spock tests in a Maven project with existing JUnit tests

For more details on how to set up your IDE for Spock testing, see appendix A.

With the Spock tests in place, the next question you might have is how to run them. You'll be happy to know that Spock comes with a test runner called *Sputnik* (from Spock and JUnit) that runs on top of the existing JUnit runner, thus keeping full backward compatibility.

You can run any Spock test as you run any JUnit test:

- From your development environment
- From the command line
- From Maven/Gradle or any other build system that supports JUnit tests
- From an automated script or build server environment (as explained in chapter 7)

> **The Spock Web Console**
>
> You can also run Spock tests without installing anything at all, with the Spock Web Console. If you visit https://meetspock.appspot.com/, you can play with the Spock syntax and get a feel for how easy it is to write Spock tests by using only your browser.
>
> The Spock Web Console is based on the excellent Groovy Web Console (https://groovyconsole.appspot.com/) that offers a Groovy playground on the web, ready for you to explore from the comfort of your web browser.

1.6.3   *Spock adoption path in a Java project*

Because Spock is compatible with JUnit runners, it can be introduced gradually in an existing Java code base. Assuming you start with a 100% Java project, as shown at the top left of figure 1.14, Spock can run alongside JUnit tests in the same code base.

It's possible to rewrite all tests in Spock if that's what you want. Spock can work as a superset of JUnit, as you'll see in chapter 3. That situation is shown in the third scenario, depicted at the far right of figure 1.14.

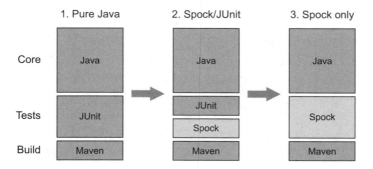

Figure 1.14   Gradual invasion of Spock tests in an existing Java project with JUnit tests

For this book, I assume that you have no prior experience with Groovy. Chapter 2 is fully devoted to Groovy features, and I'll also be careful to explain which new syntax is a feature of Spock and which is a feature of Groovy.

1.7 Comparing Spock and JUnit

Comparing JUnit and Spock in a single section is difficult because both tools have a different philosophy when it comes to testing. JUnit is a Spartan library that provides the absolutely necessary thing you need to test and leaves additional functionality (such as mocking and stubbing) to external libraries.

Spock takes a holistic approach, providing a superset of the capabilities of JUnit, while at the same time reusing its mature integration with tools and development environments. Spock can do everything that JUnit does and more, keeping backward compatibility as far as test runners are concerned.

What follows is a brief tour of some Spock highlights. Chapter 3 compares similar functionality between Spock and JUnit. If you're not familiar with JUnit, feel free to skip the comparisons and follow the Spock examples.

1.7.1 Writing concise code with Groovy syntax

Spock is written in Groovy, which is less verbose than Java. Spock tests are more concise than the respective JUnit tests. This advantage isn't specific to Spock itself. Any other Groovy testing framework would probably share this trait. But at the moment, only Spock exists in the Groovy world. Figure 1.15 shows this advantage in a visual way.

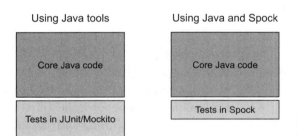

Figure 1.15   Amount of code in an application with JUnit and Spock tests

Less code is easier to read, easier to debug, and easier to maintain in the long run. Chapter 3 goes into more detail about how Groovy supports less-verbose code than Java.

1.7.2 Mocking and stubbing with no external library

JUnit doesn't support mocking and stubbing on its own. Several Java frameworks fill this position. The main reason that I became interested in Spock in the first place is

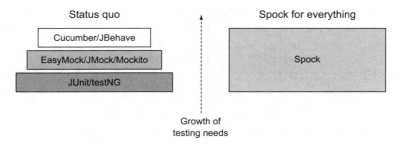

Figure 1.16   Spock is a superset of JUnit.

that it comes "batteries included," with mocking and stubbing supported out of the box. As figure 1.16 shows, it does even more than that.

I'll let this example explain:

David goes into a software company and starts working on an existing Java code base. He's already familiar with JUnit (the de facto testing framework for Java). While working on the project, he needs to write some unit tests that need to run in a specific order. JUnit doesn't support this, so David also includes TestNG in the project.

Later he realizes that he needs to use mocking for some special features of the software (for example, the credit card billing module), so he spends time researching all the available Java libraries (there are many). He chooses Mockito and integrates it into the code base.

Months pass, and David learns all about behavior-driven development in his local dev meeting. He gets excited! Again he researches the tools and selects JBehave for his project in order to accomplish BDD.

Meanwhile, Jane is a junior developer who knows only vanilla Java. She joins the same company and gets overwhelmed the first day because she has to learn three or four separate tools just to understand all the testing code.

In an alternate universe, David starts working with Spock as soon as he joins the company. Spock has everything he needs for all testing aspects of the application. He never needs to add another library or spend time researching stuff as the project grows.

Jane joins the same company in this alternate universe. She asks David for hints on the testing code, and he replies, "Learn Spock and you'll understand all testing code." Jane is happy because she can focus on a single library instead of three.

You'll learn more about stubbing/mocking/spying in chapter 6. The semantics of Spock syntax are covered in chapter 4.

1.7.3   *Using English sentences in Spock tests and reports*

The next listing presents a questionable JUnit test (I see these all the time). It contains cryptic method names that don't describe what's being tested.

Listing 1.7 A JUnit test with method names unrelated to business value

```java
public class ClientTest {
    @Test
    public void scenario1()  {

        CreditCardBilling billing = new CreditCardBilling();
        Client client client = new Client();
        billing.chargeClient(client,150);
        assertTrue("expect bonus",client.hasBonus());
    }
    @Test
    public void scenario2()  {

        CreditCardBilling billing = new CreditCardBilling();
        Client client client = new Client();
        billing.chargeClient(client,150);
        client.rejectsCharge();
        assertFalse("expect no bonus",client.hasBonus());
    }
```

Nontechnical people can't understand the test.

A test method with a generic name

Only programmers can understand this code. Also, if the second test breaks, a project manager (PM) will see the report and know that "scenario2" is broken. This report has no value for the PM, because he doesn't know what scenario2 does without looking at the code.

Spock supports an English-like flow. The next listing presents the same example in Spock.

Listing 1.8 A Spock test with methods that explain the business requirements

```groovy
class BetterSpec extends spock.lang.Specification{

    def "Client should have a bonus if he spends more than 100 dollars"() {
        when: "a client buys something with value at least 100"
        def client = new Client();
        def billing = new CreditCardBilling();
        billing.chargeClient(client,150);

        then: "Client should have the bonus option active"
        client.hasBonus() == true
    }
    def "Client loses bonus if he does not accept the transaction"() {
        when: "a client buys something and later changes mind"
        def client = new Client();
        def billing = new CreditCardBilling();
        billing.chargeClient(client,150);
        client.rejectsCharge();

        then: "Client should have the bonus option inactive"
        client.hasBonus() == false
    }
}
```

Business description of test

Human-readable test result

Even if you're not a programmer, you can read the English text in the code (the sentences inside quotation marks) and understand the following:

- The client should get a bonus if he spends more than 100 dollars.
- When a client buys something with a value of at least 100, then the client should have the bonus option active.
- The client loses the bonus if he doesn't accept the transaction.
- When a client buys something and later changes his mind, then the client should have the bonus option inactive.

This is readable. A business analyst could read the test and ask questions about other cases. (What happens if the client spends $99.99? What happens if he changes his mind the next day rather than immediately?)

If the second test breaks, the PM will see in the report a red bar with the title "Client loses bonus if he doesn't accept the transaction." He instantly knows the severity of the problem (perhaps he decides to ship this version if he considers it noncritical).

For more information on Spock reporting and how Spock can be used as part of an enterprise delivery process, see chapter 7.

1.8   Summary

- Spock is an alternative test framework written in the Groovy programming language.
- A test framework automates the boring and repetitive process of manual testing, which is essential for any large application code base.
- Although Spock is written in Groovy, it can test both Java and Groovy code.
- Spock has built-in support for mocking and stubbing without an external library.
- Spock follows the given-when-then code flow commonly associated with the BDD paradigm.
- Both Groovy and Java build and run on the JVM. A large enterprise build can run both JUnit and Spock tests at the same time.
- Spock uses the JUnit runner infrastructure and therefore is compatible with all existing Java infrastructure. For example, code coverage with Spock is possible in the same way as JUnit.
- One of the killer features of Spock is the detail it gives when a test fails. JUnit mentions the expected and actual value, whereas Spock records the surrounding running environment, mentioning the intermediate results and allowing the developer to pinpoint the problem with greater ease than JUnit.
- Spock can pave the way for full Groovy migration into a Java project if that's what you want. Otherwise, it's possible to keep your existing JUnit tests in place and use Spock only in new code.
- Spock tests have the ability to include full English sentences in their code structures, allowing for easy documentation.

Groovy knowledge for Spock testing

This chapter covers

- Understanding the connection between Java and Groovy
- Learning Groovy conventions
- Comparing JUnit asserts and Groovy power asserts
- Using Groovy utilities for common testing needs
- Obtaining test data with Groovy

Learning a new programming language is usually a daunting task. You must study a new syntax, new concepts, and new libraries all at once to be productive. If you've spent too many years with a single language, several concepts are so entrenched that having to "unlearn" them poses a big barrier to any alternative (even if it's objectively better). With Groovy, this isn't the case because Groovy is a cousin language to Java. Much of your current knowledge can be reused and extended instead of thrown away.

This chapter gives you a crash course in the essentials of Groovy. It's important to know your way around Groovy code before writing Spock tests. I've seen several

Java developers who jump into Spock, but write the same JUnit-like tests as they did before.

Because the subject of this book is the Spock testing framework (and by extension other relevant testing topics), all Groovy capabilities listed are those relevant to unit tests only. Groovy has many more features aimed at writing production code (and not unit test code). Explaining all of Groovy's concepts is impossible in a single chapter; extensive books already exist on vanilla Groovy that you should consult if you decide to use it outside Spock unit tests.

Apart from *Groovy in Action* by Dierk Konig and Paul King (Manning, 2015), which is the major source for all things Groovy, I also recommend *Making Java Groovy* by Ken Kousen (Manning, 2013), which emphasizes the augmenting role of Groovy compared to Java.

2.1   *What you need to know about Groovy*

If you already know Java, you have knowledge in three distinct areas:

- The syntax/keywords of the Java language
- The Java Development Kit (JDK) that contains many helpful collections and utilities
- The Java runtime (Java Virtual Machine)

It would be a mistake to think that learning Groovy is like learning a new programming language from scratch. Groovy was designed as a companion to Java.

Groovy offers the productivity boost of a dynamic language (think Python or Ruby) because it doesn't have as many restrictions as Java. But at the same time, it runs in the familiar JVM and can take advantage of all Java libraries. It completely removes some bulky features of Java and always attempts to minimize boilerplate code by providing only the gist of what you're doing.

Java is mature as a platform, but as a language, it lags behind in some areas (for example, concurrent facilities or, until recently, functional constructs) that usually are filled by external frameworks. Groovy closes this gap and provides a modern language aimed at productive code sessions in a stable and mature ecosystem of libraries.

Groovy syntax is a superset of Java syntax. Almost all Java code (with some minor exceptions) is valid Groovy code as well. The Groovy Development Kit, or GDK (www.groovy-lang.org/gdk.html), is an enhanced version of the JDK. And most important of all, Groovy runs on the JVM exactly like Java does!

For those reasons, your journey into the magic world of Groovy should be a pleasant adventure in a different yet familiar land. If Java isn't the only language you speak and you have some experience with other dynamic languages such as Python or Ruby, picking up the basics of Groovy will be an even easier matter.

In a nutshell, Groovy

- Is a dynamic language (Java is static)
- Is a strongly typed language (same as Java)

- Is object-oriented (same as Java)
- Comes with the GDK (Java has the JDK)
- Runs on the JVM (same as Java)
- Favors concise code (Java is considered verbose compared to Groovy)
- Offers its own libraries (for example, web and object relational frameworks)
- Can use any existing Java library as-is (Java can also call Groovy code)
- Has closures (Java 8 has lambda expressions)
- Supports duck typing[1] (Java has strict inheritance)

You'll explore the most important concepts in the next sections and see side-by-side Java and Groovy code where appropriate. I spent a lot of time thinking about which of the Groovy features to showcase in this chapter. I decided to split Groovy features into four categories—essential, useful, advanced, and everything else:

- Sections 2.1 and 2.2 contain knowledge that I consider *essential* for Spock tests.
- Sections 2.3 and 2.4 contain Groovy features that you'll find *useful* in your everyday contact with Spock but aren't otherwise essential.
- Section 2.5 contains some *advanced* Groovy features that you may need in your Spock tests in about 20%[2] of cases.
- Finally, the rest of Groovy features were left out of this book (even if some of them are essential for writing production code and not unit tests). I invite you to look at the official Groovy web page for more details that I haven't included here (and there are a lot).

What is the biggest difficulty while learning Groovy as a Java programmer?

If Java is the only language you know, then the biggest barrier (in my opinion) to learning Groovy is Groovy's dynamic nature. Java provides a direct mapping between a source file and a class. If you know the source code, you know everything there is to know about a class.

In Groovy, a class/object can change during runtime in ways that are impossible in Java. For example, it's possible to add new methods to a Groovy object (that weren't in its source code), delegate existing methods to other objects, or even create completely new classes during runtime out of thin air. If you thought that Java introspection was a fancy trick, Groovy has a complete repertoire of magic tricks that will leave your head spinning with all the possibilities.

Fortunately, these Groovy features aren't essential for unit tests, so you don't need to be overwhelmed with too much information while you're learning Spock. If you decide to use Groovy in production code and not just Spock tests, some of its capabilities will certainly amaze you if you've never worked with a dynamic language before.

---

[1] You can learn more about duck typing on Wikipedia at http://en.wikipedia.org/wiki/Duck_typing.
[2] This number is not scientific in any way.

2.1.1 Groovy as a companion to Java

Your first contact with Groovy is probably with the new syntax. Sometimes when I look at Groovy code, I think the syntax is a subset of Java, because Groovy does away with many redundant Java features. Other times I think that Groovy syntax is a superset of Java because it adds capabilities into existing well-known Java structures.

The fact is that Groovy code is more expressive. I promised in the previous chapter that writing your unit tests in Groovy would result in less code than Java. Now it's time to look at this promise.

How to use the code listings

You can find almost all this book's code listings at https://github.com/kkapelon/java-testing-with-spock. For brevity, the book sometimes points you to the source code (especially for long listings).

I use the Eclipse IDE in my day-to-day work, as shown in the screenshots throughout the book. You can find specific instructions for installing Spock (including the optional Groovy installation) and the Eclipse IDE (plus some information on alternative IDEs) in appendix A.

Let's start with the Groovy basics: automatic creation of getters and setters as well as default visibility modifiers, as shown in the next listing.

Listing 2.1   Groovy class conventions

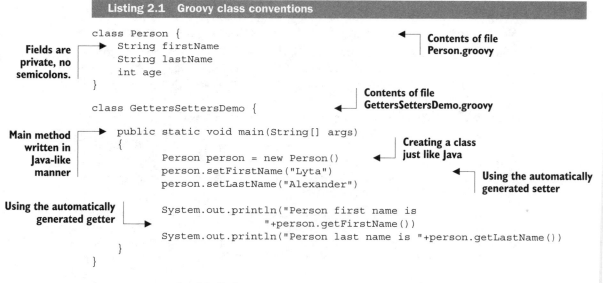

As you can see in this listing,

- Classes are public by default.
- Fields are private by default.

- Getters and setters are automatically created during runtime and thus don't need to be included in the class declarations.
- Semicolons are optional and should only be used in case of multiple statements in the same line.[3]

These are some of the basic conventions that allow Groovy to cut back on the amount of boilerplate. The biggest gain comes from the removal of getters and setters. You're free to define a getter/setter if you need to implement it in a different way than the default. Even though the `Person.groovy` class is written in idiomatic Groovy, the `GettersSettersDemo` is still Java-like.

You can reduce even further the amount of code by using the Groovy way of field accessing, as shown in the following listing.

Listing 2.2 Groovy field conventions

```
class GettersSettersDemo2 {

    public static void main(String[] args)        This still calls
    {                                             person.setFirstName()
        Person person = new Person()              behind the scenes.
        person.firstName = "Marcus"
        person.lastName = "Cole"

        println("Person first name is "+person.firstName)
        println("Person last name is "+person.lastName)
    }
}
```

This still calls person.getFirstName() behind the scenes.

All Groovy objects inherit the println method that outputs messages to console.

As seen in this listing, Groovy not only supports the autogeneration of getters and setters, but also allows using only the name of the field instead of the method. The getter or the setter is implicitly called according to the surrounding context. Finally, as a shortcut to `System.out.println`, Groovy makes available the `println` method to any object.

You're not finished yet. You can further refine the code by completely removing the main method and employing Groovy strings to finally reach the state of idiomatic Groovy shown in the next listing.

Listing 2.3 A complete Groovy script

```
class Person {                      The Person class is defined in the
    String firstName                file GettersSettersDemo3.groovy.
    String lastName
    int age
    String rank
}                                   All code outside the class
                                    is the "main" method.
Person person = new Person()
person.firstName = "Susan "
```

---

[3] I'm personally against writing multiple statements in the same line.

Parentheses are optional for nonvoid methods.

The $ character performs string interpolation as JSP/JSTL does.

```
person.lastName = "Ivanova"
person.rank = "Commander "

println "Person first name is $person.firstName"
println "Person last name is $person.lastName"
println "Person rank is $person.rank"
```

In Groovy, the class name isn't required to match the name of the source file. The main method is also optional. All code that's in the top level of the file is treated as a Groovy script. You can completely discard the helper class and use a single Groovy file that holds both the declaration of the class and its usage.

The last piece of the puzzle is the way `println` is structured. Here I use the interpolation capability of Groovy. The property after the $ is evaluated and inserted directly into the string (which is a Groovy string, as you'll see later in this chapter). Note that this capability is possible on all strings, not only for those that are printed to the console. Also Groovy makes parentheses optional when calling a method with at least one argument.

At this point, you should already see the benefits of Groovy as far as the amount of code is concerned. The following listing shows a complete Spock test that showcases all Groovy features explained so far. It's a trivial test that will verify a custom string representation of the `Person` class.

Listing 2.4   A Spock test using concise Groovy code

Assigning values to fields

Spock assertion

Class defined in the same file as Spock test

Method that will be tested

String interpolation

```
class PersonSpec extends spock.lang.Specification{

    def "Testing getters and setters"() {
        when: "a person has both first name and last name"
        SimplePerson person = new SimplePerson()
        person.firstName = "Susan"
        person.lastName = "Ivanova"

        then: "its title should be surname, name"
        person.createTitle() == "Ivanova, Susan"
    }

}

class SimplePerson {
    String firstName
    String lastName

    String createTitle()
    {
        return "$lastName, $firstName"
    }
}
```

Here you define a single Groovy class that contains the Spock test and the class under test for demonstration purposes. The method that's tested uses string interpolation: the fields are replaced with their value inside the resulting text.

In this Spock test, both the class under test and the unit test itself are written in Groovy. In the next section, you'll see how Spock tests that are written in Groovy can test Java code.

2.1.2 Accessing Java classes in a Groovy script

In the previous section, you got a small taste of how easy it is to write Groovy code compared to the Java verbose approach. The comparison focused on the syntax of the language. This section compares the way these languages interact during runtime.

Groovy comes with its own compiler (called `groovyc`) that reads source Groovy files and creates Java bytecode. That's all you need to know in order to understand how Groovy works with Java. As figure 2.1 shows, Groovy source code is converted to the same bytecode already used by Java files.

Then the bytecode is loaded in the JVM exactly like any other Java class. The JVM doesn't care about the original source of a class. It runs each Java or Groovy class in the same way, offering them both the same capabilities and services.

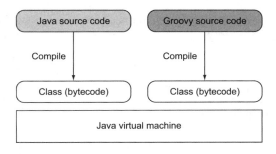

Figure 2.1   Both Java and Groovy compile in Java bytecode.

This is an important point to remember. Even though as a developer you may feel that Groovy is much more flexible than Java or that Groovy does too many things behind the scenes, it all boils down to the same bytecode of the same JVM. There isn't a "Groovy virtual machine." The Groovy runtime is a single Java archive (JAR) file. Adding Groovy capabilities into an existing Java project is as simple as adding the Groovy JAR into the classpath. Normally, your build system takes care of this inclusion, making the process of running both Groovy and Java code in the same project an effortless task.

After all is said and done, creating and accessing Java objects in Groovy code is exactly the same as in Java code.[4] The following listing shows a Spock test (in Groovy); the class under test is written with Java.

> **Listing 2.5   Creating and using a Java class from Groovy**

```
public class MilitaryPerson {          ◄─┐ Class under
    private String firstName;            │ test is Java code.
    private String lastName;
    private String rank;
```

---

[4]   It's also possible to access Groovy code from Java code, but this isn't needed for Spock testing.

```
public String createTitle()
{
        return lastName+", "+firstName +" ("+rank+")";
}

public String getFirstName() {
        return firstName;
}
   ...more getters and setters here..
}
```

Java method that will be tested

Spock test in Groovy

```
class MilitaryPersonSpec extends spock.lang.Specification{

def "Testing getters and setters of a Java class"() {
        when: "a person has both first, last name and rank"
        MilitaryPerson person = new MilitaryPerson()
        person.firstName = "Susan"
        person.lastName = "Ivanova"
        person.setRank("Commander");

        then: "its title should be surname, name (rank)"
        person.createTitle() == "Ivanova, Susan (Commander)"
}

}
```

Creating a Java class in Groovy code

Accessing Java fields using Groovy conventions

Java way for accessing fields is also still available.

Calling a Java method in Groovy code

That's the beauty of Java and Groovy integration. Everything works as expected:

- Groovy code can create Java classes with the new keyword.
- Groovy code can call Java methods.
- Groovy classes can extend Java classes.
- Groovy classes can implement Java interfaces.

It doesn't get any easier than this!

2.1.3   *Declaring variables and methods in Groovy*

One of the first questions every Java developer asks when seeing a Spock test is about the use of the def keyword. This keyword is one of the central concepts of Groovy that characterize it as dynamically typed.[5] You can find all the details in the Groovy specification if you feel adventurous, but for the purpose of writing Spock tests, the meaning of def is "I won't declare a type here; please do it automatically for me."

Thus in Groovy the following listing is possible.

Listing 2.6   Groovy optional typing in variables

Java way of declaring

```
String firstName = "Susan"
def lastName = "Ivanova"
def fullName = "$firstName $lastName"
println fullName
```

Groovy optional typing

fullName is also a string.

_____

[5] Or optionally typed, because Groovy still supports the Java way of explicit types.

As shown in this listing, Groovy supports the usual Java way of declaring things. It also adds its own way, with the type of the object inferred by the context. An alternative way to run Groovy files is using the command line and the `groovy` executable. The listing results in this output:

```
> groovy DefDemo.groovy
Susan Ivanova
```

Is def like Object?

When you're learning Groovy, it's easy to think that `def` is an alias for `Object`. Even though it might seem to work that way, it doesn't, and you can find some big differences with Java if you use `def` in the wrong way in production code. A suggestion that many Groovy developers embrace is to always declare the type of a variable if you know how it will be used. The same suggestion is true for Spock tests, too.

It's interesting to note that the `def` keyword can also be applied in methods, as shown in the following listing. This can trim the size of Spock test methods even further (after omitting the visibility modifier).

Listing 2.7 Groovy optional typing in methods

```
def createName(String firstName,String lastName)          ◄─┐ Using def for
{                                                             │ return type
    return "$lastName, $firstName"
}

def createMilitaryName(def firstName,def lastName, def rank)  ◄─┐ Using def for
{                                                                │ arguments as well
    return "$lastName, $firstName ($rank)"
}

def fullName = createName "Susan","Ivanova"
println fullName                                     Parentheses are optional if at
                                                         least one argument is used.
def militaryName = createMilitaryName "Susan","Ivanova","Commander"
println militaryName
```

This listing outputs the following:

```
> groovy DefDemo2.groovy
Ivanova, Susan
Ivanova, Susan (Commander)
```

Remember that Groovy also supports the Java syntax, so mixing both styles of typing is easy. You can gradually convert to Groovy syntax when you feel comfortable with this notation. Now that you know how the `def` keyword works, you can see in the following listing how it applies to Spock tests.

Listing 2.8   Using dynamic typing in Spock methods

```
class DefDemoSpec extends spock.lang.Specification{

    public void trivialSum1() {                               ◄─── Java way of
        when: "number is one"                                      declaring methods
        int number =1;

        then: "number plus number is two"
        number + number ==2;
    }
    def trivialSum2() {                                       ◄─┐ Groovy way of
        when: "number is one"                                   │ method declaration
        int number = 1

        then: "number plus number is two"
        number + number ==2
    }
    def "Testing a trivial sum"() {                           ◄─┐ Full string for
        when: "number is one"                                   │ method name
        def number =1                                         ◄─┐ Optional typing
                                                                │ of Groovy
        then: "number plus number is two"
        number + number ==2
    }
}
```

Still using semicolons → (points to `int number =1;` / `number + number ==2;`)

Semicolons optional → (points to `int number = 1` / `number + number ==2`)

As shown in this listing, the def keyword is part of standard Groovy. It's also possible to use full strings for method names. The final result is the Spock DSL for unit tests (and not a standard Groovy feature). I've written the same unit test in three possible ways. Even though the syntax is different, they run in exactly the same way as far as Spock is concerned.

2.1.4   *Writing less code with Groovy*

Groovy still has many tricks under its belt for reducing Java code. For example, the return keyword is also optional. The last evaluated statement in a method is the result of the method in that case. In a similar manner, the def keyword in arguments is also optional. The example from listing 2.7 can be further simplified by using these two rules.

Groovy syntax is indeed a refreshing experience when you come from the Java world. Several things that Java considers essential are simply discarded by Groovy, freeing the programmer from boilerplate code that can be automatically created or understood by the runtime.

While learning Spock, you'll find several ways to reduce the amount of code, but this doesn't need to happen right away. My proposal is to follow a gradual learning curve, as shown in figure 2.2.

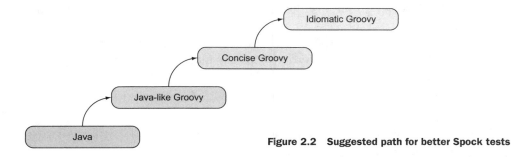

Figure 2.2   Suggested path for better Spock tests

You already know Java. Your first Spock tests should focus on understanding Spock concepts, so continuing to write "Java-like" Groovy is fine. Once you understand how Spock works, you can apply the shortcuts Groovy offers (as illustrated in the previous sections) to reduce the amount of code and simplify your Spock tests. When you're confident using Spock, you can apply core Groovy techniques (for example, closures) to write idiomatic Groovy and get completely out of the Java mindset.

A common mistake of Java programmers is writing Spock tests using example code without understanding which feature is Spock-specific and which is offered by Groovy. This can make your Spock journey harder than it should be, so don't fall into that trap. Make sure that you know how Spock works before applying cool Groovy tricks that dazzle you.

You've seen the basic syntax of Groovy and use of the def keyword. Now it's time to explore Spock asserts.

2.2   *Groovy Power assert as a replacement for JUnit asserts*

With the def mystery solved, the second striking feature of Spock tests is the lack of assert statements for evaluating results. All JUnit tests end with one or more assert statements[6] that define the expected result of the computation. If the expected result doesn't match the actual one, the test will fail. JUnit comes with an extensive API for assert statements, and it's considered a good practice to create your own extensions, dealing with the business domain of your application.

I mentioned in the previous chapter that unlike JUnit, Spock doesn't have assert methods. In this section, you'll see how Spock deals with assertions and how they can help you in case of test failures. I'll also continue with the general theme of this chapter: reducing the amount of code needed when using Groovy instead of Java.

2.2.1   *Understanding how Groovy handles asserts*

In theory, Groovy asserts function in a similar way to Java asserts. They expect a Boolean variable (or an expression that evaluates to a Boolean), evaluate it, and if it's true,

---

6   Not having an assert (or verify) statement is a huge antipattern, because the test never fails.

the assertion passes successfully. Spock runs assertions in the same way. If all assertions pass, the unit test succeeds.

In practice, however, Java is very strict regarding `true`/`false`. Only Boolean variables can be tested for assertions. Groovy takes a more relaxed[7] approach to this, allowing all objects to be treated as Booleans.

Groovy treats all objects[8] as `true` unless

- The object is an empty string.
- The object is a null reference.
- The object is the zero number.
- The object is an empty collection (map, list, array, and so on).
- The object is the `false` Boolean (obviously).
- The object is a regex matcher that fails.

The following listing shows some examples, with Groovy assertions demonstrating the rules of Groovy `true`/`false`.

Listing 2.9   Groovy can convert everything to a Boolean

```
assert true
assert !false

assert true || false            Boolean variables
assert true && !false           work like Java.

String firstName = "Susan"
assert firstName                              A nonempty string is true.

def lastName = "Ivanova"
assert lastName

String empty = ""
assert !empty                   An empty string is false.

Person person = new Person()
assert person;                  A valid reference is true.

Person nullReference = null
assert !nullReference;          A null reference is false.

int answerToEverything = 42     A nonzero number is true.
assert answerToEverything

int zero=0                      A zero number is false.
assert !zero

Object[] array= new Object[3];  A nonempty collection is true.
assert array
```

---

[7] Or error-prone, if you wish. Some of the old C traps are now possible with Groovy as well (but not all).

[8] Closures are also "true."

Creation of regular expression

```
Object[] emptyArray= new Object[0];          ◄──── An empty collection is false.
assert !emptyArray

Pattern myRegex = ~/needle/
assert myRegex.matcher("needle in haystack")        Regex is true if it
assert !myRegex.matcher("Wrong haystack")           matches at least once.

println "Script has finished because all asserts pass"
```

If you run the preceding example, all asserts evaluate to true, and the final line is printed in the console.

GROOVY TRUTH

The way Groovy handles `true/false` statements (called *Groovy truth* in Groovy parlance) can be used in Spock to trim the assert statement into a shorter form instead of converting it explicitly to Boolean variables.

> **Fun with Groovy truth**
>
> This is valid Groovy code: `boolean flag = -45`. Even though this line doesn't even compile in Java, in Groovy the number –45 is a nonzero number, and therefore the variable flag is now `true`.

The next listing presents a Spock example with both approaches, using both an explicit Boolean evaluation (Java) and automatic "casting" to `true/false` (Groovy). The class under test is a trivial string tokenizer that counts word occurrences.

Listing 2.10   Groovy truth used in Spock tests

```
class GroovyTruthSpec extends spock.lang.Specification{

    def "demo for Groovy truth"() {                        Class under test
        when: "a line of text is processed"               is a Java class.
        WordDetector wordDetector = new WordDetector();  ◄──
        wordDetector.parseText("Understanding is a three edged sword:
                        your side, their side, and the truth");

        then: "word frequency should be correct"
        wordDetector.wordsFound() > 0                      Using Java-like asserts with
        wordDetector.duplicatesFound().size() > 0          explicit conversion to Boolean

        wordDetector.wordsFound()                  ◄── Any positive number is
        wordDetector.duplicatesFound()                 automatically seen as true.
    }
}
```

Calling a Java method

Any nonempty collection is automatically seen as true.

As an exercise, locate examples in chapter 1 that don't use Groovy truth rules in the assert statements and rewrite them now that you know that Groovy can convert everything to a Boolean variable.[9]

---

[9] Groovy strings also get an additional `toBoolean()` method that treats only true, y, and 1 as true.

2.2.2   Using Groovy assertions in Spock tests

In the previous section, you saw how to use Groovy truth to simplify your assert statements. I admit that this is another feature that looks mainly like sugarcoating, and you might not be impressed by the amount of code reduced. This is understandable, but the advantage of Groovy assertions isn't the application of Groovy truth rules.

The killer feature of Groovy (and therefore Spock) is the information it gives when an assert fails. You've seen some hints of this in chapter 1, using assertions that expect numbers (code listings 1.2 and 1.3). In complex expressions, Groovy shows all intermediate results. Figure 2.3 shows the Eclipse JUnit window in both cases, but you get similar output if you run your unit tests in the command line or any other compatible tool with JUnit.

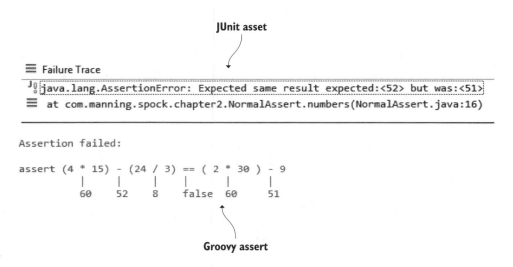

Figure 2.3   Groovy assert shows much more information than a JUnit assert.

The magic of this feature is that it works with all objects and not just primitives. Groovy has no such distinction: everything is an object as far as Groovy is concerned.

What == means in Groovy

In Groovy, the `==` operator isn't testing identity like Java. It calls the `equals()` method of the object. Identity in Groovy is handled by the `is` keyword. Thus `object1.is(object2)` is the Groovy way of testing identity. You should be aware of this difference if you use objects in both sides of the assert statement. (If you perform only simple assertions with scalar values—as you should—then this difference doesn't matter.)

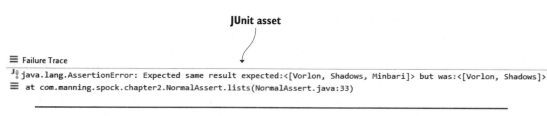

```
≡ Failure Trace
J⁰₈ java.lang.AssertionError: Expected same result expected:<[Vorlon, Shadows, Minbari]> but was:<[Vorlon, Shadows]>
≡ at com.manning.spock.chapter2.NormalAssert.lists(NormalAssert.java:33)
```

```
Caught: Assertion failed:

assert all.subList(0, all.indexOf("Humans")) == firstOnes
       |   |               |   |                |  |
       |   |               |   3                |  [Vorlon, Shadows]
       |   |               |                    false
       |   |               [Vorlon, Shadows, Minbari, Humans, Drazi]
       |   [Vorlon, Shadows, Minbari]
       [Vorlon, Shadows, Minbari, Humans, Drazi]
```

Figure 2.4 Groovy assert with lists compared to JUnit assert

Figure 2.4 is a more complex example of a failed Groovy assert with lists. Again notice how Groovy shows all intermediate operations, whereas JUnit reports only the final result.

A Groovy Power assert works for your own objects as well, as shown in figure 2.5.

This Spock feature is crucial for continuous delivery environments. As a developer, you can understand exactly what goes wrong when a test fails. A well-configured build server keeps all the results from unit tests and provides reports for the failed ones.

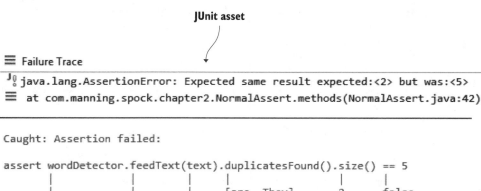

```
≡ Failure Trace
J⁰₈ java.lang.AssertionError: Expected same result expected:<2> but was:<5>
≡ at com.manning.spock.chapter2.NormalAssert.methods(NormalAssert.java:42)
```

```
Caught: Assertion failed:

assert wordDetector.feedText(text).duplicatesFound().size() == 5
       |                    |       |                |      |   |
       |                    |       |       [are, They]     2   false
       |                    |       They are alone. They are a dying race.
       |                    com.manning.spock.chapter2.WordDetector@552ee43b
       com.manning.spock.chapter2.WordDetector@552ee43b
```

Figure 2.5 Groovy assert with the Java class shown in listing 2.10

Because Groovy (and by extension Spock) shows you the running context, you can, in several cases, fix the bug right away instead of spending time with a debugger in order to reproduce it. For enterprise environments in which running an integration test is a lengthy process, this extra context for failing tests is a time-saver that can easily persuade any Java developer to switch from JUnit.

I'll show you how to further enhance the output of Groovy Power asserts in chapter 4. For now, I'll continue with some useful Groovy features that have helped me in several Spock tests.

2.3   *Groovy features useful to Spock tests*

Now you have all the essential knowledge needed in order to write your own Spock assertions. The rest of this chapter continues with the theme of reducing unit test code size with the expressiveness provided by Groovy compared to Java. All the following techniques are optional, and you can still use normal Java code in your Spock tests if your organization needs a more gradual change. Each application is different, so it's hard to predict all the ways that Groovy can help you with unit tests. The following selection is my personal preference.

2.3.1   *Using map-based constructors*

If there's one feature of Groovy that I adore, it's object creation. Most unit tests create new classes either as test data or as services or helper classes used by the class under test. In a large Java application, a lot of statements are wasted creating such objects. The next listing presents a Java example of testing a class that takes as its argument a list of persons.

Listing 2.11   JUnit test with multiple object creation statements

```
Employee trainee = new Employee();                          ◄──  Java object that will be
trainee.setAge(22);                                              used as test input
trainee.setFirstName("Alice");
trainee.setLastName("Olson");           Filling of fields one by one
trainee.setInTraining(true);

                                                           Second Java object
Employee seasoned = new Employee();                     ◄── for test input
seasoned.setAge(45);
seasoned.setFirstName("Alex");          Filling of different
seasoned.setMiddleName("Jones");        fields one by one
seasoned.setLastName("Corwin");

List<Employee> people = Arrays.asList(trainee,seasoned);
                                                               Class under
Department department = new Department();               ◄──   test
department.assign(people);           ◄──── Test data is used.
[...rest of test]
```

Java needs more than 10 statements to create the two objects that will be used for test input. This boilerplate code is too noisy when compared with the code that tests the `Department` class.

EASY OBJECT CREATION WITH GROOVY CONSTRUCTORS

This is a well-known problem for Java developers. Sometimes special constructors are created for business domain objects to allow for easy testing. I consider this an antipattern. This technique not only shifts verbosity from unit tests to core code, but also has its own shortcomings in the case of multiple constructors. In the preceding example, the `Employee` class would be polluted with at least two constructors (one that sets the trainee flag and one that ignores it).

Groovy comes to the rescue! Map-based constructors are autogenerated for your Java objects, allowing your Spock tests to initialize any number of fields as well, as shown in the following listing.

Listing 2.12 Spock test with map-based constructors

```
when:
Employee trainee = new                          Java object created with
    Employee(age:22,firstName:"Alice",lastName:"Olson",inTraining:true)   ◀── specific field values
Employee seasoned = new
    Employee(middleName:"Jones",lastName:"Corwin",age:45,firstName:"Alex")

List<Employee> people = Arrays.asList(trainee,seasoned)

Department department = new Department()        ◀── Class under test
department.assign(people)                        ◀── Test data is used.
[...rest of test]
```

Another Java object with different field values → (points to `Employee seasoned = new`)

Without changing a single line of Java code in the `Employee` class file, I've used the map-based constructors, whereby each field is identified by name and the respective value is appended after the semicolon character. Notice that the order of the fields and the set of the fields are completely arbitrary. With this technique,[10] you can create a Java object with all possible combinations of its fields in any order that you like!

2.3.2 Using maps and lists in Groovy

The syntax shown in the previous section isn't specific to constructors. This is the Groovy way of initializing a map. You can use it for creating a map in a single statement. The following listing presents an example.

Listing 2.13 Groovy versus Java maps

```
Map<String,Integer> wordCounts = new HashMap<>();
wordCounts.put("Hello",1);                       Manually filling a
wordCounts.put("Java",1);                         map (Java way)
wordCounts.put("World",2);

Map<String,Integer> wordCounts2 = ["Hello":1,"Groovy":1,"World":2]
```

Groovy can create and initialize a map. → (points to `Map<String,Integer> wordCounts2`)

---

[10] Groovy supports even-more-concise constructors. They sacrifice clarity, so I refrain from showing them here.

You can create any kind of map like these, even those with keys and values that are classes on their own. For Groovy, it makes no difference (see the following listing).

Listing 2.14 Groovy maps with nonscalar keys and values

```
Employee person1 = new
    Employee(firstName:"Alice",lastName:"Olson",age:30)        Creating a Java
Employee person2 = new                                          object by using
    Employee(firstName:"Jones",lastName:"Corwin",age:45)        map-based
                                                                constructors
Address address1 = new Address(street:"Marley",number:25)
Address address2 = new Address(street:"Barnam",number:7)

Map<Employee,Address> staffAddresses = new HashMap<>();
staffAddresses.put(person1, address1);
staffAddresses.put(person2, address2);          Filling a map manually (the Java way)

Map<Employee,Address> staffAddresses2 =              Creating and initializing
    [(person1):address1,(person2):address2]          a map (the Groovy way)
```

As shown in listing 2.13, when classes are used for the keys of the map, you need to use extra parentheses. If you don't, the classes are assumed to be strings. Also, this concise Groovy syntax creates by default a `LinkedHashMap`.

In a similar way to maps, Groovy supports a concise syntax for lists. If you've ever wondered why it's so easy to create an array in Java in a single statement but not a list, you'll be happy to discover that Groovy has you covered. The following listing shows the comparison between Groovy and Java lists.

Listing 2.15 Groovy versus Java lists

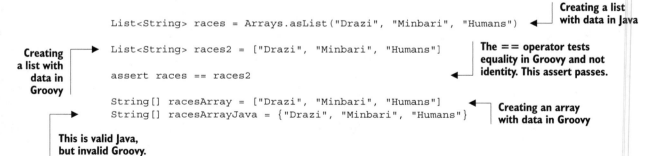

```
                                                          Creating a list
                                                          with data in Java
List<String> races = Arrays.asList("Drazi", "Minbari", "Humans")

Creating      List<String> races2 = ["Drazi", "Minbari", "Humans"]      The == operator tests
a list with                                                             equality in Groovy and not
data in       assert races == races2                                    identity. This assert passes.
Groovy
              String[] racesArray = ["Drazi", "Minbari", "Humans"]      Creating an array
              String[] racesArrayJava = {"Drazi", "Minbari", "Humans"}  with data in Groovy

This is valid Java,
but invalid Groovy.
```

Because the syntax of arrays and lists is similar in Groovy, you might find yourself using arrays less and less as you gain experience with Groovy. Notice that the usual way of declaring arrays in Java is one of the few cases where valid Java is invalid Groovy. If you try to create an array in Groovy by using the Java notation, you'll get an error, because Groovy uses the same syntax for closures, as you'll see later in this chapter.

Using the knowledge you've gained from the preceding sections, you can completely rewrite the JUnit test from listing 2.11, as the following listing shows.

Listing 2.16 Creating Groovy lists and maps in test code

```
List<Employee> people = [
    new Employee(age:22,firstName:"Alice",lastName:"Olson",
                    inTraining:true),
    new Employee(middleName:"Jones",lastName:"Corwin",age:45,
                    firstName:"Alex")
                ]

Department department = new Department()
department.assign(people)
[...rest of test]
```

Groovy initialization of a list, using map-based constructor objects

Java class under test

Use of test data

By following Groovy conventions, I've replaced 11 Java statements with 1. The unit test is much more readable because it's clearly split as far as test data creation and test data usage are concerned.

ACCESSING LISTS IN GROOVY BY USING ARRAY INDEX NOTATION

So far, I've demonstrated only how maps and lists are initialized. Let's see how Groovy improves their usage as well, as shown in the next listing.

Listing 2.17 Using Groovy lists

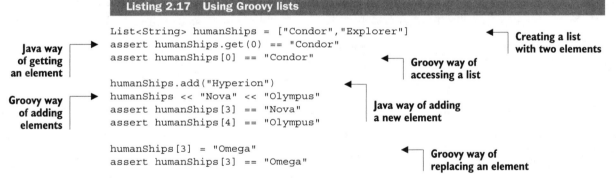

```
List<String> humanShips = ["Condor","Explorer"]
assert humanShips.get(0) == "Condor"
assert humanShips[0] == "Condor"

humanShips.add("Hyperion")
humanShips << "Nova" << "Olympus"
assert humanShips[3] == "Nova"
assert humanShips[4] == "Olympus"

humanShips[3] = "Omega"
assert humanShips[3] == "Omega"
```

Java way of getting an element

Groovy way of adding elements

Creating a list with two elements

Groovy way of accessing a list

Java way of adding a new element

Groovy way of replacing an element

Notice how writing and reading to a list uses the same syntax, and only the context defines the exact operation. Again, this syntax is optional, and you're free to use the Java way of doing things even in Spock tests.

Groovy offers the same array-like syntax for maps as well, as shown in the following listing.

Listing 2.18 Using Groovy maps

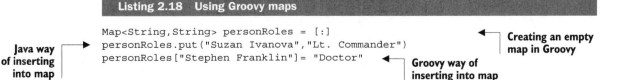

```
Map<String,String> personRoles = [:]
personRoles.put("Suzan Ivanova","Lt. Commander")
personRoles["Stephen Franklin"]= "Doctor"
```

Java way of inserting into map

Creating an empty map in Groovy

Groovy way of inserting into map

Groovy way of accessing map

```
assert personRoles.get("Suzan Ivanova") == "Lt. Commander"
assert personRoles["Stephen Franklin"] == "Doctor"

personRoles["Suzan Ivanova"]= "Commander"
assert personRoles["Suzan Ivanova"] == "Commander"
```

◄── **Java way of accessing map**

◄── **Groovy way of replacing element**

Lists and maps are one of the many areas where Groovy augments existing Java collections. Groovy comes with its own GDK that sits on top of the existing JDK. You should spend some time exploring the GDK according to your own unit tests and discovering more ways to reduce your existing Java code.

So far, you've seen how Groovy enhances classes, fields, and collections. Let's see how Groovy strings compare to Java strings.

2.3.3   *Interpolating text with Groovy strings*

I demonstrated Groovy strings (`GStrings`) at the beginning of this chapter by taking a single Java class and converting it to idiomatic Groovy in a gradual way. At the most basic level, Groovy strings allow for quick text templates of object properties, but they also can handle full expressions, as shown in the following listing.

Listing 2.19   Using Groovy strings

```
SimpleDepartment sales =
    new SimpleDepartment(name:"Sales",location:"block C")
SimpleEmployee employee =
    new SimpleEmployee(fullName:"Andrew Collins",age:37,department:sales)

System.out.println("Age is "+employee.getAge())
println "Age is $employee.age"

System.out.println("Department location
    is at "+employee.getDepartment().getLocation())
println "Department location is at $employee.department.location"

println "Person is adult ${employee.age > 18}"
println "Amount in dollars is \$300"
println 'Person is adult ${employee.age > 18}'
```

◄── **Creating Java objects with map-based constructors**

Groovy way of accessing fields ──►

◄── **Java way of accessing fields**

Using {} for full expressions ──►

Escaping the $ character ───┘

◄── **Disabling evaluation altogether with single quotes**

When run, this code prints the following:

```
>groovy GroovyStrings.groovy
Age is 37
Age is 37
Department location is at block C
Department location is at block C
Person is adult true
Amount in dollars is $300
Person is adult ${employee.age > 18}
```

Groovy string interpolation is certainly powerful, but for unit tests, their multiline capability is more interesting. Similar to other scripting languages, Groovy allows you to split a big string with newlines, as shown in the next listing.

Listing 2.20 Using Groovy multiline strings

```
def "Another demo for Groovy multiline strings"() {
    when: "a paragraph is processed"
    String input = '''I want you to know you were right. I didn't want \
        to admit that. Just pride I guess. You get my age, you \
        get kinda set in your ways. It had to be \
        done. Don't blame yourself for what happened later.'''
    WordDetector wordDetector = new WordDetector();
    wordDetector.parseText(input);

    then: "word count should be correct"
    wordDetector.wordsFound() == 34
}
```

Creation of a multiline string ▶

◀ **Using the multiline string**

This is a great feature for unit tests that require text input of three to four lines that can be embedded directly on the source file. Multiline strings also support text interpolation if you use double quotes instead of single, but inside unit tests, it's clearer if they're pure text (without text interpolation). For more lines of text, I also advise using a separate text file, as demonstrated in the next section.

2.4   Reading a test dataset from an external source

One of the challenges I face when creating a new unit test (especially in test-driven development, as the test is created before the implementation code) is finding correct test input. For basic unit tests in which only a single class is tested, you might get away with trivial data created on the spot.

For integration tests, however, which test multiple code modules, your selection of test data needs more thought. Once you have enough tests for the happy paths of your code, it's time to examine all corner cases and strange scenarios. Creating effective test data is a separate skill of its own, but a good source of such data can be found on an existing running system. Often, test data can also be obtained from issues reported by the users of the software. These types of data are as real as they get, so they're excellent candidates for your unit tests.

Unfortunately, useful test data is often trapped in the transport medium (for example, XML files) that must be processed before they can be used directly in a unit test. Groovy comes with excellent facilities for extracting test data from external files, and you should take advantage of these techniques in your Spock tests. Using the Java approach will also work, but again in a much more verbose way.

2.4.1   Reading a text file

Reading a text file in Java usually requires a basic understanding of buffered readers or any other Java file API that was added with each new Java version.[11] Groovy does away with all the unneeded craft and allows you to read a file in the simplest way possible:

```
String testInput = new File("src/test/resources/quotes.txt").text
```

---

[11] Or coming from an external library such as Apache Commons.

A normal file is opened. Groovy adds the `.getText()` method that reads its text. You could also specify the encoding if it's not the default. This simplicity is handy because it can be used straight in a Spock test. The following listing shows an example.

Listing 2.21 Reading test data from a file in a Spock test

```
def "demo for reading a text file"() {
    when: "a paragraph is processed"
    WordDetector wordDetector = new WordDetector();
    String inputText = new File("src/test/resources/quotes.txt").text
    wordDetector.parseText(inputText);

    then: "word frequency should be correct"
    wordDetector.wordsFound() == 78
}

def "demo for reading a text file line by line"() {
    when: "a paragraph is processed"
    List<String> inputText = new
    File("src/test/resources/quotes.txt").readLines()
    WordDetector wordDetector = new WordDetector();
    for(String line:inputText)
    {
        wordDetector.feedText(line)
    }

    then: "word count should be correct"
    wordDetector.wordsFound() == 78
}
```

Reading the whole text file → (points to `String inputText = new File(...)`)

Reading a file line by line ← (points to `File("src/test/resources/quotes.txt").readLines()`)

Notice the expressive code. It has no boilerplate for autoclosing streams or anything like that. I'll show you more examples of file reading in chapter 5, where Groovy code is both shorter and easier to understand than the Java way. In chapter 5, I'll show you data-driven Spock tests in which the same test is evaluated for multiple (similar) sets of input test data.

2.4.2 Reading an XML file

XML is the lingua franca of large enterprise applications. One of the original marketing points of Java was the handling of XML files. Business web services usually produce some sort of XML dialect, and several custom file formats are XML files under the hood. As with Java, Groovy supports several ways, but explaining them all is outside the scope of this chapter.

This section demonstrates the `XmlSlurper` way of reading XML files with Groovy. You can use this technique either when you want to read test data from an XML file, or when your Java class writes XML and you want to quickly verify its correctness.[12]

---

[12] For more-complex XML verification cases, you can also use a dedicated XML diff library such as XMLUnit.

Let's assume that your XML file is the following:

```
<staff>
    <department name="sales">
            <employee>
                    <firstName>Orlando</firstName>
                    <lastName>Boren</lastName>
                    <age>24</age>
            </employee>
            <employee>
                    <firstName>Diana</firstName>
                    <lastName>Colgan</lastName>
                    <age>28</age>
            </employee>
    </department>
</staff>
```

The next listing provides the respective Groovy code.

Listing 2.22   Reading XML in Groovy

```
def xmlRoot = new
    XmlSlurper().parse('src/main/resources/employee-data.xml')    ◄─── Creating the XmlSlurper object
assert xmlRoot.department.size() ==1                              ◄───
assert xmlRoot.department.@name =="sales"                              Checking the number
assert xmlRoot.department.employee.size() ==2                     ◄─── of children XML nodes
assert xmlRoot.department.employee[0].firstName =="Orlando"  ◄───
assert xmlRoot.department.employee[0].lastName =="Boren"          Accessing XML content
assert xmlRoot.department.employee[0].age ==24                   of the first child
assert xmlRoot.department.employee[1].firstName =="Diana"   ◄───
assert xmlRoot.department.employee[1].lastName =="Colgan"         Accessing XML content
assert xmlRoot.department.employee[1].age ==28                   of the second child
```

Accessing an XML property → (points to `assert xmlRoot.department.@name =="sales"`)

Here you can see the expressive Groovy power in all its glory. Reading the XML file is a single line. Then you use an XPath-like expression to retrieve XML content. I won't even bother to write the Java code for the same example. XML reading (and writing) in Java has always contained boilerplate code, which is taken for granted by Java developers. Groovy discards all this and keeps only the substance.

2.4.3   *Reading a JSON file*

Groovy reads JavaScript Object Notation (JSON) in a similar way to how it reads XML. XML might be dominant in legacy enterprise applications, but newer web services tend to use JSON. Groovy covers them both with ease.

Let's assume that your JSON file is the following:

```
{
  "staff": {
    "department": {
      "name": "sales",
      "employee": [
```

```
    {
      "firstName": "Orlando",
      "lastName": "Boren",
      "age": "24"
    },
    {
      "firstName": "Diana",
      "lastName": "Colgan",
      "age": "28"
    }
  ]
    }
  }
}
```

The next listing presents the respective Groovy code (almost the same as the XML one).

Listing 2.23   Reading JSON in Groovy

```
def jsonRoot =                                              ◀──  Creating the
    new JsonSlurper().parse(new                                  JsonSlurper object
            File('src/main/resources/employee-data.json'))
assert jsonRoot.staff.department.name =="sales"
assert jsonRoot.staff.department.employee.size() ==2
assert jsonRoot.staff.department.employee[0].firstName =="Orlando"   ◀──  Accessing
assert jsonRoot.staff.department.employee[0].lastName =="Boren"           first element
assert jsonRoot.staff.department.employee[0].age =="24"                   of the array
assert jsonRoot.staff.department.employee[1].firstName =="Diana"
assert jsonRoot.staff.department.employee[1].lastName =="Colgan"
assert jsonRoot.staff.department.employee[1].age =="28"
```

Accessing
Json field

Checking
the size of
JSon array

Accessing
second
element of
the array

With Groovy, obtaining test data from JSON is easy. The syntax is even simpler than XML in some ways.

2.5   *Advanced Groovy features useful to testing*

I hope that this chapter serves as a gentle introduction to Groovy, and that if you were scared by the syntax of Spock tests in chapter 1, you're now more confident about how things work. In several ways, Groovy simplifies Java code by leaving only the gist and discarding the bloat.

Explaining all the things Groovy can do in a single chapter is impossible. Groovy has several advanced constructs for core programming that blow away any Java code you've already seen. This last section presents some advanced concepts that you might use in your Spock tests.

Don't be alarmed if the code shown is more complex than the previous examples. You can skip this part and come back again when you have more experience with Groovy and become comfortable with Spock tests. That being said, the following techniques are in no way essential to Spock tests. They have their uses at times, but you should always make sure that your unit tests aren't overengineered.

Don't fall into the trap of using cool Groovy tricks in Spock tests to impress your Java friends! Keep Spock tests simple and understandable.

2.5.1 *Using Groovy closures*

The official Groovy book (*Groovy in Action*) assigns a whole chapter to explain closures, so I'm not going to try to do the same in these paragraphs. You might already know closures from other programming languages.[13] If not, spend some time researching them because they're universally helpful (even outside the context of Groovy).

Closures are in many ways similar to methods. Unlike Java methods, they can be passed around as arguments to other methods or become partially evaluated instead of called directly. Java 8 also comes with lambda expressions, which serve as a stepping stone to functional programming concepts. If you've already worked with Java 8, Groovy closures will come naturally to you.

Closures in Groovy are denoted by the -> character and are contained in {}. The following listing presents some examples.

Listing 2.24 Groovy closures

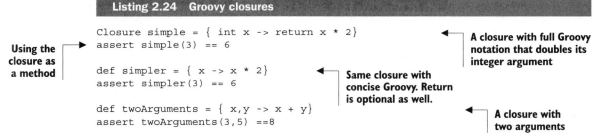

Using the closure as a method

```
Closure simple = { int x -> return x * 2}
assert simple(3) == 6

def simpler = { x -> x * 2 }
assert simpler(3) == 6

def twoArguments = { x,y -> x + y}
assert twoArguments(3,5) ==8
```

A closure with full Groovy notation that doubles its integer argument

Same closure with concise Groovy. Return is optional as well.

A closure with two arguments

Closures are the Swiss army knife of Groovy. They're used almost everywhere, and it's hard to deal with Groovy code without stumbling upon them. Prior to Java 8, they were one of the main advantages of Groovy over Java, and even after Java 8, they still offer great value and simplicity. Closures are so powerful in Groovy that you can use them directly to implement interfaces or as exit points in switch statements.

The Groovy GDK augments the existing JDK with several new methods that accept closures for arguments. For example, a handy Groovy method for unit testing is the every() method available in collections. Assume that you have a Java class that gets a list of image names from a text file and returns only those that end in a specific file extension. Closures can be employed in the Groovy assert, as shown in the next listing.

Listing 2.25 Using Groovy closures in Spock tests

Creation of Java class under test

```
def "Testing Jpeg files"() {
    when: "only jpeg files are selected from a list of filenames"
    FileExtensionFilter myFilter = new FileExtensionFilter()
```

---

[13] You may have seen function pointers, function references, higher-order methods, and code blocks in other languages. They're not, strictly speaking, the same thing as closures, but the main concepts are similar.

List that will be passed to class under test →

```
myFilter.addValidExtension("jpeg")
myFilter.addValidExtension("jpg")
```
Setup file extensions that will be accepted

```
List<String> testInput = ["image1.jpg","image2.png","image3.jpeg",
    "image4.gif","image5.jpg","image6.tiff"]
```

Using a closure to test each element of the list →

```
List<String> result = myFilter.filterFileNames(testInput)
```
← **Result of method call is another list.**

```
    then: "result should not contain other types"
    result.every{ filename -> filename.endsWith("jpeg") ||
        filename.endsWith("jpg")}
}
```

In this Spock test, the assertion is a single line because all elements of the list are checked one by one automatically by the closure. The closure takes as an argument a string and returns `true` if the string ends in `jpg` (using both three- and four-letter notations).

Other methods useful to unit tests (apart from `every()` shown in the preceding listing) are as follows:

- `any(closure)`—Returns `true` if at least one element satisfies closure
- `find(closure)`—Finds the first element that satisfies closure
- `findAll(closure)`—Finds all elements that satisfy closure

You should consult the Groovy official documentation (www.groovy-lang.org/gdk.html) for more details.

2.5.2   *Creating test input with ObjectGraphBuilders*

One of the arguments against unit tests (and integration tests, in particular) is the effort required to come up with "real" test data. In a complex business application, the data that's moved around is rarely a single object. Usually it's a collection of objects, a tree structure, a graph, or any other complex structure.

This makes writing integration tests a lengthy process because about 80% of the code can be consumed by creating the test input for the class under test. Test input code generation is one of the first candidates for code reuse inside unit tests. In sufficiently large enterprise projects, test input generation might need a separate code module of its own, outside the production code.

Groovy to the rescue! Groovy comes with a set of builders that allow you to create test data by using a fancy DSL. Instead of creating the data manually, you declare the final result. As an example, assume that your domain contains the classes in the following listing.

Listing 2.26   Domain classes in Java

```
public class AssetInventory {
    private List<Ship> ships = new ArrayList<>();
    [...getters and setters here...]
}
```
← **Lists are already initialized**

```java
public class Ship {
    private String name;
    private List<CrewMember> crewMembers = new ArrayList<>();
    private String destination;
    private List<Cargo> cargos= new ArrayList<>();
[...getters and setters here...]
}

public class CrewMember {
    private String firstName;
    private String lastName;
    private int age;
[...getters and setters here...]
}
public class Cargo {
    private String type;
    private CargoOrder cargoOrder;      ◄──  Name of fields is the
    private float tons;                       same as class name.
[...getters and setters here...]
}
public class CargoOrder {
    private String buyer;
    private String city;
    private BigDecimal price;
[...getters and setters here...]
}
```

This is a typical business domain. If you look closely enough, you'll see that it follows certain rules:

- Each child field has the same name of the class (CargoOrder cargoOrder).
- Each list is already initialized.
- Each list field has the plural name of its class (Ship > ships).

Because of these rules, it's possible to create a deep hierarchy of this domain by using an ObjectGraphBuilder, as shown in the next listing.

Listing 2.27 Using a Groovy builder for quick object creation

```
Creating     ──► ObjectGraphBuilder builder = new ObjectGraphBuilder()
the builder      builder.classNameResolver = "com.manning.spock.chapter2.assets"  ◄──  Instructing the
                                                                                       builder of that
Using the    ──► AssetInventory shipRegistry = builder.assetInventory() {              domain Java package
builder for          ship ( name: "Sea Spirit", destination:"Chiba") {
the top-level            crewMember(firstName:"Michael", lastName:"Curiel",age:43)
object                   crewMember(firstName:"Sean", lastName:"Parker",age:28)      ◄──
                         crewMember(firstName:"Lillian ", lastName:"Zimmerman",age:32)
                         cargo(type:"Cotton", tons:5.4) {
Children node    ──►         cargoOrder ( buyer: "Rei                                 Map-based
automatically                    Hosokawa",city:"Yokohama",price:34000)              constructors
created and              }
attached to parent       cargo(type:"Olive Oil", tons:3.0) {
                             cargoOrder ( buyer: "Hirokumi
                                 Kasaya",city:"Kobe",price:27000)
```

```
                }
        }
        ship ( name: "Calypso I", destination:"Bristol") {
                crewMember(firstName:"Eric", lastName:"Folkes",age:35)
                crewMember(firstName:"Louis", lastName:"Lessard",age:22)
                cargo(type:"Oranges", tons:2.4) {
                        cargoOrder ( buyer: "Gregory
                                Schmidt",city:"Manchester",price:62000)
                }
        }
        ship ( name: "Desert Glory", destination:"Los Angeles")
        {
                crewMember(firstName:"Michelle", lastName:"Kindred",age:38)
                crewMember(firstName:"Kathy", lastName:"Parker",age:21)
                cargo(type:"Timber", tons:4.8) {
                        cargoOrder ( buyer: "Carolyn
                        Cox",city:"Sacramento",price:18000)
                }
        }
}
assert shipRegistry.ships.size == 3
assert shipRegistry.ships[0].name == "Sea Spirit"
assert shipRegistry.ships[1].crewMembers.size == 2
assert shipRegistry.ships[1].crewMembers[0].firstName == "Eric"
assert shipRegistry.ships[2].cargos[0].type=="Timber"
assert shipRegistry.ships[2].cargos[0].cargoOrder.city=="Sacramento"
```

This creates a ship registry with three ships, seven people, and four cargo orders, all in about 30 lines of Groovy code. Creating the same tree with Java code would need more than 120 lines of code (for brevity, you can find the code in the source of this book). In this case, Groovy reduces code lines by 75%.

The other important point is the visual overview of the tree structure. Because the ObjectGraphBuilder offers a declarative DSL for the object creation, you can get an overview of the tree structure by looking at the code.

If your domain classes don't follow the preceding rules, you can either change them (easiest) or inject the ObjectBuilder with custom resolvers to override default behavior. Consult the official Groovy documentation for examples with custom resolvers. By default, the ObjectGraphBuilder will treat as plural (for collections) the class name plus *s* (*ship* becomes *ships*). It also supports special cases with words that end in *y* (*daisy* becomes *daisies*, *army* becomes *armies*, and so forth).

2.5.3 *Creating test input with Expando*

Spock includes comprehensive mocking and stubbing capabilities, as you'll see in chapter 6. For simple cases, you can also get away with using vanilla Groovy. Groovy shines when it comes to dynamic object creation.

As a final example of Groovy power, I'll demonstrate how Groovy can create objects on the spot. Assume that you have an interface of this DAO:

```
public interface AddressDao {
    Address load(Long id);
}
```

You also have a business service that uses this DAO as follows:

```
public class Stamper {
    private final AddressDao addressDao;

    public Stamper(AddressDao addressDao)
    {
            this.addressDao = addressDao;
    }

    public boolean isValid(Long addressID)
    {
            Address address = addressDao.load(addressID);
            return address.getStreet()!= null &&
                        address.getPostCode()!= null;
    }
}
```

This business service checks `Address` objects (a POJO) and considers them valid if they have both a street and a postal code. You want to write a Spock test for this service. Of course, you could mock the `AddressDao`, as you'll see in chapter 6. But with Groovy, you can dynamically create an object that mimics this service, as shown in the following listing.

Listing 2.28 Using Expando to mock interfaces

```
def "Testing invalid address detection"() {
    when: "an address does not have a postcode"
    Address address = new Address(country:"Greece",number:23)      ◀── Creating the
                                                                        test data
    def dummyAddressDao = new Expando()            ◀── Creating the load
    dummyAddressDao.load = { return address}           method dynamically

    Stamper stamper = new Stamper(dummyAddressDao as AddressDao)   ◀──

    then: "this address is rejected"                       Using the Groovy
    !stamper.isValid(1)                                    dynamic object in place
}                                                          of the Java interface

def "Testing invalid and valid address detection"() {
    when: "two different addresses are checked"
    Address invalidAddress = new Address(country:"Greece",number:23)   Covers
    Address validAddress = new Address(country:"Greece",              both cases
            number:23,street:"Argous", postCode:"4534")

    def dummyAddressDao = new Expando()
    dummyAddressDao.load = { id -> return                ◀── Using the closure argument
            id==2?validAddress:invalidAddress}               to return either test input

    Stamper stamper = new Stamper(dummyAddressDao as AddressDao)

    then: "Only the address with street and postcode is accepted"
    !stamper.isValid(1)
    stamper.isValid(2)
}
```

Creating the empty Groovy dynamic object

Tricking the class under test to use the Expando— the argument is irrelevant.

Call class under test— argument is used in Expando closure.

The magic line here is the one with the as keyword. This keyword performs casting in Groovy but in a much more powerful way than Java. The Expando class has no common inheritance with the AddressDao, yet it can still work as one because of duck typing (both objects have a load() method, and that's enough for Groovy).

Although this is a common use of Expando classes, they have several other uses that you might find interesting. The combination of duck typing and dynamic object creation will certainly amaze you.[14] The next listing presents another example where I use an Expando for integer generation (which could be used as test data in a Spock test).

Listing 2.29   Using a Groovy Expando as test-data generator

Creating field that will hold next number

Using the Expando in the place of an iterator

Creating empty Groovy dynamic object

Creating field that will hold max value returned

Imitation of iterator interface method

Adding custom method not defined in iterator interface

Calling the custom method to change the state of the iterator

Using the Expando after resetting it

```
Expando smartIterator = new Expando()
smartIterator.counter = 0;
smartIterator.limit = 4;
smartIterator.hasNext = { return counter < limit}
smartIterator.next = {return counter++}
smartIterator.restartFrom = {from->counter = from}

for(Integer number:smartIterator as Iterator<Integer>)
{
    println "Next number is $number"
}

println "Reset smart iterator"
smartIterator.restartFrom(2)#

for(Integer number:smartIterator as Iterator<Integer>)
{
    println "Next number is $number"
}
```

When you run this code, you'll get the following:

```
>groovy ExpandoDemo.groovy
Next number is 0
Next number is 1
Next number is 2
Next number is 3
Reset smart iterator
Next number is 2
Next number is 3
```

After the iterator is restarted, you can use it again as usual, even though the previous run reached the limit of numbers generated. Notice also that you don't implement in the Expando class the remove() method defined by the iterator Java interface. The code doesn't use it, so the Expando object doesn't need to declare it. But because of

---

[14] Just don't get carried away. Expando overuse is not a healthy habit.

duck typing, this Expando still passes as an iterator even though it implements only two out of three required methods.

2.6 *Summary*

- Groovy is a language that also runs in the JVM.
- Groovy source is compiled into Java bytecode.
- Using Java classes from Groovy code happens with the new keyword exactly like Java.
- Groovy is mostly compatible with Java syntax.
- In Groovy, classes are public by default, and fields are private by default.
- Groovy autogenerates getters and setters.
- In Groovy, semicolons and the return keyword are optional.
- Groovy supports optional typing: you can declare the type of a variable (as in Java) or use the def keyword to leave it to the runtime.
- Groovy treats all objects as true unless the object is an empty string, an empty collection, 0, null, or false.
- Spock uses Groovy assertions instead of JUnit assert calls.
- Groovy allows you to create objects by using maps of fields/values inside the constructor.
- Groovy strings employ automatic templating, similar to JSTL.
- Groovy comes with extensive utilities that read XML and JSON files.
- Groovy supports closures that can be used to reduce the code lines in assert statements.
- An ObjectGraphBuilder can be used to quickly create a tree-like structure of your business domain.
- You can use Expando to dynamically create Groovy objects during runtime.

A tour of Spock functionality

This chapter covers

- Understanding the given-when-then Spock syntax
- Testing datasets with data-driven tests
- Introducing mocks/stubs with Spock
- Examining mock behavior

With the Groovy basics out of the way, you're now ready to focus on Spock syntax and see how it combines several aspects of unit testing in a single and cohesive package.

Different applications come with different testing needs, and it's hard to predict what parts of Spock will be more useful to you beforehand. This chapter covers a bit of all major Spock capabilities to give you a bird's-eye view of how Spock works. I won't focus on all the details yet because these are explained in the coming chapters.

The purpose of this chapter is to act as a central hub for the whole book. You can read this chapter and then, according to your needs, decide which of the coming chapters is of special interest to you. If, for example, in your current application you have tests with lots of test data that spans multiple input variables, you can skip straight to the chapter that deals with data-driven tests (chapter 5).

The following sections briefly touch on these three aspects of Spock:

- Core testing of Java code (more details in chapter 4)
- Parameterized tests (more details in chapter 5)
- Isolation of the class under test (more details in chapter 6)

To illustrate these concepts, a series of increasingly complex, semi-real scenarios are used, because some Spock features aren't evident with trivial unit tests. For each scenario, I'll also compare the Spock unit test with a JUnit test (if applicable).

3.1 Introducing the behavior-testing paradigm

Let's start with a full example of software testing. Imagine you work as a developer for a software company that creates programs for fire-control systems, as shown in figure 3.1.

The processing unit is connected to multiple fire sensors and polls them continuously for abnormal readings. When a fire is discovered, the alarm sounds. If the fire starts spreading and another detector is triggered, the fire brigade is automatically called. Here are the complete requirements of the system:

- If all sensors report nothing strange, the system is OK and no action is needed.
- If one sensor is triggered, the alarm sounds (but this might be a false positive because of a careless smoker who couldn't resist a cigarette).
- If more than one sensor is triggered, the fire brigade is called (because the fire has spread to more than one room).

Your colleague has already implemented this system, and you're tasked with unit testing. The skeleton of the Java implementation is shown in listing 3.1.

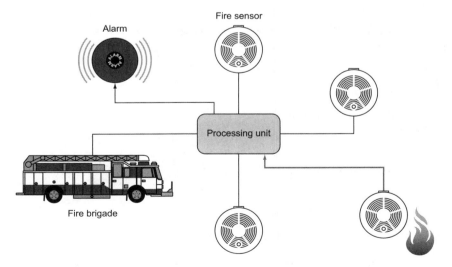

Figure 3.1   A fire-monitoring system controlling multiple detectors

> **How to use the code listings**
>
> You can find almost all code listings for this book at https://github.com/kkapelon/java-testing-with-spock.
>
> For brevity, the book sometimes points you to the source code (especially for long listings). I tend to use the Eclipse IDE in my day-to-day work. If you didn't already install Spock and Eclipse in chapter 2, you can find installation instructions in appendix A.

This fire sensor is regularly injected with the data from the fire sensors, and at any given time, the sensor can be queried for the status of the alarm.

Listing 3.1   A fire-control system in Java

```java
public class FireEarlyWarning {                    ◄─┐ The main class that
                                                      │ implements monitoring
    public void feedData(int triggeredFireSensors)
    {
            [...implementation here...]             ◄── Redacted for brevity—see
    }                                                   source code for full code

    public WarningStatus getCurrentStatus()         ◄─┐ Status report
    {                                                  │ getter method
            [...implementation here...]
    }
}

public class WarningStatus {                        ◄─┐ Contents of status
    public boolean isAlarmActive() {                   │ report (status class)
            [...implementation here...]
    }
                                                    ◄─┐ If true, the fire
    public boolean isFireDepartmentNotified() {        │ brigade is called.
            [...implementation here...]
    }

}
```

Annotations:
- **Method called every second by sensor software** → `public void feedData(int triggeredFireSensors)`
- **If true, the alarm sounds.** → `public boolean isAlarmActive() {`

The application uses two classes:

- The *polling class* has all the intelligence and contains a getter that returns a status class with the present condition of the system.
- The *status class* is a simple object that holds the details.[1]

---

[1] This is only the heart of the system. Code for contacting the fire brigade or triggering the alarm is outside the scope of this example.

Your colleague has finished the implementation code, and has even written a JUnit test[2] as a starting point for the test suite you're supposed to finish. You now have the full requirements of the system and the implementation code, and you're ready to start unit testing.

3.1.1 *The setup-stimulate-assert structure of JUnit*

You decide to look first at the existing JUnit test your colleague already wrote. The code is shown in the following listing.

Listing 3.2 A JUnit test for the fire-control system

```
@Test
public void fireAlarmScenario() {                          ◄──┐ JUnit test case
    FireEarlyWarning fireEarlyWarning = new FireEarlyWarning();
    int triggeredSensors = 1;

    fireEarlyWarning.feedData(triggeredSensors);            ◄──┘ Create an event.
    WarningStatus status = fireEarlyWarning.getCurrentStatus();

    assertTrue("Alarm sounds", status.isAlarmActive());
    assertFalse("No notifications", status.isFireDepartmentNotified());
}
```

Setup needed for the test — first block.
Create an event.
Examine results of the event. — assert block.

This unit test covers the case of a single sensor detecting fire. According to the requirements, the alarm should sound, but the fire department isn't contacted yet. If you closely examine the code, you'll discover a hidden structure between the lines. All good JUnit tests have three code segments:

1 In the *setup phase*, the class under test and all collaborators are created. All initialization stuff goes here.

2 In the *stimulus phase*, the class under test is tampered with, triggered, or otherwise passed a message/action. This phase should be as brief as possible.

3 The *assert phase* contains only read-only code (code with no side effects), in which the expected behavior of the system is compared with the actual one.

Notice that this structure is *implied* with JUnit. It's never enforced by the framework and might not be clearly visible in complex unit tests. Your colleague is a seasoned developer and has clearly marked the three phases by using the empty lines in listing 3.2:

- The setup phase creates the `FireEarlyWarning` class and sets the number of triggered sensors that will be evaluated (the first two statements in listing 3.2).

- The stimulus phase passes the triggered sensors to the fire monitor and also asks it for the current status (the middle two statements in listing 3.2).

- The assert phase verifies the results of the test (the last two statements).

---

[2] Following the test-driven development (TDD) principles of writing a unit test for a feature before the feature implementation.

This is good advice to follow, but not all developers follow this technique. (It's also possible to demarcate the phases with comments.)

Because JUnit doesn't clearly distinguish between the setup-stimulate-assert phases, it's up to the developer to decide on the structure of the unit test. Understanding the structure of a JUnit test isn't always easy when more-complex testing is performed. For comparison, the following listing shows a real-world result.[3]

Listing 3.3   JUnit test with complex structure (real example)

```
private static final String MASTER_NAME = "mymaster";
private static HostAndPort sentinel = new HostAndPort("localhost",26379);

@Test
public void sentinelSet() {
    Jedis j = new Jedis(sentinel.getHost(), sentinel.getPort());

    try {
        Map<String, String> parameterMap = new HashMap<String,
                                                        String>();
        parameterMap.put("down-after-milliseconds",
            String.valueOf(1234));
        parameterMap.put("parallel-syncs", String.valueOf(3));
        parameterMap.put("quorum", String.valueOf(2));
        j.sentinelSet(MASTER_NAME, parameterMap);

        List<Map<String, String>> masters = j.sentinelMasters();
        for (Map<String, String> master : masters) {
            if (master.get("name").equals(MASTER_NAME)) {
                assertEquals(1234, Integer.parseInt(master
                        .get("down-after-milliseconds")));
                assertEquals(3,
                        Integer.parseInt(master.get("parallel-
                        syncs")));
                assertEquals(2,
                        Integer.parseInt(master.get("quorum")));
            }
        }

        parameterMap.put("quorum", String.valueOf(1));
        j.sentinelSet(MASTER_NAME, parameterMap);
    } finally {
        j.close();
    }
}
```

After looking at the code, how long did it take you to understand its structure? Can you easily understand which class is under test? Are the boundaries of the three

---

[3]   This unit test is from the jedis library found on GitHub. I mean no disrespect to the authors of this code, and I congratulate them for offering their code to the public. The rest of the tests from jedis are well-written.

phases really clear? Imagine that this unit test has failed, and you have to fix it immediately. Can you guess what has gone wrong simply by looking at the code?

Another problem with the lack of clear structure of a JUnit test is that a developer can easily mix the phases in the wrong[4] order, or even write multiple tests into one. Returning to the fire-control system in listing 3.2, the next listing shows a bad unit test that tests two things at once. The code is shown as an antipattern. Please don't do this in your unit tests!

Listing 3.4 A JUnit test that tests two things—*don't do this*

```
@Test
public void sensorsAreTriggered() {
    FireEarlyWarning fireEarlyWarning = new FireEarlyWarning();     ◄─┤ Setup phase
    fireEarlyWarning.feedData(1);
    WarningStatus status = fireEarlyWarning.getCurrentStatus();

    assertTrue("Alarm sounds", status.isAlarmActive());            ◄─┤ First assert phase
    assertFalse("No notifications", status.isFireDepartmentNotified());
    fireEarlyWarning.feedData(2);

    WarningStatus status2 = fireEarlyWarning.getCurrentStatus();
    assertTrue("Alarm sounds", status2.isAlarmActive());           ◄─┐ Second assert
    assertTrue("Fire Department is notified",                        │ phase
                      status2.isFireDepartmentNotified());
}
```

Stimulus phase → `fireEarlyWarning.feedData(1);` ... `WarningStatus status = fireEarlyWarning.getCurrentStatus();`

Another stimulus phase—this is bad practice. → `fireEarlyWarning.feedData(2);`

This unit test asserts two different cases. If it breaks and the build server reports the result, you don't know which of the two scenarios has the problem.

Another common antipattern I see all too often is JUnit tests with no assert statements at all! JUnit is powerful, but as you can see, it has its shortcomings. How would Spock handle this fire-control system?

3.1.2 *The given-when-then flow of Spock*

Unlike JUnit, Spock has a clear test structure that's denoted with labels (*blocks* in Spock terminology), as you'll see in chapter 4, which covers the lifecycle of a Spock test. Looking back at the requirements of the fire-control system, you'll see that they can have a one-to-one mapping with Spock tests. Here are the requirements again:

- If all sensors report nothing strange, the system is OK and no action is needed.
- If one sensor is triggered, the alarm sounds (but this might be a false positive because of a careless smoker who couldn't resist a cigarette).
- If more than one sensor is triggered, the fire brigade is called (because the fire has spread to more than one room).

---

[4] Because "everything that can go wrong, will go wrong," you can imagine that I've seen too many antipatterns of JUnit tests that happen because of the lack of a clear structure.

Spock can directly encode these sentences by using full English text inside the source test of the code, as shown in the following listing.

Listing 3.5   The full Spock test for the fire-control system

```
class FireSensorSpec extends spock.lang.Specification{

def "If all sensors are inactive everything is ok"() {
    given: "that all fire sensors are off"
    FireEarlyWarning fireEarlyWarning = new FireEarlyWarning()
    int triggeredSensors = 0

    when: "we ask the status of fire control"
    fireEarlyWarning.feedData(triggeredSensors)
    WarningStatus status = fireEarlyWarning.getCurrentStatus()

    then: "no alarm/notification should be triggered"
    !status.alarmActive
    !status.fireDepartmentNotified
}

def "If one sensor is active the alarm should sound as a precaution"() {
    given: "that only one fire sensor is active"
    FireEarlyWarning fireEarlyWarning = new FireEarlyWarning()
    int triggeredSensors = 1

    when: "we ask the status of fire control"
    fireEarlyWarning.feedData(triggeredSensors)
    WarningStatus status = fireEarlyWarning.getCurrentStatus()

    then: "only the alarm should be triggered"
    status.alarmActive
    !status.fireDepartmentNotified
}

def "If more than one sensor is active then we have a fire"() {
    given: "that two fire sensors are active"
    FireEarlyWarning fireEarlyWarning = new FireEarlyWarning()
    int triggeredSensors = 2

    when: "we ask the status of fire control"
    fireEarlyWarning.feedData(triggeredSensors)
    WarningStatus status = fireEarlyWarning.getCurrentStatus()

    then: "alarm is triggered and the fire department is notified"
    status.alarmActive
    status.fireDepartmentNotified
}
}
```

Clear explanation of what this test does

Setup phase

Stimulus phase

Assert phase

Spock follows a given-when-then structure that's enforced via labels inside the code. Each unit test can be described using plain English sentences, and even the labels can be described with text descriptions.

FireSensorSpec

⚠	If all sensors are inactive everything is ok	0.008
⚠	If one sensor is active the alarm should sound as a precaution	0.001
⚠	If more than one sensor is active then we have a fire	0.001

Figure 3.2   Surefire report with Spock test description

This enforced structure pushes the developer to think before writing the test, and also acts as a guide on where each statement goes. The beauty of the English descriptions (unlike JUnit comments) is that they're used directly by reporting tools. A screenshot of a Maven Surefire report is shown in figure 3.2 with absolutely no modifications (Spock uses the JUnit runner under the hood). This report can be created by running `mvn surefire-report:report` on the command line.

The first column shows the result of the test (a green tick means that the test passes), the second column contains the description of the test picked up from the source code, and the third column presents the execution time of each test (really small values are ignored). More-specialized tools can drill down in the labels of the blocks as well, as shown in figure 3.3. The example shown is from Spock reports (https://github.com/renatoathaydes/spock-reports).

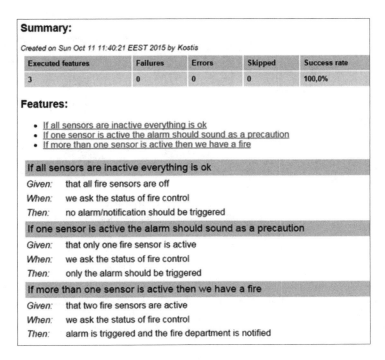

Figure 3.3   Spock report with all English sentences of the test

Spock isn't a full BDD tool,[5] but it certainly pushes you in that direction. With careful planning, your Spock tests can act as living business documentation.

You've now seen how Spock handles basic testing. Let's see a more complex testing scenario, where the number of input and output variables is much larger.

3.2   *Handling tests with multiple input sets*

With the fire-control system in place, you're tasked with a more complex testing assignment. This time, the application under test is a monitor system for a nuclear reactor. It functions in a similar way to the fire monitor, but with more input sensors. The system[6] is shown in figure 3.4.

The components of the system are as follows:

- Multiple fire sensors (input)
- Three radiation sensors in critical points (input)
- Current pressure (input)
- An alarm (output)

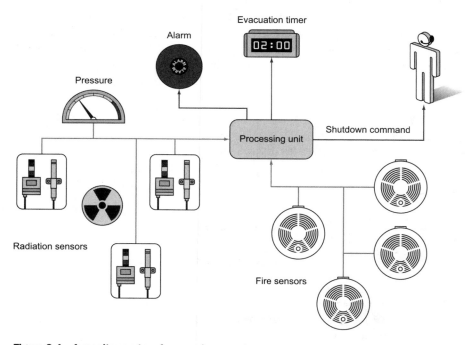

Figure 3.4   A monitor system for a nuclear reactor

---

[5] See JBehave (http://jbehave.org/) or Cucumber JVM (http://cukes.info/) to see how business analysts, testers, and developers can define the test scenarios of an enterprise application.

[6] This system is imaginary. I'm in no way an expert on nuclear reactors. The benefits of the example will become evident in the mocking/stubbing section of the chapter.

- An evacuation command (output)
- A notification to a human operator that the reactor should shut down (output)

The system is already implemented according to all safety requirements needed for nuclear reactors. It reads sensor data at regular intervals and depending on the readings, it can alert or suggest corrective actions. Here are some of the requirements:

- If pressure goes above 150 bars, the alarm sounds.
- If two or more fire alarms are triggered, the alarm sounds and the operator is notified that a shutdown is needed (as a precautionary measure).
- If a radiation leak is detected (100+ rads from any sensor), the alarm sounds, an announcement is made that the reactor should be evacuated within the next minute, and a notification is sent to the human operator that a shutdown is needed.

You speak with the technical experts of the nuclear reactor, and you jointly decide that a minimum of 12 test scenarios will be examined, as shown in table 3.1.

Table 3.1   Scenarios that need testing for the nuclear reactor

Sample inputs			Expected outputs		
Current pressure	Fire sensors	Radiation sensors	Audible alarm	A shutdown is needed	Evacuation within *x* minutes
150	0	0, 0, 0	No	No	No
150	1	0, 0, 0	Yes	No	No
150	3	0, 0, 0	Yes	Yes	No
150	0	110.4 ,0.3, 0.0	Yes	Yes	1 minute
150	0	45.3 ,10.3, 47.7	No	No	No
155	0	0, 0, 0	Yes	No	No
170	0	0, 0, 0	Yes	Yes	3 minutes
180	0	110.4 ,0.3, 0.0	Yes	Yes	1 minute
500	0	110.4 ,300, 0.0	Yes	Yes	1 minute
30	0	110.4 ,1000, 0.0	Yes	Yes	1 minute
155	4	0, 0, 0	Yes	Yes	No
170	1	45.3 ,10.f, 47.7	Yes	Yes	3 minutes

The scenarios outlined in this table are a classic example of *parameterized* tests. The test logic is always the same (take these three inputs and expect these three outputs), and the test code needs to handle different sets of variables for only this single test logic.

In this example, we have 12 scenarios with 6 variables, but you can easily imagine cases with much larger test data. The naive way to handle testing for the nuclear reactor would be to write 12 individual tests. That would be problematic, not only because of code duplication, but also because of future maintenance. If a new variable is added in the system (for example, a new sensor), you'd have to change all 12 tests at once.

A better approach is needed, preferably one that decouples the test code (which should be written once) from the sets of test data and expected output (which should be written for all scenarios). This kind of testing needs a framework with explicit support for parameterized tests.

Spock comes with built-in support for parameterized tests with a friendly DSL[7] syntax specifically tailored to handle multiple inputs and outputs. But before I show you this expressive DSL, allow me to digress a bit into the current state of parameterized testing as supported in JUnit (and the alternative approaches).

Many developers consider parameterized testing a challenging and complicated process. The truth is that the limitations of JUnit make parameterized testing a challenge, and developers suffer because of inertia and their resistance to changing their testing framework.

3.2.1 Existing approaches to multiple test-input parameters

The requirements for the nuclear-reactor monitor are clear, the software is already implemented, and you're ready to test it. What's the solution if you follow the status quo?

The recent versions of JUnit advertise support for parameterized tests. The official way of implementing a parameterized test with JUnit is shown in the following listing. The listing assumes that −1 in evacuation minutes means that no evacuation is needed.

Listing 3.6   Testing the nuclear reactor scenarios with JUnit

```
@RunWith(Parameterized.class)                          ◀─┐ Specialized runner needed
public class NuclearReactorTest {                         │ for parameterized tests is
    private final int triggeredFireSensors;               │ created with @RunWith.
    private final List<Float> radiationDataReadings;
    private final int pressure;

    private final boolean expectedAlarmStatus;
    private final boolean expectedShutdownCommand;         Outputs become
    private final int expectedMinutesToEvacuate;           class fields.

    public NuclearReactorTest(int pressure, int triggeredFireSensors,
        List<Float> radiationDataReadings, boolean expectedAlarmStatus,
        boolean expectedShutdownCommand, int expectedMinutesToEvacuate) {

        this.triggeredFireSensors = triggeredFireSensors;
        this.radiationDataReadings = radiationDataReadings;
        this.pressure = pressure;
        this.expectedAlarmStatus = expectedAlarmStatus;
        this.expectedShutdownCommand = expectedShutdownCommand;
        this.expectedMinutesToEvacuate = expectedMinutesToEvacuate;
```

Inputs become class fields. (annotation pointing to the private final int/List fields)

Special constructor with all inputs and outputs (annotation pointing to the constructor)

---

[7] A DSL is a programming language targeted at a specific problem as opposed to a general programming language like Java. See http://en.wikipedia.org/wiki/Domain-specific_language.

```
        }

@Test
public void nuclearReactorScenario() {                          Unit test that will
    NuclearReactorMonitor nuclearReactorMonitor = new           use parameters
                          NuclearReactorMonitor();

    nuclearReactorMonitor.feedFireSensorData(triggeredFireSensors);
    nuclearReactorMonitor.feedRadiationSensorData(radiationDataReadings);
    nuclearReactorMonitor.feedPressureInBar(pressure);
    NuclearReactorStatus status = nuclearReactorMonitor.getCurrentStatus();

    assertEquals("Expected no alarm", expectedAlarmStatus,
                 status.isAlarmActive());
    assertEquals("No notifications", expectedShutdownCommand,
                 status.isShutDownNeeded());
    assertEquals("No notifications", expectedMinutesToEvacuate,
                 status.getEvacuationMinutes());
}
                                                                Source of
@Parameters                                                     test data
public static Collection<Object[]> data() {
        return Arrays.asList(new Object[][] {
            { 150, 0, new ArrayList<Float>(), false, false, -1 },
            { 150, 1, new ArrayList<Float>(), true, false, -1 },
            { 150, 3, new ArrayList<Float>(), true, true, -1 },
            { 150, 0, Arrays.asList(110.4f, 0.3f, 0.0f), true,
                                                  true, 1 },
            { 150, 0, Arrays.asList(45.3f, 10.3f, 47.7f), false,
                                                  false, -1 },
            { 155, 0, Arrays.asList(0.0f, 0.0f, 0.0f), true, false,
                                                  -1 },
            { 170, 0, Arrays.asList(0.0f, 0.0f, 0.0f), true, true,
                                                  3 },
            { 180, 0, Arrays.asList(110.4f, 0.3f, 0.0f), true,
                                                  true, 1 },
            { 500, 0, Arrays.asList(110.4f, 300f, 0.0f), true,
                                                  true, 1 },
            { 30, 0, Arrays.asList(110.4f, 1000f, 0.0f), true,
                                                  true, 1 },
            { 155, 4, Arrays.asList(0.0f, 0.0f, 0.0f), true, true,
                                                  -1 },
            { 170, 1, Arrays.asList(45.3f, 10.3f, 47.7f), true,
                                                  true, 3 }, });

    }

}
```

Two-dimensional array with test data → `public static Collection<Object[]> data() {`

If you look at this code and feel it's too verbose, you're right! This listing is a true testament to the limitations of JUnit. To accomplish parameterized testing, the following constraints specific to JUnit need to be satisfied:

- The test class must be polluted with fields that represent inputs.
- The test class must be polluted with fields that represent outputs.

- A special constructor is needed for all inputs and outputs.
- Test data comes into a two-dimensional object array (which is converted to a list).

Notice also that because of these limitations, it's impossible to add a second parameterized test in the same class. JUnit is so strict that it forces you to have a single class for each test when multiple parameters are involved. If you have a Java class that needs more than one parameterized test and you use JUnit, you're out of luck.[8]

The problems with JUnit parameterized tests are so well known that several independent efforts have emerged to improve this aspect of unit testing. At the time of writing, at least three external projects[9] offer their own syntax on top of JUnit for a friendlier and less cluttered code.

Parameterized tests are also an area where TestNG (http://testng.org) has been advertised as a better replacement for JUnit. TestNG does away with all JUnit limitations and comes with extra annotations (@DataProvider) that truly decouple test data and test logic.

Despite these external efforts, Spock comes with an even better syntax for parameters (Groovy magic again!). In addition, having all these improved efforts external to JUnit further supports my argument that Spock is a "batteries-included" framework providing everything you need for testing in a single package.

3.2.2   Tabular data input with Spock

You've seen the hideous code of JUnit when multiple parameters are involved. You might have also seen some improvements with TestNG or extra JUnit add-ons. All these solutions attempt to capture the values of the parameters by using Java code or annotations.

Spock takes a step back and focuses directly on the original test scenarios. Returning to the nuclear-monitoring system, remember that what you want to test are the scenarios listed in table 3.1 (written in a human-readable format).

Spock allows you to do the unthinkable. You can directly embed this table as-is inside your Groovy code, as shown in the next listing. Again I assume that −1 in evacuation minutes means that no evacuation is needed.

Listing 3.7   Testing the nuclear reactor scenarios with Spock

```
class NuclearReactorSpec extends spock.lang.Specification{

def "Complete test of all nuclear scenarios"() {          ◀─┐ Human-readable
    given: "a nuclear reactor and sensor data"              │ test description
    NuclearReactorMonitor nuclearReactorMonitor =new
            NuclearReactorMonitor()
```

---

8   There are ways to overcome this limitation, but I consider them hacks that make the situation even more complicated.

9   https://code.google.com/p/fuzztester/wiki/FuzzTester; https://github.com/Pragmatists/junitparams; https://github.com/piotrturski/zohhak.

Usage of test inputs

```
when: "we examine the sensor data"
nuclearReactorMonitor.feedFireSensorData(fireSensors)
nuclearReactorMonitor.feedRadiationSensorData(radiation)
nuclearReactorMonitor.feedPressureInBar(pressure)
NuclearReactorStatus status = nuclearReactorMonitor.getCurrentStatus()
```

Usage of test outputs

```
then: "we act according to safety requirements"
status.alarmActive == alarm
status.shutDownNeeded == shutDown
status.evacuationMinutes == evacuation
```

Source of parameters

Definition of inputs and outputs

```
where: "possible nuclear incidents are:"
```

pressure	fireSensors	radiation		alarm	shutDown	evacuation
150	0	[]		false	false	-1
150	1	[]		true	false	-1
150	3	[]		true	true	-1
150	0	[110.4f ,0.3f, 0.0f]		true	true	1
150	0	[45.3f ,10.3f, 47.7f]		false	false	-1
155	0	[0.0f ,0.0f, 0.0f]		true	false	-1
170	0	[0.0f ,0.0f, 0.0f]		true	true	3
180	0	[110.4f ,0.3f, 0.0f]		true	true	1
500	0	[110.4f ,300f, 0.0f]		true	true	1
30	0	[110.4f ,1000f, 0.0f]		true	true	1
155	4	[0.0f ,0.0f, 0.0f]		true	true	-1
170	1	[45.3f ,10.3f, 47.7f]		true	true	3

```
    }

}
```

Tabular representation of all scenarios

Spock takes a different approach to parameters. Powered by Groovy capabilities, it offers a descriptive DSL for tabular data. The key point of this unit test is the where: label (in addition to the usual given-then-when labels) that holds a definition of all inputs/outputs used in the other blocks.

In the where: block of this Spock test, I copied verbatim the scenarios of the nuclear-reactor monitor from the table. The || notation is used to split the inputs from outputs. Reading this table is possible even by nontechnical people. Your business analyst can look at this table and quickly locate missing scenarios.

Adding a new scenario is easy:

- You can append a new line at the end of the table with a new scenario, and the test will pick the new scenario upon the next run.
- The parameters are strictly contained inside the test method, unlike JUnit. The test class has no need for special constructors or fields. A single Spock class can hold an unlimited number of parameterized tests, each with its own tabular data.

The icing on the cake is the amount of code. The JUnit test has 82 lines of Java code, whereas the Spock test has 38 lines. In this example, I gained 50% code reduction by using Spock, and kept the same functionality as before (keeping my promise from chapter 1 that Spock tests will reduce the amount of test code in your application).

Chapter 5 shows several other tricks for Spock parameterized tests, so feel free to jump there directly if your enterprise application is plagued by similar JUnit boilerplate code.

We'll close our Spock tour with its mocking/stubbing capabilities.

3.3 *Isolating the class under test*

JUnit doesn't support mocking (faking external object communication) out of the box. Therefore, I usually employ Mockito[10] when I need to fake objects in my JUnit tests.

If you've never used mocking in your unit tests, fear not, because this book covers both theory and practice (with Spock). I strongly believe that mocking is one of the pillars of well-written unit tests and I'm always puzzled when I see developers who neglect or loathe mocks and stubs.

The literature on mocking hasn't reached a single agreement on naming the core concepts. Multiple terms exist, such as these:

- Mocks/stubs
- Test doubles
- Fake collaborators

All these usually mean the same thing: dummy objects that are injected in the class under test, replacing the real implementations.

- A *stub* is a fake class that comes with preprogrammed return values. It's injected in the class under test so that you have absolute control of what's being tested as input.
- A *mock* is a fake[11] class that can be examined after the test is finished for its interactions with the class under test (for example, you can ask it whether a method was called or how many times it was called).

Things sometimes get more complicated because a mock can also function as a stub if that's needed.[12] The rest of this book uses the mock/stub naming convention because Spock closely follows this pattern. The next examples show both.

3.3.1 *The case of mocking/stubbing*

After finishing with the nuclear-reactor monitor module, you're tasked with testing the temperature sensors of the same reactor. Figure 3.5 gives an overview of the system.

---

[10] Many mock frameworks are available for Java, but Mockito is the easiest and most logical in my opinion. Some of its ideas have also found their way into Spock itself. See https://github.com/mockito/mockito.

[11] Don't sweat the naming rules. In my day job, I name all these classes as mocks and get on with my life.

[12] The two hardest problems in computer science are naming things and cache invalidation.

Even though at first glance this temperature monitor is similar to the previous system, it has two big differences:

- The system under test—the temperature monitor—doesn't directly communicate with the temperature sensors. It obtains the readings from another Java system, the temperature reader (implemented by a different software company than yours).
- The requirements for the temperature monitor indicate that the alarm should sound if the difference in temperature readings (either up or down) is greater than 20 degrees.

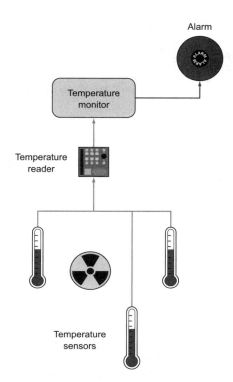

Figure 3.5   A monitor that gets temperatures via another system

You need to write unit tests for the temperature monitor. The implementation code to be tested is shown in the next listing.

Listing 3.8   Java classes for the temperature monitor and reader

```
public class TemperatureReadings {              ◄── Simple class that
                                                     contains temperatures
    private long sensor1Data;
    private long sensor2Data;          Current
    private long sensor3Data;          temperature

    [...getters and setters here]
}

public interface TemperatureReader {            ◄── Interface implemented
    TemperatureReadings getCurrentReadings();        by the reader software
}

public class TemperatureMonitor {               ◄── The class
                                                     under test
    private final TemperatureReader reader;     ◄── Injected field
    private TemperatureReadings lastReadings;        of reader
    private TemperatureReadings currentReadings;  ◄── Latest temperature
                                                       readings
}
```

Method called by the class under test → `TemperatureReadings getCurrentReadings();`

Previous temperature readings → `private TemperatureReadings lastReadings;`

```
                 public TemperatureMonitor(final TemperatureReader reader)
                 {
                        this.reader = reader;
                 }

                 public boolean isTemperatureNormal()
                 {
                        [...implementation here that compares readings...]
                 }

                 public void readSensor()
                 {
                        lastReadings = currentReadings;
                        currentReadings = reader.getCurrentReadings();
                 }

         }
```

Constructor injection → `this.reader = reader;`

Method that needs unit tests ← `public boolean isTemperatureNormal()`

Called automatically at regular intervals ← `public void readSensor()`

Communication with temperature reader | `lastReadings = currentReadings;` `currentReadings = reader.getCurrentReadings();`

The specifications are based on temperature readings. Unlike the previous example that used fixed values (for example, if pressure is more than 150, do this), here you have to test consecutive readings (that is, take an action only if temperature is higher compared to the previous reading).

Reading the specifications, it's obvious you need a way to "trick" the class under test to read temperature readings of your choosing. Unfortunately, the temperature monitor has no way of directly obtaining input. Instead, it calls another Java API from the reader software.[13] How can you "trick" the `TemperatureMonitor` class to read different types of temperatures?

SOLUTIONS FOR FAKING INPUT FROM COLLABORATING CLASSES
A good start would be to contact the software company that writes the temperature-reader software and ask for a debug version of the module, which can be controlled to give any temperature you choose, instead of reading the real hardware sensors. This scenario might sound ideal, but in practice it's difficult to achieve, either for political reasons (the company won't provide what you ask) or technical reasons (the debug version has bugs of its own).

Another approach would be to write your own dummy implementation of `TemperatureReader` that does what you want. I've seen this technique too many times in enterprise projects, and I consider it an antipattern. This introduces a new class that's used exclusively for unit tests and must be kept in sync with the specifications. As soon as the specifications change (which happens a lot in enterprise projects), you must hunt down all those dummy classes and upgrade them accordingly to keep the stability of unit tests.

The recommended approach is to use the built-in mocking capabilities of Spock. Spock allows you to create a replacement class (or interface implementation) on the

---

[13] Notice that in this case I used constructor injection, but setter injection could also work.

spot and direct it to do your bidding while the class under test still thinks it's talking to a real object.

3.3.2 Stubbing fake objects with Spock

To create a unit test for the temperature-monitoring system, you can do the following:

1 Create an implementation of the `TemperatureReader` interface.
2 Instruct this smart implementation to return fictional readings for the first call.
3 Instruct this smart implementation to return other fictional readings for the second call.
4 Connect the class under test with this smart implementation.
5 Run the test, and see what the class under test does.

In Spock parlance, this "smart implementation" is called a *stub*, which means a fake class with canned responses. The following listing shows stubbing in action, as previously outlined.

Listing 3.9   Stubbing with Spock

```
class CoolantSensorSpec extends spock.lang.Specification{

    def "If current temperature difference is within limits everything is
                    ok"() {
        given: "that temperature readings are within limits"
        TemperatureReadings prev = new
                TemperatureReadings(sensor1Data:20,
                sensor2Data:40,sensor3Data:80)
        TemperatureReadings current = new
                TemperatureReadings(sensor1Data:30,
                sensor2Data:45,sensor3Data:73);
        TemperatureReader reader = Stub(TemperatureReader)

        reader.getCurrentReadings() >>> [prev, current]

        TemperatureMonitor monitor = new TemperatureMonitor(reader)

        when: "we ask the status of temperature control"
        monitor.readSensor()
        monitor.readSensor()

        then: "everything should be ok"
        monitor.isTemperatureNormal()
    }

    def "If current temperature difference is more than 20 degrees the
                    alarm should sound"() {
        given: "that temperature readings are not within limits"
        TemperatureReadings prev = new
                TemperatureReadings(sensor1Data:20,
                sensor2Data:40,sensor3Data:80)
        TemperatureReadings current = new
```

Annotations:
- **Premade temperature readings** → (points to the two `TemperatureReadings` objects)
- **Dummy interface implementation** → `TemperatureReader reader = Stub(TemperatureReader)`
- **Instructing the dummy interface to return premade readings** → `reader.getCurrentReadings() >>> [prev, current]`
- **Class under test is injected with dummy interface** → `TemperatureMonitor monitor = new TemperatureMonitor(reader)`
- **Class under test calls dummy interface** → `monitor.readSensor()`
- **Assertion after two subsequent calls** → `monitor.isTemperatureNormal()`

```
                    TemperatureReadings(sensor1Data:30,
                        sensor2Data:10,sensor3Data:73);
            TemperatureReader reader = Stub(TemperatureReader)
            reader.getCurrentReadings() >>> [prev,current]
            TemperatureMonitor monitor = new TemperatureMonitor(reader)

            when: "we ask the status of temperature control"
            monitor.readSensor()
            monitor.readSensor()

            then: "the alarm should sound"
            !monitor.isTemperatureNormal()
        }
    }
```

The magic line is the Stub() call, shown here:

```
TemperatureReader reader = Stub(TemperatureReader)
```

Spock, behind the scenes, creates a dummy implementation of this interface. By default the implementation does nothing, so it must be instructed how to react, which is done with the second important line, the >>> operator:

```
reader.getCurrentReadings() >>> [prev, current]
```

This line indicates the following:

- The first time the getCurrentReadings() method is called on the dummy interface, return the instance named prev.
- The second time, return the object named current.

The >>> operator is normally called an *unsigned shift operator*[14] in Java, but Spock overloads it (Groovy supports operator overloading) to provide canned answers to a stub. Now the dummy interface is complete. The class under test is injected with the Spock stub, and calls it without understanding that all its responses are preprogrammed. As far as the class under test is concerned, the Spock stub is a real implementation.

The final result: you've implemented the unit test for the temperature reader complying with the given requirements, even though the class under test never communicates with the temperature sensors themselves.

3.3.3   *Mocking collaborators*

For simplicity, all the systems in these examples so far only recommend the suggested action (for example, the alarm should sound). They assume that another external system polls the various monitors presented and then takes the action.

In the real world, systems are rarely this simple. Faking the input data is only half the effort needed to write effective unit tests. The other half is faking the output

---

[14] http://docs.oracle.com/javase/tutorial/java/nutsandbolts/op3.html.

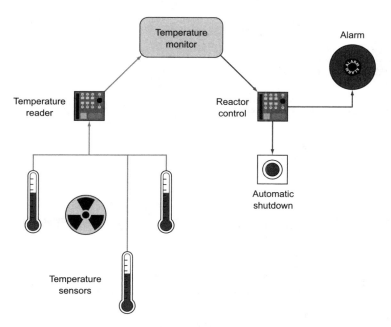

Figure 3.6   A full system with input and output and side effects

parameters. In this case, you need to use mocking in the mix as well. To see how this works, look at the extended temperature-monitor system shown in figure 3.6.

Assume that for this scenario, business analysis has decided that the temperature control of the reactor is mission critical and must be completely automatic. Instead of sounding an alarm and contacting a human operator, the system under test is fully autonomous, and will shut down the reactor on its own if the temperature difference is higher than 50 degrees. The alarm still sounds if the temperature difference is higher than 20 degrees, but the reactor doesn't shut down in this case, allowing for corrective actions by other systems.

Shutting down the reactor and sounding the alarm happens via an external Java library (over which you have no control) that's offered as a simple API. The system under test is now injected with this external API as well, as shown in the following listing.

Listing 3.10   Java classes for the temperature monitor, reader, and reactor control

```
public class TemperatureReadings {                  Simple class that
                                                    contains temperatures
    private long sensor1Data;           Current
    private long sensor2Data;           temperature
    private long sensor3Data;

    [...getters and setters here]
}
```

Method called
by the class
under test

```java
public interface TemperatureReader {
    TemperatureReadings getCurrentReadings();
}
```

Interface implemented by
the reader software

```java
public class ReactorControl {
    public void activateAlarm()
    {
            [...implementation here...]
    }

    public void shutdownReactor()
    {
            [...implementation here...]
    }
}
```

Class with
side effects

```java
public class ImprovedTemperatureMonitor {

    private final TemperatureReader reader;
    private TemperatureReadings lastReadings;
    private TemperatureReadings currentReadings;
    private final ReactorControl reactorControl;

    public ImprovedTemperatureMonitor(final TemperatureReader reader, final
                ReactorControl reactorControl)
    {
            this.reactorControl = reactorControl;
            this.reader = reader;
    }

    private boolean isTemperatureDiffMoreThan(long degrees)
    {
            [...implementation here that compares readings...]
    }

    public void readSensor()
    {
            lastReadings = currentReadings;
            currentReadings = reader.getCurrentReadings();

            [...sanity checks...]

            if(isTemperatureDiffMoreThan(20))
            {
                reactorControl.activateAlarm();
            }
            if(isTemperatureDiffMoreThan(50))
            {
                reactorControl.shutdownReactor();
            }
    }

}
```

Class under test

Injected field of reader
and reactor control

Class under test calls
method with side effects

Again, you're tasked with the unit tests for this system. By using Spock stubs as demonstrated in the previous section, you already know how to handle the temperature reader. This time, however, you can't easily verify the reaction of the class under test, `ImprovedTemperatureMonitor`, because there's nothing you can assert.

The class doesn't have any method that returns its status. Instead it internally calls the Java API for the external library that handles the reactor. How can you test this?

OPTIONS FOR UNIT TESTING THIS MORE-COMPLEX SYSTEM

As before, you have three options:

1 You can ask the company that produces the Java API of the reactor control to provide a "debug" version that doesn't shut down the reactor, but instead prints a warning or a log statement.

2 You can create your own implementation of `ReactorControl` and use that to create your unit test. This is the same antipattern as stubs, because it adds extra complexity and an unneeded maintenance burden to sync this fake object whenever the Java API of the external library changes. Also notice that `ReactorControl` is a concrete class and not an interface, so additional refactoring effort is required before you even consider this route.

3 You can use mocks. This is the recommended approach.

Let's see how Spock handles this testing scenario.

3.3.4 *Examining interactions of mocked objects*

As it does for stubbing, Spock also offers built-in mocking support. A *mock* is another fake collaborator of the class under test. Spock allows you to examine mock objects for their interactions after the test is finished. You pass it as a dependency, and the class under test calls its methods without understanding that you intercept all those calls behind the scenes. As far as the class under test is concerned, it still communicates with a real class.

Unlike stubs, mocks can fake input/output, and can be examined after the test is complete. When the class under test calls your mock, the test framework (Spock in this case) notes the characteristics of this call (such as number of times it was called or even the arguments that were passed for this call). You can examine these characteristics and decide if they are what you expect.

In the temperature-monitor scenario, you saw how the temperature reader is stubbed. The reactor control is also mocked, as shown in the next listing.

Listing 3.11 Mocking and stubbing with Spock

```
def "If current temperature difference is more than 20 degrees the alarm
                                   sounds"() {
    given: "that temperature readings are not within limits"
    TemperatureReadings prev = new TemperatureReadings(sensor1Data:20,
            sensor2Data:40,sensor3Data:80)
    TemperatureReadings current = new TemperatureReadings(sensor1Data:30,
            sensor2Data:10,sensor3Data:73);
```

```
                TemperatureReader reader = Stub(TemperatureReader)
```
◄—— **Creating a stub for an interface**

```
                reader.getCurrentReadings() >>> [prev, current]
```

```
                ReactorControl control = Mock(ReactorControl)
                ImprovedTemperatureMonitor monitor = new
                        ImprovedTemperatureMonitor(reader,control)
```
◄—— **Creating a mock for a concrete class**

Class under test is injected with mock and stub. ——►

```
                when: "we ask the status of temperature control"
                monitor.readSensor()
                monitor.readSensor()
```
Mock methods are called behind the scenes.

```
                then: "the alarm should sound"
                0 * control.shutdownReactor()
                1 * control.activateAlarm()
            }
```
Verification of mock calls

```
        def "If current temperature difference is more than 50 degrees the reactor
                                        shuts down"() {
            given: "that temperature readings are not within limits"
            TemperatureReadings prev = new TemperatureReadings(sensor1Data:20,
                    sensor2Data:40,sensor3Data:80)
            TemperatureReadings current = new TemperatureReadings(sensor1Data:30,
                    sensor2Data:10,sensor3Data:160);
            TemperatureReader reader = Stub(TemperatureReader)

            reader.getCurrentReadings() >>> [prev, current]

            ReactorControl control = Mock(ReactorControl)
            ImprovedTemperatureMonitor monitor = new
                    ImprovedTemperatureMonitor(reader,control)

            when: "we ask the status of temperature control"
            monitor.readSensor()
            monitor.readSensor()

            then: "the alarm should sound and the reactor should shut down"
            1 * control.shutdownReactor()
            1 * control.activateAlarm()
        }
```

The code is similar to listing 3.9, but this time the class under test is injected with two fake objects (a stub and a mock). The mock line is as follows:

```
ReactorControl control = Mock(ReactorControl)
```

Spock automatically creates a dummy class that has the exact signature of the ReactorControl class. All methods by default do nothing (so there's no need to do anything special if that's enough for your test).

You let the class under test run its way, and at the end of the test, instead of testing Spock assertions, you examine the interactions of the mock you created:

```
0 * control.shutdownReactor()
1 * control.activateAlarm()
```

- The first line says, "After this test is finished, I expect that the number of times the `shutdownReactor()` method was called is zero."
- The second line says, "After this test is finished, I expect that the number of times the `activateAlarm()` method was called is one."

This is equivalent to the business requirements that dictate what would happen depending on different temperature variations.

Using both mocks and stubs, you've seen how it's possible to write a full test for the temperature system without shutting down the reactor each time your unit test runs. The reactor scenario might be extreme, but in your programming career, you may already have seen Java modules with side effects that are difficult or impossible to test without the use of mocking. Common examples are as follows:

- Charging a credit card
- Sending a bill to a client via email
- Printing a report
- Booking a flight with an external system

Any Java API that has severe side effects is a natural candidate for mocking. I've only scratched the surface of what's possible with Spock mocks. In chapter 6, you'll see many more advanced examples that also demonstrate how to capture the arguments of mocked calls and use them for further assertions, or even how a stub can respond differently according to the argument passed.

Mocking with Mockito

For comparison, I've included in the GitHub source code the same test with JUnit/Mockito in case you want to compare it with listing 3.11 and draw your own conclusions. Mockito was one of the inspirations for Spock, and you might find some similarities in the syntax. Mockito is a great mocking framework, and much thought has been spent on its API. It sometimes has a strange syntax in more-complex examples (because it's still limited by Java conventions). Ultimately, however, it's Java's verbosity that determines the expressiveness of a unit test, regardless of Mockito's capabilities.

For example, if you need to create a lot of mocks that return Java maps, you have to create them manually and add their elements one by one before instructing Mockito to use them. Within Spock tests, you can create maps in single statements (even in the same line that stubbing happens), as you've seen in Chapter 2.

Also, if you need a parameterized test with mocks (as I'll show in the next section), you have to combine at least three libraries (JUnit plus Mockito plus JUnitParams) to achieve the required result.

3.3.5   *Combining mocks and stubs in parameterized tests*

As a grand finale of this Spock tour, I'll show you how to easily combine parameterized tests with mocking/stubbing in Spock. I'll again use the temperature scenario introduced in listing 3.10. Remember the requirements of this system:

- If the temperature difference is larger than 20 degrees (higher or lower), the alarm sounds.
- If the temperature difference is larger than 50 degrees (higher or lower), the alarm sounds and the reactor shuts down automatically.

We have four cases as far as temperature is concerned, and three temperature sensors. Therefore, a full coverage of all cases requires at least 12 unit tests. Spock can combine parameterized tests with mocks/stubs, as shown in the following listing.

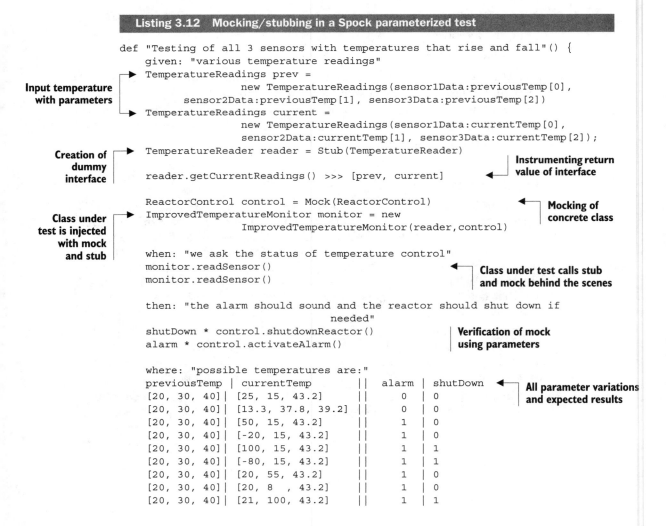

Listing 3.12   Mocking/stubbing in a Spock parameterized test

```
def "Testing of all 3 sensors with temperatures that rise and fall"() {
    given: "various temperature readings"
    TemperatureReadings prev =
                new TemperatureReadings(sensor1Data:previousTemp[0],
            sensor2Data:previousTemp[1], sensor3Data:previousTemp[2])
    TemperatureReadings current =
                new TemperatureReadings(sensor1Data:currentTemp[0],
            sensor2Data:currentTemp[1], sensor3Data:currentTemp[2]);
    TemperatureReader reader = Stub(TemperatureReader)

    reader.getCurrentReadings() >>> [prev, current]

    ReactorControl control = Mock(ReactorControl)
    ImprovedTemperatureMonitor monitor = new
                ImprovedTemperatureMonitor(reader,control)

    when: "we ask the status of temperature control"
    monitor.readSensor()
    monitor.readSensor()

    then: "the alarm should sound and the reactor should shut down if
                                needed"
    shutDown * control.shutdownReactor()
    alarm * control.activateAlarm()

    where: "possible temperatures are:"
    previousTemp | currentTemp        ||  alarm | shutDown
    [20, 30, 40]| [25, 15, 43.2]      ||    0   | 0
    [20, 30, 40]| [13.3, 37.8, 39.2]  ||    0   | 0
    [20, 30, 40]| [50, 15, 43.2]      ||    1   | 0
    [20, 30, 40]| [-20, 15, 43.2]     ||    1   | 0
    [20, 30, 40]| [100, 15, 43.2]     ||    1   | 1
    [20, 30, 40]| [-80, 15, 43.2]     ||    1   | 1
    [20, 30, 40]| [20, 55, 43.2]      ||    1   | 0
    [20, 30, 40]| [20, 8  , 43.2]     ||    1   | 0
    [20, 30, 40]| [21, 100, 43.2]     ||    1   | 1
```

Annotations:
- Input temperature with parameters
- Creation of dummy interface
- Instrumenting return value of interface
- Class under test is injected with mock and stub
- Mocking of concrete class
- Class under test calls stub and mock behind the scenes
- Verification of mock using parameters
- All parameter variations and expected results

```
        [20, 30, 40]|  [22, -40, 43.2]      ||      1  | 1
        [20, 30, 40]|  [20, 35, 76]         ||      1  | 0
        [20, 30, 40]|  [20, 31  ,13.2]      ||      1  | 0
        [20, 30, 40]|  [21, 33, 97]         ||      1  | 1
        [20, 30, 40]|  [22, 39, -22]        ||      1  | 1
}
```

This code combines everything you've learned in this chapter. It showcases the following:

- The expressiveness of Spock tests (clear separation of test phases)
- The easy tabular format of parameters (matching business requirements)
- The ability to fake both input and output of the class under test

As an exercise, try replicating this functionality using Java and JUnit in fewer lines of code (statements). As I promised you at the beginning of the book, Spock is a cohesive testing framework that contains everything you need for your unit tests, all wrapped in friendly and concise Groovy syntax.

3.4   Summary

- Spock tests have a clear structure with explicit given-when-then blocks.
- Spock tests can be named with full English sentences.
- JUnit reporting tools are compatible with Spock tests.
- Spock tests allow for parameterized tests with the `where:` block.
- Parameters in Spock tests can be written directly in a tabular format (complete with header).
- Unlike JUnit, Spock can have an unlimited number of parameterized tests in the same class.
- A stub is a fake class that can be programmed with custom behavior.
- A mock is a fake class that can be examined (after the test is finished) for its interactions with the class under test (which methods were called, what the arguments were, and so forth).
- Spock can stub classes/interfaces and instrument them to return whatever you want.
- The triple-right-shift/unsigned shift (>>>) operator allows a stub to return different results each time it's called.
- Spock can mock classes/interfaces and automatically record all invocations.
- Spock can verify the number of times a method of a mock was called.
- Combining stubs, mocks, and multiple parameters in the same Spock test is easy.

Part 2

Structuring Spock tests

This part contains the principal Spock knowledge. With the foundations out of the way, you're ready to see the Spock syntax in all its glory, particularly the different parts of a Spock unit test and how they can be combined for various cases.

Chapter 4—the central chapter of the whole book—shows the individual parts of a Spock unit test (which are called *blocks*), their purpose, significance, and expected structure. This chapter also explains the lifecycle of a Spock test, the documentation annotations, and the facilities offered by Spock that affect the readability of a unit test. Make sure that you've mastered the topics of this chapter before moving on to the rest of the book.

Chapter 5 focuses on parameterized tests. *Parameterized tests* are unit tests that always test the same scenario with different input and output parameters. Depending on your application, you may have one or two parameterized tests (among your vanilla unit tests), or you may be overwhelmed with parameterized tests of multiple parameter combinations. Parameterized tests in Spock are a breath of fresh air compared to existing solutions, as Spock allows you to directly embed into source code the business description of input/output parameters.

Chapter 6 focuses on the mocking capabilities of Spock. Unlike other test frameworks, Spock has built-in support for creating mocks without the need of an external library. The way it sets up mocks and instructs them on their expected behavior is one of the huge changes that set it apart from its competitors. If you've already worked with Mockito, you'll truly appreciate the simplicity of Spock mocking. Again, depending on your application, you may need mocking in a few special cases or in all your unit tests.

Writing unit tests with Spock

This chapter covers

- Working with Spock blocks
- Understanding the lifecycle of a test
- Improving readability of Spock tests
- Using reusable JUnit features

All the Spock tests you've seen so far have been presented to you as a finished unit test, with no explanation of how to reach that particular code structure. You're probably eager to create your own Spock tests from scratch. In this chapter, you'll see all the building blocks that compose a Spock test and how they fit together (various combinations are possible).

You'll also learn about the lifecycle of a Spock test and how to interact with its various phases. Finally, you'll see some tricks for handling lengthy Spock tests and making them more readable (a common issue in large enterprise projects).

4.1 Understanding Spock from the ground up

At the lowest level, a Spock test method is highly characterized by its individual *blocks*. This term is used for the code labels inside a test method. You've already seen the given-when-then blocks multiple times in the previous chapters, as shown in the following listing.

Listing 4.1   Spock blocks inside a test method

```
def "Adding two and three results in 5"() {        ◄────── Spock test
    given: "the integers two and three"  ◄──────              method
    int a = 3
    int b = 2                          The given: block
                                       and its description
    when: "they are added"
    int result = a + b
                                       The when:
                                       block and its
                                       description
    then: "the result is five"    ◄────── The then: block
    result == 5                          and its description
}
```

Apart from the given-when-then blocks, Spock offers several other blocks that express different test semantics. The full list is shown in table 4.1.

Table 4.1   Available Spock blocks

Spock block	Description	Expected usage
given:	Creates initial conditions	85%
setup:	An alternative name for given:	0% (I use given:)
when:	Triggers the action that will be tested	99%
then:	Examines results of test	99%
and:	Cleaner expression of other blocks	60%
expect:	Simpler version of then:	20%
where:	Parameterized tests	40%
cleanup:	Releases resources	5%

The last column shows the percentage of your unit tests that should contain each block. This number isn't scientific, and is based only on my experience. Depending on your application, your numbers will be different, but you can get an overall indication of the importance of each block.

4.1.1   *A simple test scenario*

I hope you enjoyed the nuclear reactor example of the previous chapter. In this chapter, you'll get down to earth with a more common[1] system that needs testing. The Java

---

[1] ...and more boring. I know some of you were waiting for the software that tracks trajectories of nuclear missiles in order to launch countermeasures (as teased in chapter 1). Sorry to disappoint you.

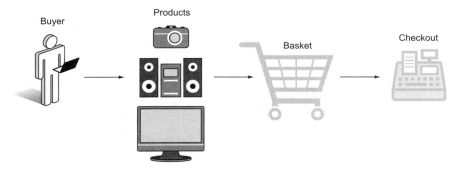

Figure 4.1   Buying products in an electronic shop

system you'll test is an electronic shop that sells computer products via a website, which I guess is more familiar to you than the internals of a nuclear reactor. You can see an overview of the system in figure 4.1.

I'll show you most Spock blocks by testing the base scenario, in which a user adds one or more products in an electronic basket. The basket keeps the total weight (for shipping purposes) and the price of all products selected by the user. The class under test is that electronic basket. The collaborator class is the product, as shown in the following listing.

Listing 4.2   Java skeleton for an electronic basket

```java
public class Product {                          All products sold are
    private String name;                        defined with this class.
    private int price;
    private int weight;
    [...getters and setters here]
}

public class Basket {

    public void addProduct(Product product)      Triggered by the UI when
    {                                            the user selects a product
        addProduct(product,1);
    }

    public void addProduct(Product product, int times)
    {
        [...code redacted for brevity]
    }
                                                 Needed for shipping
    public int getCurrentWeight()                calculations
    {
        [...code redacted for brevity]
    }
```

```
public int getProductTypesCount()
{
        [...code redacted for brevity]
}
```
}

Needed for sale analytics

Notice that this code is used only for illustration purposes. A production-ready e-shop would be much different. Now let's see all Spock blocks that you can use in your unit tests.

4.1.2   *The given: block*

You've already seen the given: block multiple times in previous chapters of the book. The given: block should contain all initialization code that's needed to prepare your unit test. The following listing shows a unit test that deals with the weight of the basket after a product is selected by the user.

Listing 4.3   The given-when-then triad

```
def "A basket with one product has equal weight"() {
    given: "an empty basket and a TV"
    Product tv = new Product(name:"bravia",price:1200,weight:18)
    Basket basket = new Basket()

    when: "user wants to buy the TV"
    basket.addProduct(tv)

    then: "basket weight is equal to the TV"
    basket.currentWeight == tv.weight
    }
```

Prepare the unit test.

Trigger the action that will be tested.

Examine the results.

The given: block sets up the scene for the test, as shown in figure 4.2. Its function is to get everything ready just before the method(s) that will be tested is/are called.

Sometimes it's tempting to place this initialization code in the when: block instead, and completely skip the given: block. Although you can have Spock tests without a given: block, I consider this a bad practice[2] because it makes the test less readable.

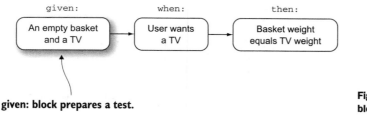

given: block prepares a test.

Figure 4.2   The given: **block prepares a test.**

---

[2] An exception to this rule is a simple test with just the expect: block. That's why I have 85% in expected usage of the given: block.

> ### Rewrite credit card billing example with a given: block
>
> As a quick exercise, look at listing 1.8 in chapter 1 (the example with credit card billing) and rewrite it correctly, by properly constructing a `given:` block. Some examples in chapter 2 are also missing the `given:` block. Try to find them and think how you should write them correctly.

Unfortunately, in large enterprise projects, the code contained in the `given:` block can easily get out of hand. Complex tests require a lot of setup code, and often you'll find yourself in front of a huge `given:` block that's hard to read and understand. You'll see some techniques for managing that initialization code in a more manageable manner later in this chapter and also in chapter 8.

4.1.3 The setup: block

The `setup:` block is an alias for the `given:` block. It functions in exactly the same way. The following listing contains the same unit test for the basket weight.

Listing 4.4 Using the setup alias

```
def "A basket with one product has equal weight (alternative)"() {
    setup: "an empty basket and a TV"
    Product tv = new Product(name:"bravia",price:1200,weight:18)
    Basket basket = new Basket()

    when: "user wants to buy the TV"
    basket.addProduct(tv)

    then: "basket weight is equal to the TV"
    basket.currentWeight == tv.weight
}
```

Prepare the unit test. (points to the setup lines)

Trigger the action that will be tested. (points to the when lines)

Examine the results. (points to the then lines)

Using `setup:` or `given:` is a semantic choice and makes absolutely no difference to the underlying code or how the Spock test will run. Choosing between `setup:` and `given:` for the initialization code is a purely personal preference (see figure 4.3).

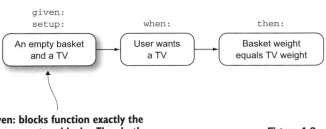

given: blocks function exactly the same as setup: blocks. They both prepare a test.

Figure 4.3 The `given:` and `setup:` blocks do exactly the same thing in Spock tests.

I tend to use the `given:` block, because I believe that the sentence flow is better (given-when-then). Also, the `setup:` block might be confusing with some of the life-cycle methods that you'll see later in this chapter.

4.1.4 The when: block

The `when:` block is arguably the most important part of a Spock test. It contains the code that sets things in motion by triggering actions in your class under test or its collaborators (figure 4.4). Its code should be as short as possible, so that anybody can easily understand what's being tested.

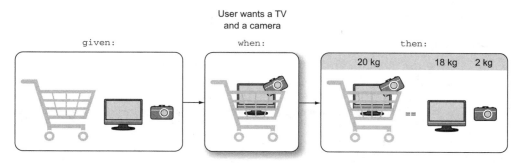

Figure 4.4   The `when:` block triggers the test and should be as simple as possible.

When I read an existing Spock test, I sometimes find myself focusing directly on the `when:` block, in order to understand the meaning of the test (bypassing completely the `given:` block).

> ### The importance of the when: block
>
> Every time you finish writing a Spock test, your first impulse should be to check the contents of the `when:` block. It should be as simple as possible. If you find that it contains too much code or triggers too many actions, consider refactoring its contents.
>
> Put yourself in the shoes of the next developer who comes along and sees your Spock test. How long will it take to understand the actions performed by the `when:` block?

In listing 4.4, the `when:` block is a single statement, so it's easy to understand what's being tested. Even though the e-shop example is basic, the same concept should apply to your `when:` blocks. The contents should be one "action." This action doesn't have to be a single statement, but it must capture a single concept in your unit test. To explain this idea better, the following listing shows a bad use of a when: block.

Listing 4.5   A nontrivial when: block—*don't do this*

```
def "Test index assign"() {
    setup:
        List<String> list = ["IDCODIGO", "descripcion", "field_1",
            "FAMILIA", "MARCA" ]
        ArticuloSunglassDescriptor.reset()

    when:                                          ◄─┐ when: block with no text description
        Integer ix = 0                               │ and unclear trigger code
        for (String tag in list) {
            for (ArticuloSunglassDescriptor descriptor in
                ArticuloSunglassDescriptor.values()) {
                if (descriptor.equals(tag)) {
                    descriptor.index = ix
                    break
                }
            }
            ix++
        }


    then:
        ArticuloSunglassDescriptor.family.index == 3

}
```

The code comes from a Spock test I found in the wild.[3] How long does it take you to understand what this Spock test does? Is it easy to read the contents of the when: block?

What's the class under test here? Notice also that all three blocks (setup-when-then) have no text description (another practice that I find controversial). This makes understanding the test even harder.

You'll see some techniques for refactoring when: blocks later in this chapter. For now, keep in mind that the code inside the when: block should be short and sweet, as seen in the following listing.

Listing 4.6   Descriptive when: blocks

```
def "A basket with two products weights as their sum"() {
    given: "an empty basket, a TV and a camera"
    Product tv = new Product(name:"bravia",price:1200,weight:18)
```

---

[3] Again I mean no disrespect to the author of the code. If you're reading this, I thank you for providing a real Spock test available on the internet for my example.

```
    Product camera = new Product(name:"panasonic",price:350,weight:2)
    Basket basket = new Basket()

    when: "user wants to buy the TV and the camera"
    basket.addProduct(tv)
    basket.addProduct(camera)

    then: "basket weight is equal to both camera and tv"
    basket.currentWeight == (tv.weight + camera.weight)
}
```

← **when: block with text description and clear trigger code**

Even though the when: block is two statements here, they both express the same concept (adding a product to a basket). Understanding the when: block in this example is easy.

4.1.5   *The then: block*

The then: block is the last part of the given-when-then trinity. It contains one or more Groovy assertions (you've seen them in chapter 2) to verify the correct behavior of your class under test, as shown in figure 4.5.

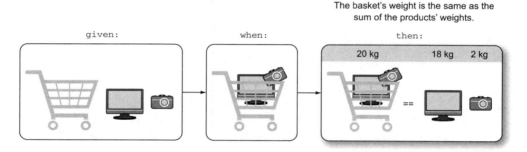

Figure 4.5   The then: **block verifies the behavior of the class under test.**

Again, you're not limited to a single statement, but all assertions should examine the same thing. If you have unrelated assertions that test different things, your Spock test should break up into smaller ones.

Note also that Spock has an automatic safeguard against Groovy asserts that aren't really asserts (a common mistake). Assume that I wrote my Spock test like the following listing.

Listing 4.7   Invalid then: **block**

```
def "A basket with two products weights as their sum"() {
    given: "an empty basket, a TV and a camera"
    Product tv = new Product(name:"bravia",price:1200,weight:18)
    Product camera = new Product(name:"panasonic",price:350,weight:2)
```

```
Basket basket = new Basket()
when: "user wants to buy the TV and the camera"
basket.addProduct(tv)
basket.addProduct(camera)

then: "basket weight is equal to both camera and tv"
basket.currentWeight = (tv.weight + camera.weight)
}
```

Mistake! It should be == instead of =.

Running this test prints the following:

```
>mvn test
> BasketWeightSpec.groovy: 45: Expected a condition, but found an
assignment. Did you intend to write '==' ? @ line 45, column 3.
[ERROR] basket.currentWeight = (tv.weight + camera.weight)
```

This is a nice touch of Spock, and although it's not bulletproof, it provides effective feedback when you start writing your first Spock tests.

4.1.6 The and: block

The and: block is a strange one indeed. It might seem like syntactic sugar at first sight because it has no meaning on its own and just extends other blocks, but it's important as far as semantics are concerned. It allows you to split all other Spock blocks into distinctive parts, as shown in the next listing, making the code more understandable.

Listing 4.8 Using and: to split the given: block

```
def "A basket with three products weights as their sum"() {
    given: "an empty basket"
    Basket basket = new Basket()

    and: "several products"
    Product tv = new Product(name:"bravia",price:1200,weight:18)
    Product camera = new Product(name:"panasonic",price:350,weight:2)
    Product hifi = new Product(name:"jvc",price:600,weight:5)

    when: "user wants to buy the TV and the camera and the hifi"
    basket.addProduct tv
    basket.addProduct camera
    basket.addProduct hifi

    then: "basket weight is equal to all product weight"
    basket.currentWeight == (tv.weight + camera.weight + hifi.weight)
}
```

given: block deals only with the class under test.

and: block creates the collaborators.

Here you use the and: block to distinguish between the class under test (the Basket class) and the collaborators (the products), as illustrated in figure 4.6. In larger Spock tests, this is helpful because, as I said already, the initialization code can quickly grow in size in a large enterprise application.

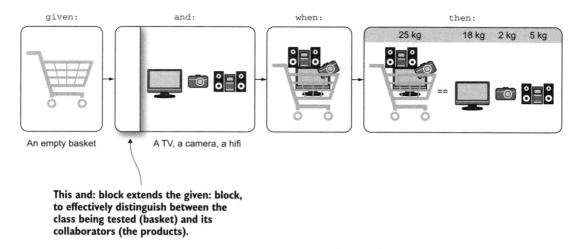

This and: block extends the given: block, to effectively distinguish between the class being tested (basket) and its collaborators (the products).

Figure 4.6   The `and:` block allows you to include collaborator classes in a test.

It's also possible to split the `when:` block, as shown in the following listing.

Listing 4.9   Using `and:` to split the `when:` block

```
def "A basket with three products weights as their sum (alternate)"() {
    given: "an empty basket, a TV,a camera and a hifi"
    Basket basket = new Basket()
    Product tv = new Product(name:"bravia",price:1200,weight:18)
    Product camera = new Product(name:"panasonic",price:350,weight:2)
    Product hifi = new Product(name:"jvc",price:600,weight:5)

    when: "user wants to buy the TV.."          ◀── Original
    basket.addProduct tv                              when: block

    and: "..the camera.."                       ◀──
    basket.addProduct camera                          Extension of
                                                      when: block
    and: "..and the wifi"                       ◀──
    basket.addProduct hifi

    then: "basket weight is equal to all product weight"
    basket.currentWeight == (tv.weight + camera.weight + hifi.weight)
}
```

This example might be trivial, but it also showcases the capability to have more than one and: block. It's up to you to decide how many you need. In the case of the when: block, always keep in mind the rule outlined in the previous section: if your and:

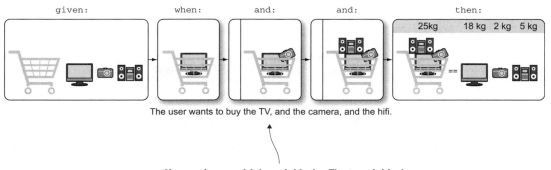

The user wants to buy the TV, and the camera, and the hifi.

You can have multiple and: blocks. These and: blocks split up the when: blocks into related triggers.

Figure 4.7 You can concatenate multiple and: blocks to a when: block.

blocks that come after when: perform unrelated triggers, you need to simplify the when: block. Figure 4.7 demonstrates this scenario.

The most controversial usage of the and: block occurs when it comes after a then: block, as shown in the next listing.

Listing 4.10 Using and: as an extension to a then: block

```
def "A basket with three products has correct weight and count
                       (controversial)"() {
    given: "an empty basket, a TV,a camera and a hifi"
    Basket basket = new Basket()
    Product tv = new Product(name:"bravia",price:1200,weight:18)
    Product camera = new Product(name:"panasonic",price:350,weight:2)
    Product hifi = new Product(name:"jvc",price:600,weight:5)

    when: "user wants to buy the TV and the camera and the hifi"
    basket.addProduct tv
    basket.addProduct camera
    basket.addProduct hifi

    then: "the basket weight is equal to all product weights"
    basket.currentWeight == (tv.weight + camera.weight + hifi.weight)

    and: "it contains 3 products"
    basket.productTypesCount == 3
}
```

Original then: block ⟶ (pointing to the then: block)

Extension of then: block ⟵ (pointing to the and: block)

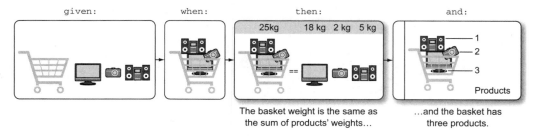

The basket weight is the same as
the sum of products' weights...

...and the basket has
three products.

Figure 4.8   Using an `and:` block with a `then:` block is possible but controversial. You could be testing two unrelated things.

In this example, I use the `and:` block to additionally verify the number of products inside the basket, as illustrated in figure 4.8.

Whether this check is related to the weight of the basket is under discussion. Obviously, if the number of products inside the basket is wrong, its weight will be wrong as well; therefore, you could say that they should be tested together.

Another approach is to decide that the basket weight and number of products are two separate things that need their own respective tests, as shown in figure 4.9.

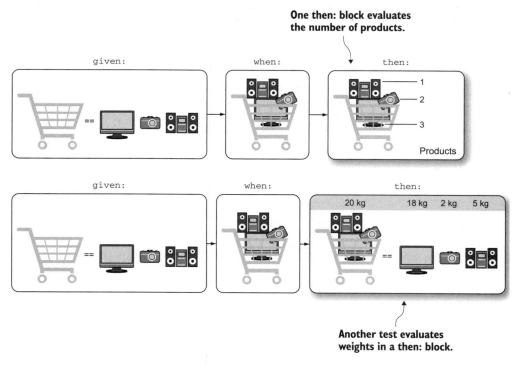

One then: block evaluates
the number of products.

Another test evaluates
weights in a then: block.

Figure 4.9   Instead of using an `and:` block with a `then:` block, consider writing two separate tests.

There's no hard rule on what's correct and what's wrong here. It's up to you to decide when to use an and: block after a then: block. Keep in mind the golden rule of unit tests: they should check one thing.[4] My advice is to avoid using and: blocks after then: blocks, unless you're sure of the meaning of the Spock test. The and: blocks are easy to abuse if you're not careful.

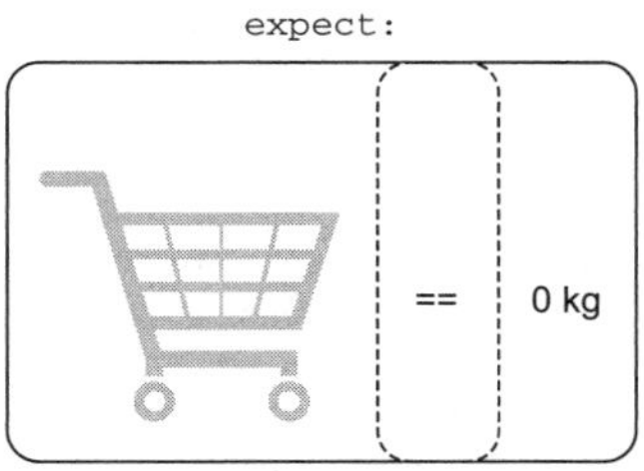

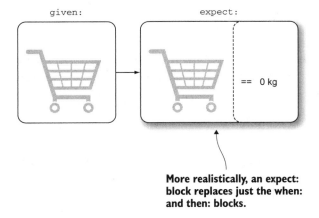

Figure 4.10 An expect: block can replace given:, when:, and then: blocks.

4.1.7 *The expect: block*

The expect: block is a jack-of-all-trades in Spock tests. It can be used in many semantic ways, and depending on the situation, it might improve or worsen the expressiveness of a Spock test.

At its most basic role, the expect: block combines the meaning of given-when-then. Like the then: block, it can contain assertions and will fail the Spock test if any of them don't pass. It can be used for simple tests that need no initialization code (figure 4.10), and their trigger can be tested right away, as shown in the following listing.

Listing 4.11 Trivial tests with the expect: block

```
def "An empty basket has no weight"() {
    expect: "zero weight when nothing is added"
    new Basket().currentWeight == 0
}
```
◄─── **Only the expect: block is present.**

More preferably, the expect: block should replace only the when: and then: blocks, as shown in figure 4.11.

More realistically, an expect: block replaces just the when: and then: blocks.

Figure 4.11 An expect: usually replaces a when: and a then: block.

---

4 Alternatively, a unit test should fail for a single reason.

This is my preferred use of the `expect:` block, as shown in the following listing.

Listing 4.12 `expect:` block replaces `when:` and `then:`

```
def "An empty basket has no weight (alternative)"() {
    given: "an empty basket"
    Basket basket = new Basket()

    expect: "that the weight is 0"          ◄─┤ expect: block performs
    basket.currentWeight == 0                   the assertion of the test
}
```

Because the `expect:` block accepts Groovy assertions, it can be used in other creative ways that distinguish it from the `then:` block that typically ends a Spock test. The following listing shows a given-expect-when-then test (as seen in the excellent presentation "Idiomatic Spock"[5] found at https://github.com/robfletcher/idiomatic-spock).

Listing 4.13 Using `expect:` for preconditions

```
def "A basket with two products weights as their sum (precondition)"() {
    given: "an empty basket, a TV and a camera"
    Product tv = new Product(name:"bravia",price:1200,weight:18)
    Product camera = new Product(name:"panasonic",price:350,weight:2)
    Basket basket = new Basket()

    expect:"that nothing should be inside"    ◄─┐ expect: block performs
    basket.currentWeight == 0                     intermediate assertions
    basket.productTypesCount == 0

    when: "user wants to buy the TV and the camera"
    basket.addProduct tv
    basket.addProduct camera
                                                  ┐ then: block examines
    then: "basket weight is equal to both camera and tv" ◄─┘ the final result
    basket.currentWeight == (tv.weight + camera.weight)
}
```

In this example, you use the `expect:` block to verify the initial state of the basket before adding any product. This way, the test fails faster if a problem with the basket occurs.

4.1.8 *The cleanup: block*

The `cleanup:` block should be seen as the "finally" code segment of a Spock test. The code it contains will always run at the end of the Spock test, regardless of the result (even if the test fails). The following listing shows an example of this.

---

[5] The presentation is by Robert Fletcher, but the specific example of `expect:` is by Luke Daley (co-author of the Spock framework and creator of Geb, which you'll see in chapter 7).

Listing 4.14   Using `cleanup:` to release resources even if test fails

```
def "A basket with one product has equal weight"() {
    given: "an empty basket and a TV"
    Product tv = new Product(name:"bravia",price:1200,weight:18)
    Basket basket = new Basket()

    when: "user wants to buy the TV"
    basket.addProduct(tv)

    then: "basket weight is equal to the TV"
    basket.currentWeight == tv.weight

    cleanup: "refresh basket resources"
    basket.clearAllProducts()
}
```

then: block examines the final result.

cleanup: block will always run, even if then: fails.

Assume for a moment that the implementation of the basket also keeps temporary files for the current contents for reliability purposes (or sends analytics to another class—you get the idea). The basket comes with a `clearAllProducts()` method that empties the basket and releases the resources (deletes temporary files) it holds. By placing this method in the `cleanup:` block, you ensure that this method always runs, even if the code stops at the `then:` block because of failure.

The `cleanup:` block concludes all possible Spock blocks. Continuing with the bottom-up approach, let's see where these blocks go in your source code.

The where: block is shown in chapter 5

If you've been paying close attention, you must have noticed that I haven't said anything about the `where:` block. The `where:` block is used exclusively for parameterized tests. There are so many things to discuss about parameterized Spock testing that it has its own chapter. Chapter 5 covers parameterized tests and the possible forms of the `where:` block, so keep reading to get the full picture on all Spock blocks.

4.2   *Converting requirements to Spock tests*

Spock blocks embody the low-level mechanics of unit tests. You should also pay equal attention to the methods and classes that contain them. In large enterprise projects, organization and naming of unit tests play a crucial role in easy maintenance and effortless refactoring.

Spock also offers metadata that you can use to annotate your tests for extra clarity. The advantage that this metadata has over normal Java comments is that it can be extracted by reporting tools.

4.2.1   *Explaining the feature examined in a Spock test*

A unique characteristic of Spock test methods is the capability to name them by using full English sentences. This is a huge advantage for Spock tests because it makes reading tests so much easier (even for nontechnical colleagues).

I've used this technique since the first chapter and consider it a groundbreaking feature of Spock, compared to the status quo. The following listing provides an example.

Listing 4.15   Test method describes exactly what is being tested

```
def "A basket with one product has equal weight"() {          ◄──┐ Full English text
    given: "an empty basket and a TV"
    Product tv = new Product(name:"bravia",price:1200,weight:18)
    Basket basket = new Basket()

    when: "user wants to buy the TV"
    basket.addProduct(tv)

    then: "basket weight is equal to the TV"
    basket.currentWeight == tv.weight
}
```

It's your job to make sure that this text is understandable (even out of context). Ideally, it should match the specifications given by business analysts. If you don't have detailed specifications (and you should), the method name should describe what's being tested in a nontechnical way.

The names of Spock methods will appear in test results and coverage reports, so always assume that somebody will read this text without having direct access to the code of the implementation.

4.2.2   *Marking the class under test inside a Spock test*

In most unit tests, initialization code prepares multiple classes and input data. The class that will be tested and evaluated has more importance than its collaborators, which are the classes that communicate with it, but not under test (either because they have their own tests or because they're assumed to be correct).

To distinguish this special class, Spock offers the @Subject annotation, as shown is the next listing. In this example, the class under test is the Basket class.

Listing 4.16   Marking the class under test

```
def "A basket with two products weights as their sum (better)"() {
    given: "an empty basket"
    @Subject                                        The subject of this test
    Basket basket = new Basket()                    is the Basket class.

    and: "several products"
    Product tv = new Product(name:"bravia",price:1200,weight:18)
    Product camera = new Product(name:"panasonic",price:350,weight:2)

    when: "user wants to buy the TV and the camera and the hifi"
    basket.addProduct tv
    basket.addProduct camera

    then: "basket weight is equal to all product weight"
    basket.currentWeight == (tv.weight + camera.weight)
}
```

In this simple example, it might be easy to understand that the `Basket` class is the one being tested (especially by looking at the `when:` and `then:` blocks), but in larger unit tests, the class under test might not be obvious.

At the time of writing, there's no reporting tool that takes into account the `@Subject` annotation, but you should use it anyway to improve readability by other programmers. In current reporting tools, you can't see which class is under test and you're forced to look at the source code to identify it. Hopefully, this limitation will be amended soon by newer versions of test reporting tools.

4.2.3 Describing the Spock unit test as a whole

You now have multiple test methods (*features* in Spock terminology) and want to group them in a Groovy class. This class is a *specification*, as you can see in the following listing.

> Listing 4.17 Writing a Spock specification

Description in full English sentence →

```
@Title("Unit test for basket weight")
class BasketWeightSpec extends spock.lang.Specification{   ◄—— Groovy class extends
                                                               Specification.
    [...test methods here redacted for brevity...]

}
```

The class that contains all the test methods is a Groovy class that must extend `spock.lang.Specification`. This makes it a Spock test. The name of the class can be anything, but it's good practice to end the name in `Spec` (for example, `BasketWeight-Spec`). You can pick any ending you want, as long as it's the same on all your Spock tests, because it makes it easier for the build system (e.g., Maven) to detect Spock tests.

For technical reasons, Spock can't allow you to name the class with full English text like the test methods. To remedy this limitation, it instead offers the `@Title` annotation, which you can use to give a human-readable explanation of the features that make up this specification.

> **Naming .groovy files using the expected Java convention**
>
> Unlike Java, Groovy doesn't require the name of the class and the name of the file on the disk to be the same. You can place the `BasketWeightSpec` class in a file called MyBasketWeightUnitTest.groovy if that's what you want. For simplicity, I still urge you to use the Java convention because it makes navigating Spock tests much easier. Therefore, the `BasketWeightSpec` class should be placed in a file named Basket-WeightedSpec.groovy.

As an extra bonus, Spock also offers the `@Narrative` annotation, which can provide even more text that describes what the test does, as shown in the following listing.

This listing uses a Groovy multiline string that allows you to insert as many lines of text as you want (a feature that your business analysts might love). In Groovy, multiline strings need triple quotes.

Listing 4.18 also shows the application of the @Subject annotation on the whole class. If you find that all your test methods focus on the same class (which is the usual case), you can apply the @Subject annotation at the top of the Spock test instead of placing it multiple times in the test methods. The class under test is then used as an argument (no need to add the .class extension).

Notice that for brevity I omit the @Title and @Narrative annotations (and usually @Subject as well) in this book's examples. You should always attempt to include them in your Spock tests. I tend to look at @Title and @Subject as a compulsory requirement for a Spock test. @Narrative is good to have, but not essential for all kinds of tests.

4.2.4   *Revising our view of a Spock test*

Because I started explaining Spock elements by using a bottom-up approach, now that we've reached the top, let's see how to revise all parts of a Spock test, as shown in figure 4.12.

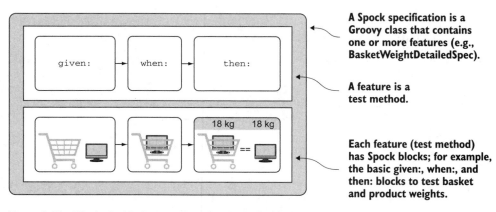

Figure 4.12   Blocks inside features (test methods) inside Specification (Groovy class)

A Spock test is a Groovy class that extends `spock.lang.Specification`. It should be marked with the `@Title` annotation to explain its purpose.

The Spock test contains one or more test methods (*features* in Spock terminology) that examine various aspects of the class under test. Test methods can be named directly with full English sentences. The class under test should be marked with the `@Subject` annotation, either in each test method individually or at the top of the specification.

Finally, each Spock feature (test method) is characterized by the Spock blocks it contains. The most basic structure is the given-when-then blocks that prepare the test, trigger the tested action, and examine the results.

This diagram is useful for our next topic: the lifecycle of a Spock specification.

4.3 *Exploring the lifecycle of a Spock test*

When you create a unit test to examine the behavior of a specific class, you'll find yourself writing the same code over and over again in the `given:` block. This makes sense because several test methods have the same initial state and only a different trigger (the `when:` block). Instead of copying and pasting this behavior (and thus violating the DRY[6] principle), Spock offers you several facilities to extract common preconditions and post-conditions of tests in their own methods.

4.3.1 *Setup and cleanup of a feature*

In the Spock test that examines your imaginary electronic basket, I've duplicated the code that creates products multiple times. This code can be extracted as shown in the following listing.

Listing 4.19 Extracting common initialization code

```
class CommonSetupSpec extends spock.lang.Specification{

        Product tv                              Common classes
        Product camera                          are placed as fields.
                                                                        This method runs
        def setup() {                                                   automatically before
                                                                        each test method.
Initialization code         tv = new Product(name:"bravia",price:1200,weight:18)
is written once.            camera = new Product(name:"panasonic",price:350,weight:2)
        }

        def "A basket with one product weights as that product"() {
                [...code redacted for brevity purposes...]                  Test methods
        }                                                                   run after
                                                                            initialization
         def "A basket with two products weights as their sum"()            code.
                [...code redacted for brevity purposes...]
        }
}
```

---

[6] This acronym stands for don't repeat yourself. See https://en.wikipedia.org/wiki/Don't_repeat_yourself for more information.

Spock will detect a special method called setup() and will run it automatically before each test method. In a similar manner, Spock offers a cleanup() method that will run after each test method finishes. A full example is shown in the following listing.

Listing 4.20   Extracting common pre/post conditions

```
@Subject(Basket)
class CommonCleanupSpec extends spock.lang.Specification{

    Product tv                                   Common classes
    Product camera                               are placed as fields.
    Basket basket

    def setup() {
            tv = new Product(name:"bravia",price:1200,weight:18)
            camera = new Product(name:"panasonic",price:350,weight:2)
            basket = new Basket()
    }

    def "A basket with one product weights as that product"() {
            when: "user wants to buy the TV"
            basket.addProduct tv

            then: "basket weight is equal to all product weight"
            basket.currentWeight == tv.weight
    }

    def "A basket with two products weights as their sum"() {
            when: "user wants to buy the TV and the camera"
            basket.addProduct tv
            basket.addProduct camera

            then: "basket weight is equal to all product weight"
            basket.currentWeight == (tv.weight + camera.weight)
    }

    def cleanup()
    {
            basket.clearAllProducts()
    }
}
```

This method will run automatically before each test method. → `def setup() {`

`def cleanup()` ← *This method will run automatically after each test method.*

As with the cleanup: block, the cleanup() method will always run, regardless of the result of the test. The cleanup() method will even run if an exception is thrown in a test method.

4.3.2   *Setup and cleanup of a specification*

The code you place inside the setup() and cleanup() methods will run once for each test method. If, for example, your Spock test contains seven test methods, the setup/cleanup code will run seven times as well. This is a good thing because it makes each test method independent. You can run only a subset of test methods, knowing they'll be correctly initialized and cleaned afterward.

But sometimes you want initialization code to run only once before all test methods. This is the usual case when you have expensive objects that will slow down the test if they run multiple times. A typical case is a database connection that you use for integration tests, but any long-lived expensive object is a good candidate for running only once.

Spock supports this case as well, as shown in the following listing.

Listing 4.21   All Spock lifecycle methods

```
class LifecycleSpec extends spock.lang.Specification{

    def setupSpec() {                                    ◄─── Initialization for
        println "Will run only once"                          expensive objects
    }

    def setup() {                                        ◄─── Common code
        println "Will run before EACH feature"                for all tests
    }

    def "first feature being tested"() {                 ◄─┐
        expect: "trivial test"                             │
        println "first feature runs"                       │
        2 == 1 +1                                          │
    }                                                      ├── Test methods
    def "second feature being tested"() {                ◄─┘
        expect: "trivial test"
        println "second feature runs"
        5 == 3 +2
    }                                                    ─┐ Common cleanup
    def cleanup() {                                      ◄─┘ code for all tests
        println "Will run once after EACH feature"
    }

    def cleanupSpec() {                                  ◄─── Finalization of
        println "Will run once at the end"                    expensive objects
    }
}
```

If you run this unit test, it will print the following:

```
Will run only once
Will run before EACH feature
first feature runs
Will run once after EACH feature
Will run before EACH feature
second feature runs
Will run once after EACH feature
Will run once at the end
```

Compatibility with JUnit lifecycle methods

If you're familiar with JUnit, you'll notice that the Spock lifecycle methods work exactly like the annotations @Before, @After, @BeforeClass, and @AfterClass. Spock honors these annotations as well, if for some reason you want to continue to use them.

Because setupSpec() and cleanupSpec() are destined to hold only long-lived objects that span all the test methods, Spock allows code in these methods to access only static fields (not recommended) and objects marked as @Shared, as you'll see in the next section.

4.3.3 *Long-lived objects with the @Shared annotation*

You can indicate to Spock which objects you want to survive across all test methods by using the @Shared annotation. As an example, assume that you augment your electronic basket with a credit card processor:

```
public class CreditCardProcessor {

    public void newDayStarted()
    {
            [...code redacted for brevity..]
    }
    public void charge(int price)
    {
            [...code redacted for brevity..]
    }

    public int getCurrentRevenue()
    {
            [...code redacted for brevity..]
    }

    public void shutDown()
    {
            [...code redacted for brevity..]
    }
}
```

CreditCardProcessor is an expensive object. It connects to a bank back end and allows your basket to charge credit cards. Even though the bank has provided dummy credit card numbers for testing purposes, the initialization of the connection is slow. It would be unrealistic to have each test method connect to the bank again. The following listing shows the solution to this problem.

Listing 4.22 Using the @Shared annotation

```
class SharedSpec extends spock.lang.Specification{

    @Shared                                             Will be created
    CreditCardProcessor creditCardProcessor;            only once

    BillableBasket basket                  ◀──  Will be created
                                                multiple times
    def setupSpec() {
        creditCardProcessor = new CreditCardProcessor()  ◀──  Expensive/slow
    }                                                          initialization
```

Shared object
can be used
normally.

```
def setup() {
    basket = new BillableBasket()
    creditCardProcessor.newDayStarted()
    basket.setCreditCardProcessor(creditCardProcessor)
}

def "user buys a single product"() {
    given: "an empty basket and a TV"
    Product tv = new Product(name:"bravia",price:1200,weight:18)

    and: "user wants to buy the TV"
    basket.addProduct(tv)

    when: "user checks out"
    basket.checkout()

    then: "revenue is the same as the price of TV"
    creditCardProcessor.currentRevenue == tv.price
}

def "user buys two products"() {
    given: "an empty basket and a camera"
    Product camera = new
                Product(name:"panasonic",price:350,weight:2)

    and: "user wants to two cameras"
    basket.addProduct(camera,2)

    when: "user checks out"
    basket.checkout()

    then: "revenue is the same as the price of both products"
    creditCardProcessor.currentRevenue == 2 * camera.price
}

def cleanup() {
    basket.clearAllProducts()
}

def cleanupSpec() {
    creditCardProcessor.shutDown()
}
}
```

Fast/cheap
initialization

Will run
multiple times

Will run
only once

Here you mark the expensive credit card processor with the @Shared annotation. This ensures that Spock creates it only once. On the other hand, the electronic basket itself is lightweight, and therefore it's created multiple times (once for each test method). Notice also that the credit card processor is closed down once at the end of the test.

4.3.4   *Use of the old() method*

The old() method of Spock is a cool trick, but I've yet to find a real example that makes it worthwhile. I mention it here for completeness, and because if you don't know how it works, you might think it breaks the Spock lifecycle principles. You use it when you want your test to capture the difference from the previous state instead of the absolute value, as shown in the following listing.

Listing 4.23   Asserting with the `old()` method

```
def "Adding a second product to the basket increases its weight"() {
    given: "an empty basket"
    Basket basket = new Basket()

    and: "a tv is already added to the basket"
    Product tv = new Product(name:"bravia",price:1200,weight:18)
    basket.addProduct(tv)

    when: "user gets a camera too"
    Product camera = new Product(name:"panasonic",price:350,weight:2)
    basket.addProduct(camera)

    then: "basket weight is updated accordingly"
    basket.currentWeight == old(basket.currentWeight) + camera.weight
}
```

Product is added in given: block. →

Second product is added in when: block. ←

Checking the difference in weight →

Here you have a unit test that checks the weight of the basket after a second product is added. You could check for absolute values in the `then:` block (assert that the basket weight is the sum of two products), but instead you use the `old()` method and say to Spock, "I expect the weight to be the same as before the `when:` block, plus the weight of the camera." Figure 4.13 illustrates this.

The difference in expression is subtle, and if you find the `old()` method confusing, there's no need to use it at all.

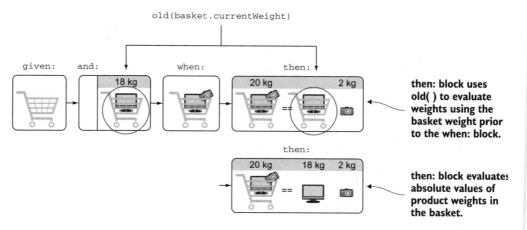

Figure 4.13   The `old()` method allows you to access values set before the `when:` block in a test.

4.4 *Writing readable Spock tests*

Despite all the cool facilities offered by Groovy, your ultimate target when writing Spock tests should be readability. Especially in large enterprise applications, the ease of refactoring is greatly affected by the quality of existing unit tests. Because unit tests also act as a live specification of the system, understanding Spock tests is crucial in cases requiring you to read a unit test to deduce the expected behavior of the code.

Knowing the basic techniques (for example, the Spock blocks) is only the first step to writing concise and understandable unit tests. The second step is to use the basic techniques effectively, avoiding the temptation of "sprinkling" unit test code with Groovy tricks that add no real purpose to the test other than showing off.[7]

4.4.1 *Structuring Spock tests*

You saw all the Spock blocks at the beginning of the chapter. The given-when-then cycle should be your mantra when you start writing your first Spock unit tests. You might quickly discover that Spock doesn't have many restrictions in regard to the number and sequence of blocks inside a test method. But just because you can mix and match Spock blocks doesn't mean that you should.

As an example, it's possible to have multiple when-then blocks in a single test method, as shown in the following listing.

Listing 4.24 Multiple when-then blocks

```
def "Adding products to a basket increases its weight"() {
    given: "an empty basket"
    Basket basket = new Basket()

    and: "a two products"
    Product tv = new Product(name:"bravia",price:1200,weight:18)
    Product camera = new Product(name:"panasonic",price:350,weight:2)

    when: "user gets the camera"
    basket.addProduct(camera)                              ◄─────  First pair of
                                                                   when-then
    then: "basket weight is updated accordingly"       ◄──┘
    basket.currentWeight == camera.weight

    when: "user gets the tv too"                           ◄─────  Second pair of when-
    basket.addProduct(tv)                                          then will be executed
                                                                   in sequence.
    then: "basket weight is updated accordingly"       ◄──┘
    basket.currentWeight == camera.weight + tv.weight
}
```

---

[7] If you really want to show off one-liners, Groovy is not for you. Learn Perl.

This pattern must be used with care. It can be used correctly as a way to test a sequence of events (as demonstrated in this listing). If used incorrectly, it might also mean that your test is testing two things and should be broken.

Use common sense when you structure Spock tests. If writing descriptions next to Spock blocks is becoming harder and harder, it might mean that your test is doing complex things.

4.4.2   *Ensuring that Spock tests are self-documenting*

I've already shown you the `@Subject` and `@Title` annotations and explained that the only reason they're not included in all examples is to save space.

What I've always included, however, are the descriptions that follow each Spock block. Even though in Spock these are optional, and a unit test will run without them, you should consider them essential and always include them in your unit tests. Take a look at the following listing for a real-world antipattern of this technique.

> **Listing 4.25   Missing block descriptions—*don't do this***

```
def "Test toRegExp(Productos3.txt)" () {                          ◄─── Unclear test
    setup:                                                             method name
    String filePattern = 'PROD{MES}{DIA}_11.TXT'
    String regexp = FileFilterUtil.toRegExpLowerCase( filePattern )
    Pattern pattern = Pattern.compile(regexp)

    expect:
    StringUtils.trimToEmpty(filename).toLowerCase().matches(pattern) ==
            match

    where:
    filename << ['PROD.05-12.11.TXT', 'prod.03-21.11.txt',
                 'PROD051211.TXT', 'prod0512_11.txt' ]
    match << [false, false, false, true ]
}
```

Blocks without descriptions (annotation pointing to `setup:`, `expect:`, and `where:`)

This test lacks any kind of human-readable text. It's impossible to understand what this test does without reading the code. It's also impossible to read it if you're a non-technical person. In this example, it's a pity that the name of the test method isn't a plain English sentence (a feature offered natively by Spock). You could improve this test by changing the block labels as follows:

```
setup: "given a naming pattern for product files"
expect: "that the file name matches regardless of spaces and capitalization"
where: "some possible file names are"
```

Always include in your Spock tests at least the block descriptions and make sure that the test method name is human-readable.

4.4.3 Modifying failure output

Readability shouldn't be constrained to successful unit tests. Even more important is the readability of failed tests. In a large application with legacy code and a suite of existing unit tests, a single change can break unit tests that you didn't even know existed.

You learned how Groovy asserts work in chapter 2 and how Spock gives you much more information when a test fails. Although Spock automatically analyzes simple types and collections, you have to provide more hints when you assert your own classes. As an example, the following listing adds one of the products in the basket twice.

Listing 4.26 Adding a product twice in the basket

```
def "Adding products to a basket increases its weight"() {
    given: "an empty basket"
    ProblematicBasket basket = new ProblematicBasket()

    and: "two different products"
    Product laptop = new Product(name:"toshiba",price:1200,weight:5)
    Product camera = new Product(name:"panasonic",price:350,weight:2)

    when: "user gets a laptop and two cameras"
    basket.addProduct(camera,2)                    ◀─┐ Two cameras
    basket.addProduct(laptop)                         │ are inserted.

    then: "basket weight is updated accordingly"
    basket.currentWeight == (2 * camera.weight) + laptop.weight
}
```

Checks the weight of three products ──▶

I've introduced a bug in the Basket class. When the test fails, you get the output shown in figure 4.14.

Because Basket.java is a class unknown to Spock, it can't give you detailed information about what went wrong. According to this result, the total weight of the basket

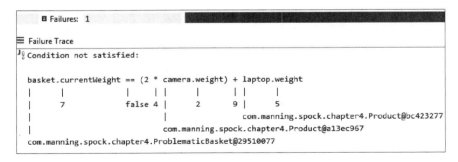

Figure 4.14 Failed Spock test with custom class

is now 7 kilograms, even though all products weigh 9 kg. To debug this unit test, you'd have to run it in a debugger and find the source of the mistake in the Basket class.

To help Spock do its magic, you can override the toString() method in your objects, because this is what Spock runs on failed tests. The following listing exposes the internal implementation of the basket in the toString() method.

Listing 4.27   Helping failure rendering in the toString() method

```
public class ProblematicBasket {

    protected Map<Product,Integer> contents = new HashMap<>();      ◄─── Key is product; value
                                                                         is how many times
    [... rest of code is redacted for brevity purposes...]               it's in the basket.

    @Override                  ◄─── Custom implementation of toString()
    public String toString()
    {
        StringBuilder builder = new StringBuilder("[ ");
        for (Entry<Product, Integer> entry:contents.entrySet())
        {
            builder.append(entry.getValue());          ◄─── Prints number of
            builder.append(" x ");                          times each product
            builder.append(entry.getKey().getName());       is in the basket
            builder.append(", ");                      ◄─── Prints product name
        }
        builder.setLength(builder.length()-2);

        return builder.append(" ]").toString();
    }

}
```

Now when the test fails, you get the output shown in figure 4.15.

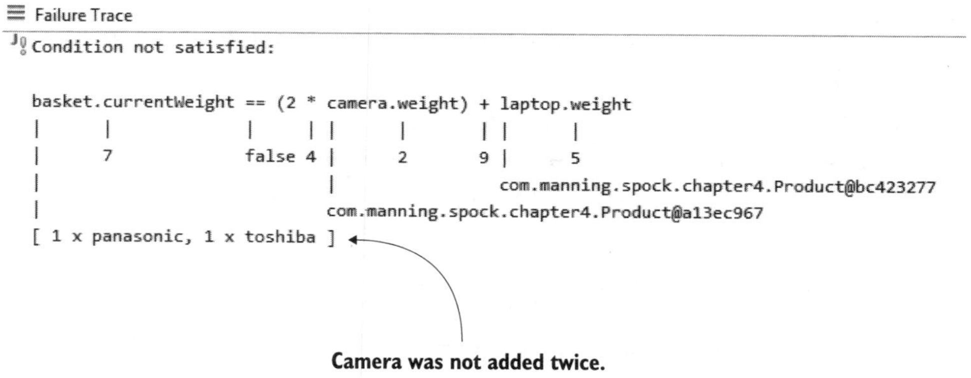

Figure 4.15   Spock failed test with custom toString() method

Seeing this result makes it much easier to understand what's gone wrong. Just by looking at the test result, you can see that even though you added two cameras in the basket, it kept only one. The bug you inserted is exactly at this place (it always adds one product in the basket, regardless of what the user said).

This kind of detail is a lifesaver when multiple tests break and it's hard to understand whether the test needs fixing or the production code you changed is against specifications. In a large enterprise application, a single code change can easily break hundreds of existing unit tests. It's critical to understand which tests broke because your change is wrong, and which tests broke because they're based on old business needs that are made obsolete by your change. In the former case, you must revise your code change (so that tests pass), whereas in the latter case, you need to update the failing unit tests themselves so that they express the new requirement.

The beauty of this Spock feature is that `toString()` is usually already implemented in domain objects for easy logging and reporting. You may be lucky enough to get this functionality for free without any changes in your Java code.

After you finish writing a Spock test, check whether you need to implement custom `toString()` methods for the classes that are used in the final assertions.

4.4.4 Using Hamcrest matchers

Hamcrest matchers[8] are a third-party library commonly used in JUnit assert statements. They offer a pseudo-language that allows for expressiveness in what's being evaluated. You might have seen them already in JUnit tests.

Spock supports Hamcrest matchers natively, as shown in the following listing.

Listing 4.28 Spock support for Hamcrest matchers

```
def "trivial test with Hamcrest"() {
    given: "a list of products"
    List<String> products= ["camera", "laptop","hifi"]          ◄── Creation of a list

    expect: "camera should be one of them"
    products hasItem("camera")                                  ◄── Checks that any item
                                                                    of the list is "camera"
    and: "hotdog is not one of them"
    products not(hasItem("hotdog"))
}
```

Chains two Hamcrest matchers → (points to `products not(hasItem("hotdog"))`)

The `hasItem()` matcher accepts a list and returns `true` if any element matches the argument. Normally, that check would require a loop in Java, so this matcher is more brief and concise.

One of the important features of Hamcrest matchers is that they can be chained together to create more-complicated expressions. Listing 4.27 also uses the `not()`

---

[8] *Hamcrest* is an anagram of the word *matchers*.

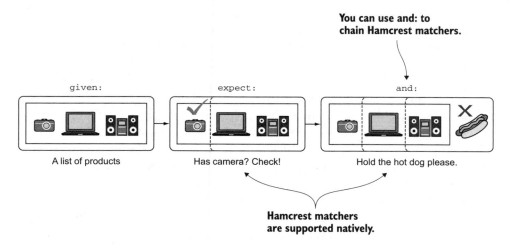

Figure 4.16   **Hamcrest matchers can be used natively within Spock tests.**

matcher, which takes an existing matcher and reverses its meaning. Figure 4.16 illustrates this test. You can find more information about other Hamcrest matchers (and how to create your own) on the official web page at http://hamcrest.org/.

Spock also supports an alternative syntax for Hamcrest matchers that makes the flow of reading a specification more natural, as shown in the next listing.

Listing 4.29   Alternative Spock support for Hamcrest matchers

```
def "trivial test with Hamcrest (alt)"() {
    given: "an empty list"
    List<String> products= new ArrayList<String>()

    when: "it is filled with products"
    products.add("laptop")
    products.add("camera")
    products.add("hifi")

    then: "camera should be one of them"         ←  expect() is useful
    expect(products, hasItem("camera"))              for then: blocks.

    and: "hotdog is not one of them"              ←  that() is useful for and:
    that(products, not(hasItem("hotdog")))           and expect: Spock blocks.
}
```

The test is exactly the same as listing 4.28, but reads better because the matcher lines are coupled with the Spock blocks. The assertions are close to human text: "expect products has item (named) camera, and that products (does) not have item (named) hotdog" (see figure 4.17).

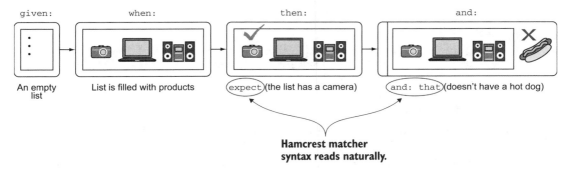

Figure 4.17 Hamcrest matchers have an alternate near-English syntax that makes them easier to read.

The `expect()` and `that()` methods are Spock syntactic sugar and have no effect on how the test runs.

> ## Compatibility with JUnit
>
> As you've seen, Spock allows you to reuse several existing JUnit facilities. I've already mentioned that JUnit lifecycle annotations (`@Before`, `@After`, and so on) are recognized by Spock. Now you've seen that integration with Hamcrest matchers is also supported. Spock even supports JUnit rules out of the box. The transition to Spock is easy because it doesn't force you to discard your existing knowledge. If your team has invested heavily in custom matchers or rules, you can use them in your Spock tests, too.

Hamcrest matchers have their uses, and they can be powerful if you create your own for your domain classes. But often they can be replaced with Groovy code, and more specifically with Groovy closures. The following listing shows the same trivial example without Hamcrest matchers.

Listing 4.30 Using Groovy closures in Spock assertions

```
def "trivial test with Groovy closure"() {
   given: "a list of products"
   List<String> products= ["camera", "laptop", "hifi"]

   expect: "camera should be one of them"
   products.any{ productName -> productName == "camera"}

   and: "hotdog is not one of them"
   products.every{ productName -> productName != "hotdog"}
}
```

Iterates over list
and passes if any
is named camera

Iterates over
list and checks
all names of
products

I consider Groovy closures more powerful because they can be created on the spot for each unit test to match exactly what's being tested. But if you have existing Hamcrest matchers from your JUnit tests, using them in Spock tests is easy, as shown in listings 4.28 and 4.29.

As a general rule, if a Hamcrest matcher already covers what you want, use it (hasItem() in the preceding example). If using Hamcrest matchers makes your example complex to read, use closures.

4.4.5   *Grouping test code further*

I mentioned at the beginning of the chapter that one of the first problems you encounter in large enterprise projects is the length of unit tests. With Spock blocks, you already have a basic structure in place because the setup-trigger-evaluate cycles are clearly marked. Even then, you'll find several times that your then: and given: blocks contain too many things, making the test difficult to read.

To better illustrate this problem, you'll add to the running example a class that represents the warehouse of the e-shop, as shown in the following listing.

Listing 4.31   An imaginary warehouse

```
public class WarehouseInventory {

    public void preload(Product product, int times){          ◄─── Loads the
            [...code redacted for brevity...]                        warehouse
    }

    public void subtract(String productName, Integer times){  ◄─── Called by the basket
                                                                    during checkout
            [...code redacted for brevity...]
    }

    public int availableOfProduct(String productName){        ◄─── Provides
            [...code redacted for brevity...]                       inventory status
    }

    public boolean isEmpty(){                                  ◄─── Returns true if
            [...code redacted for brevity...]                       no product exists
    }

    public int getBoxesMovedToday(){                          ◄─── Keeps track
            [...code redacted for brevity...]                       of sales
    }
}
```

You'll also augment the electronic basket with more (imaginary) methods that define its behavior, as shown in the following listing.

Listing 4.32   An enterprisy basket

```
public class EnterprisyBasket extends Basket{

    public void enableAutoRefresh(){                          ◄─── Classic enterprise code
            [...code redacted for brevity...]
    }
```

```
public void setNumberOfCaches(int number){
        [...code redacted for brevity...]
}

public void setCustomerResolver(DefaultCustomerResolver
                defaultCustomerResolver){
        [...code redacted for brevity...]
}

public void setWarehouseInventory(WarehouseInventory
            warehouseInventory){
        [...code redacted for brevity...]
}

public void setLanguage(String language){
        [...code redacted for brevity...]
}

public void checkout(){
        [...code redacted for brevity...]
}
```

Setter injection methods → (points to setCustomerResolver / setWarehouseInventory)

Classic enterprise code ← (points to setNumberOfCaches / setLanguage)

Removes products from inventory ← (points to checkout)

```
}
```

Now assume that you want to write a unit test for the warehouse to verify that it works correctly when a customer checks out. The Spock test is shown in the next listing.

Listing 4.33 Assertions and setup on the same object

```
def "Buying products reduces the inventory availability"() {
    given: "an inventory with products"
    Product laptop = new Product(name:"toshiba",price:1200,weight:5)
    Product camera = new Product(name:"panasonic",price:350,weight:2)
    Product hifi = new Product(name:"jvc",price:600,weight:5)
    WarehouseInventory warehouseInventory = new WarehouseInventory()
    warehouseInventory.preload(laptop,3)
    warehouseInventory.preload(camera,5)
    warehouseInventory.preload(hifi,2)

    and: "an empty basket"
    EnterprisyBasket basket = new EnterprisyBasket()
    basket.setWarehouseInventory(warehouseInventory)
    basket.setCustomerResolver(new DefaultCustomerResolver())
    basket.setLanguage("english")
    basket.setNumberOfCaches(3)
    basket.enableAutoRefresh()

    when: "user gets a laptop and two cameras"
    basket.addProduct(camera,2)
    basket.addProduct(laptop)

    and: "user completes the transaction"
    basket.checkout()
```

Object creation → (points to WarehouseInventory and EnterprisyBasket creation lines)

Object parameters ← (points to preload lines and setter lines)

```
then: "warehouse is updated accordingly"
!warehouseInventory.isEmpty()
warehouseInventory.getBoxesMovedToday() == 3
warehouseInventory.availableOfProduct("toshiba") == 2
warehouseInventory.availableOfProduct("panasonic") == 3
warehouseInventory.availableOfProduct("jvc") == 2
}
```

Assertions on the same object

You've already split the `given:` and `when:` blocks with `and:` blocks in order to make the test more-readable. But it can be improved even more in two areas:

- The final assertions test multiple things, but all on the same object.
- The `given:` block of the test has too many statements, which can be roughly split into two kinds: statements that create objects, and statements that set properties on existing objects.

In most cases (involving large Spock tests), extra properties are secondary to the object creation. You can make several changes to the test, as shown in the following listing.

Listing 4.34 Grouping similar code with Groovy and Spock

```
def "Buying products reduces the inventory availability (alt)"() {
    given: "an inventory with products"
    Product laptop = new Product(name:"toshiba",price:1200,weight:5)
    Product camera = new Product(name:"panasonic",price:350,weight:2)
    Product hifi = new Product(name:"jvc",price:600,weight:5)
    WarehouseInventory warehouseInventory = new WarehouseInventory()
    warehouseInventory.with{
            preload laptop,3
            preload camera,5
            preload hifi,2
    }

    and: "an empty basket"
    EnterprisyBasket basket = new EnterprisyBasket()
    basket.with {
            setWarehouseInventory(warehouseInventory)
            setCustomerResolver(new DefaultCustomerResolver())
            setLanguage "english"
            setNumberOfCaches 3
            enableAutoRefresh()
    }

    when: "user gets a laptop and two cameras"
    basket.with {
            addProduct camera,2
            addProduct laptop
    }

    and: "user completes the transaction"
    basket.checkout()
```

Group object setup with Groovy object.with

Remove parentheses

```
then: "warehouse is updated accordingly"
with(warehouseInventory) {
{
        !isEmpty()
        getBoxesMovedToday() == 3
        availableOfProduct("toshiba") == 2
        availableOfProduct("panasonic") == 3
        availableOfProduct("jvc") == 2
}
}
}
```

→ **Group assertions with Spock Specification.with**

First, you can group all assertions by using the Spock with() construct. This feature is specific to Spock and allows you to show that multiple assertions affect a single object. It's much clearer now that you deal specifically with the warehouse inventory at the end of this test.

The Spock with() construct is inspired from the Groovy with() construct that works on any Groovy code (even outside Spock tests). I've used this feature in the given: and when: blocks to group all setup code that affects a single object. Now it's clearer which code is creating new objects and which code is setting parameters on existing objects (indentation also helps).

Notice that the two with() constructs may share the same name but are unrelated. One is a Groovy feature, and the other is a Spock feature that works only in Spock asserts.

As an added bonus, I've also used the Groovy convention demonstrated in chapter 2, where you can remove parentheses in method calls with at least one argument. This makes the test a little more like DSL. It's not much, but it certainly helps with readability. I'll show more ways to deal with large Spock tests in chapter 8.

4.5 Summary

- Spock contains several blocks/labels to mark the phases inside a unit test. They help readability of the test and in some cases enforce the code structure. (Spock will reject assignments when an assertion was expected.)
- The given: block creates the scene for the test, the when: block triggers the tested action, and the then: block examines the result. The given-then-when structure is the suggested structure for Spock tests.
- The and: block can be used on any other block as a semantic extension.
- The expect: block is a combination of then: and when: and can be used for trivial tests or as an intermediate precondition in longer tests.
- The cleanup: block will always run at the end of a Spock test regardless of the test result. It's used to release resources.
- Spock test methods can have full sentences as names. You should always exploit this feature to better describe what your method does.
- The @Subject annotation should be used to mark the class under test. You can use it individually in each test method, or at the class level if all test methods focus on a single class.

- The `@Title` annotation should be used to explain with full English text what your Spock test does.
- The `@Narrative` annotation can be used for a longer description of a Spock test.
- Spock methods `setup()` and `cleanup()` run before and after each test method. They run as many times as test methods exist.
- Spock methods `setupSpec()` and `cleanupSpec()` run once before all test methods and once after they're finished.
- Spock supports and understands JUnit annotations such as `@Before`, `@After`, `@BeforeClass`, and `@AfterClass`.
- The `@Shared` annotation marks long-lived objects that span all test methods. The `setupSpec()` and `cleanupSpec()` methods work only with objects that are either static or marked with the `@Shared` annotation.
- The `old()` method can be used in specific cases to capture the relative change of the class state instead of comparing absolute values before and after the triggered action.
- A Spock test can have multiple `then:` blocks, which are executed in the order they're mentioned.
- All Spock blocks should have an English description next to them for readability.
- Spock calls the Java `toString()` method automatically on any involved class when a test fails. Overriding this method allows you to define what will be shown on failed tests.
- Spock natively supports Hamcrest matchers with three alternative syntax variations.
- Spock natively supports JUnit rules out of the box.
- The Groovy `object.with` construct can be used to group object parameterization inside Spock tests.
- The Spock `Specification.with` construct can be used to group assertions to a single object.

Parameterized tests

This chapter covers

- Definition of parameterized tests
- Using the `where:` block
- Understanding data tables and data pipes
- Writing custom data providers

The previous chapter presented all the Spock blocks that you can use in a unit test, except for one. I left out the `where:` block on purpose because it deserves a chapter of its own. The `where:` block is used for parameterized tests. *Parameterized tests* are unit tests that share the same test logic (for example, when the temperature goes up, the reactor must shut down), but need to run on different parameters (for example, with low temperature and then with high temperature) in order to account for all cases.

This chapter covers both some theory on when to use parameterized tests and facilities Spock offers for parameterized testing. You might already have seen parameterized tests with JUnit, so feel free to skip the first section and start reading at section 5.2 for the specific Spock features if you're already familiar with the concept of parameterized testing.

Spock is flexible when it comes to parameterized tests. If offers a complete portfo-lio of techniques adaptable to your situation, no matter the complexity of your test data. The most basic format of parameterized tests (data tables) was already demon-strated in chapter 3. This chapter also explains data pipes (the underlying mechanism of data tables) and shows how to write custom data providers with Spock, which is the most flexible solution (but needs more programming effort).

All these Spock techniques have their own advantages and disadvantages with regards to readability and flexibility of unit tests, so it's important to understand the trade-offs between them. Understanding when to use each one is one of the running themes of this chapter.

5.1   *Detecting the need for parameterized tests*

Experienced developers usually can understand the need for a parameterized test right away. But even if you're just starting with unit tests, an easy rule of thumb can show you the need for a parameterized test. Every time you start a new unit test by copying-pasting an existing one, ask yourself, "Is this test that much different from the previous one?" If you find yourself duplicating unit tests and then changing only one or two variables to create a similar scenario, take a step back and think about whether a parameterized test would be more useful. Parameterized tests will help you keep the test code DRY.[1]

Duplicating unit test code isn't a healthy habit

Anytime you copy-paste a unit test, you're creating code duplication, because you haven't thought about reusable code segments. Like production code, test code should be treated with the same "respect." Refactoring unit tests to allow them to share code via composition instead of performing a blind copy-paste should be one of your first priorities when adding new unit tests into an existing suite. More details are presented in chapter 8.

Assume, for example, that you have a single class that takes an image filename and returns `true` if the picture has an extension that's considered valid for the application:

```
public class ImageNameValidator {
    public boolean isValidImageExtension(String fileName)
    {
        [...redacted for brevity...]
    }

}
```

---

[1] This acronym stands for *don't repeat yourself.* See https://en.wikipedia.org/wiki/Don't_repeat_yourself for more information.

A first naive approach would be to write a single Spock test for every image extension that needs to be examined. This approach is shown in the following listing (and it clearly suffers from code duplication).

Listing 5.1 Duplicate tests—*don't do this*

```
def "Valid images are JPG"() {
    given: "an image extension checker and a jpg file"
    ImageNameValidator validator = new ImageNameValidator()
    String pictureFile = "scenery.jpg"

    expect: "that the filename is valid"
    validator.isValidImageExtension(pictureFile)
}

def "Valid images are JPEG"() {
    given: "an image extension checker and a jpeg file"
    ImageNameValidator validator = new ImageNameValidator()
    String pictureFile = "house.jpeg"

    expect: "that the filename is valid"
    validator.isValidImageExtension(pictureFile)
}

def "Tiff are invalid"() {
    given: "an image extension checker and a tiff file"
    ImageNameValidator validator = new ImageNameValidator()
    String pictureFile = "sky.tiff"

    expect: "that the filename is invalid"
    !validator.isValidImageExtension(pictureFile)
}
```

Each test differs in output data.

Each test differs in input data.

The original requirement is to accept JPG files only, and a single unit test is written. The customer reports that the application doesn't work on Linux because .jpeg files are used. Application code is updated, and another test method is added (by copying the existing one).

Then a business analyst requests an explicit test for *not* supporting TIFF files. You can see where this is going. In large enterprise applications, multiple developers might work on the same feature as time progresses. If each developer is blindly adding a new unit test by copy-paste (either because of a lack of time or lack of experience), the result is a Spock test, as shown in listing 5.1, that smells of code duplication from afar.

Notice that each test method by itself in listing 5.1 is well structured. Each is documented, it tests one thing, the trigger action is small, and so on. The problem stems from the collection of those test methods that need further refactoring, as they all have the exact same business logic.

5.1.1   *What are parameterized tests?*

An example of a parameterized test for this class in Spock is shown in the following listing. With a single unit test, this listing not only replaces all three tests of listing 5.1 but also adds two more cases.

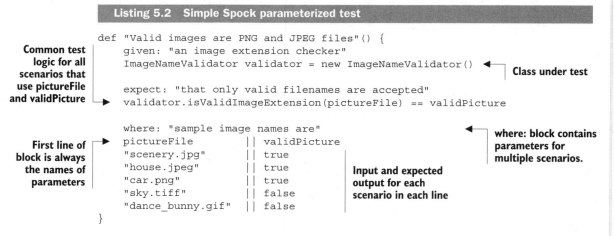

Listing 5.2   Simple Spock parameterized test

```
def "Valid images are PNG and JPEG files"() {
    given: "an image extension checker"
    ImageNameValidator validator = new ImageNameValidator()        ◄── Class under test

    expect: "that only valid filenames are accepted"
    validator.isValidImageExtension(pictureFile) == validPicture

    where: "sample image names are"
    pictureFile            || validPicture
    "scenery.jpg"          || true
    "house.jpeg"           || true
    "car.png"              || true
    "sky.tiff"             || false
    "dance_bunny.gif"      || false
}
```

Common test logic for all scenarios that use pictureFile and validPicture

First line of block is always the names of parameters

where: block contains parameters for multiple scenarios.

Input and expected output for each scenario in each line

The test method examines multiple scenarios in which the test logic is always the same (validate a filename) and only the input (jpg) and output (valid/not valid) variables change each time. The test code is fixed, whereas the test input and output data come in the form of parameters (and thus you have a parameterized test).

The idea is better illustrated in figure 5.1.

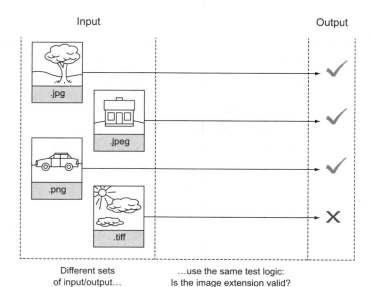

Figure 5.1   **Parameterized tests share the same test logic for different input/ output datasets.**

The test code is shared among all parameters. Instead of duplicating this common code for each scenario, you centralize it on a single test method. Then each scenario comes with its own scenario parameters that define the expected result for each input. Output 1 is expected when the test scenario is triggered with input 1, output 2 is expected if input 2 is used, and so on.

5.2 Using the where: block

The where: block, introduced in chapter 3, is responsible for holding all input and output parameters for a parameterized test. It can be combined with all other blocks shown in chapter 4, but it has to be the last block inside a Spock test, as illustrated in figure 5.2. Only an and: block might follow a where: block (and that would be rare).

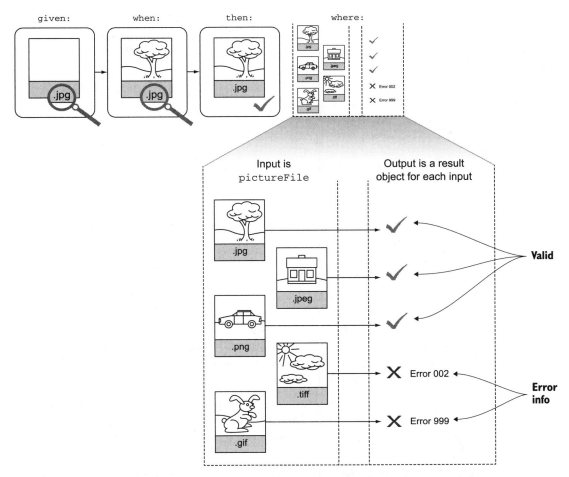

Figure 5.2 A where: **clause must be the last block in a Spock test. It contains the differing values for parameterized tests.**

The simpler given-expect-when structure was shown in listing 5.2. This works for trivial and relatively simple tests. The more usual way (and the recommended way for larger parameterized tests) is the given-when-then-where structure shown in the following listing.

Listing 5.3   The given-when-then-where structure

```
def "Valid images are PNG and JPEG files (enterprise version)"() {
    given: "an image extension checker"
    ImageNameValidator validator = new ImageNameValidator()

    when: "an image is checked"                           Input parameter
    ImageExtensionCheck imageExtensionCheck =             (pictureFile) is used
        validator.examineImageExtension(pictureFile)   ◄  in the when: block.

    then: "expect that only valid filenames are accepted"
    imageExtensionCheck.result == validPicture
    imageExtensionCheck.errorCode == error               Output parameters are
    imageExtensionCheck.errorDescription == description  checked in the then: block.

    where: "sample image names are"
    pictureFile          || validPicture | error       | description
    "scenery.jpg"        || true         | ""          | ""
    "house.jpeg"         || true         | ""          | ""
    "car.png"            || true         | ""          | ""
    "sky.tiff"           || false        | "ERROR002"  | "Tiff files are not
                                                            supported"
    "dance_bunny.gif"    || false        | "ERROR999"  | "Unsupported file
                                                            type"
}
```

where: block
is last block
in the test.

Input and output
scenarios in each
consequent line

Here I've modified the `ImageNameValidator` class to return a simple Java object named `ImageExtensionCheck` that groups the result of the check along with an error code and a human-readable description. The `when:` block creates this result object, and the `then:` block compares its contents against the parameterized variables in the `where:` block.

Notice that the `where:` block is the last one in the Spock test. If you have other blocks after the `where:` block, Spock will refuse to run the test.

Now that you know the basic use of the `where:` block, it's time to focus on its contents. So far, all the examples you've seen have used data tables. This is one of the possible variations. Spock supports the following:

- *Data tables*—This is the declarative style. Easy to write but doesn't cope with complex tests. Readable by business analysts.
- *Data tables with programmatic expressions as values*—A bit more flexible than data tables but with some loss in readability.
- *Data pipes with fully dynamic input and outputs*—Flexible but not as readable as data tables.

- *Custom data iterators*—Your nuclear option when all else fails. They can be used for any extreme corner case of data generation. Unreadable by nontechnical people.

You'll examine the details of all these techniques in turn in the rest of the chapter.

5.2.1 Using data tables in the where: block

We've now established that the where: block must be the last block in a Spock test. In all examples you've seen so far, the where: block contains a data table, as illustrated in figure 5.3.

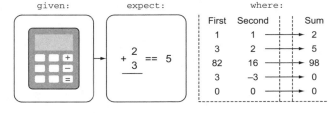

Figure 5.3 The where: block often contains a data table with defined input columns and a desired result column.

This data table holds multiple test cases in which each line is a scenario and each column is an input or output variable for that scenario. The next listing shows this format.

Listing 5.4 Using data tables in Spock

```
def "Trivial adder test"() {
    given: "an adder"
    Adder adder = new Adder()

    expect: "that it calculates the sum of two numbers"
    adder.add(first,second)==sum

    where: "some scenarios are"
    first   |second    || sum
    1       | 1        || 2
    3       | 2        || 5
    82      | 16       || 98
    3       | -3       || 0
    0       | 0        || 0
}
```

Relationship between output and input parameters: sum is based on first and second.

Scenarios that will be tested contain values for first and second and expected sum.

Names of parameters— first and second are input and sum is output.

The data table contains a header that names each parameter. You have to make sure that the names you give to parameters don't clash with existing variables in the source code (either in local scope or global scope).

You'll notice that the data table is split with either single (|) or dual (| |) pipe symbols. The single pipe denotes a column, and the double pipe shows where the input parameters stop and the output parameters start. Usually, only one column in a data table uses dual pipes.

In the simple example of listing 5.4, the output parameter is obvious. In more complex examples, such as listing 5.3 or the examples with the nuclear reactor in chapter

3, the dual pipe is much more helpful. Keep in mind that the dual pipe symbol is used strictly for readability and doesn't affect the way Spock uses the data table. You can omit it if you think that it's not needed (my recommendation is to always include it).

If you're a seasoned Java developer, you should have noticed something strange in listing 5.4.[2] The types of the parameters are never declared. The data table contains the name and values of parameters but not their type!

Remember that Groovy (as explained in chapter 2) is an optionally typed language. In the case of data tables, Spock can understand the type of input and output parameters by the context of the unit test.

But it's possible to explicitly define the types of the parameters by using them as arguments in the test method, as shown in the next listing.

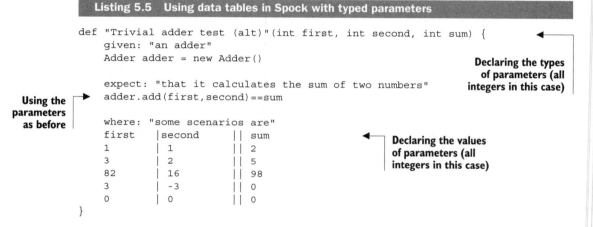

Listing 5.5 Using data tables in Spock with typed parameters

```
def "Trivial adder test (alt)"(int first, int second, int sum) {      ◀─────
    given: "an adder"
    Adder adder = new Adder()                                    Declaring the types
                                                                 of parameters (all
    expect: "that it calculates the sum of two numbers"          integers in this case)
    adder.add(first,second)==sum

    where: "some scenarios are"
    first    |second    || sum
    1        | 1        || 2            ◀─── Declaring the values
    3        | 2        || 5                 of parameters (all
    82       | 16       || 98                integers in this case)
    3        | -3       || 0
    0        | 0        || 0
}
```

Using the parameters as before

Here I've included all parameters as arguments in the test method. This makes their type clear and can also help your IDE (Eclipse) to understand the nature of the test parameters.

You should decide on your own whether you need to declare the types of the parameters. For brevity, I don't declare them in any of the chapter examples. Just make sure that all developers on your team agree on the same decision.

5.2.2 Understanding limitations of data tables

I've already stressed that the where: block must be the last block in a Spock test (and only an and: block can follow it as a rare exception). I've also shown how to declare the types of parameters (in listing 5.5) when they're not clear either to your IDE or even to Spock in some extreme cases.

Another corner case with Spock data tables is that they must have at least two columns. If you're writing a test that has only one parameter, you must use a "filler" for a second column, as shown in the next listing.

---

[2] And also in listings 5.3 and 5.2, if you've been paying attention.

Listing 5.6 Data tables with one column

```
def "Tiff, gif, raw,mov and bmp are invalid extensions"() {
    given: "an image extension checker"
    ImageNameValidator validator = new ImageNameValidator()

    expect: "that only valid filenames are accepted"
    !validator.isValidImageExtension(pictureFile)

    where: "sample image names are"
    pictureFile         || _
    "screenshot.bmp"    || _
    "IMG3434.raw"       || _
    "christmas.mov"     || _
    "sky.tiff"          || _
    "dance_bunny.gif"   || _
}
```

Output parameter is always false for this test. All images are invalid.

Underscore acts as dummy filler for the Boolean result of the test.

Perhaps some of these limitations will be lifted in future versions of Spock, but for the time being, you have to live with them. The advantages of Spock data tables still outperform these minor inconveniences.

5.2.3 *Performing easy maintenance of data tables*

The ultimate goal of a parameterized test is easy maintenance. Maintenance is affected by several factors, such as the size of the test, its readability, and of course, its comments. Unfortunately, test code doesn't always get the same attention as production code, resulting in tests that are hard to read and understand.

The big advantage of Spock and the way it exploits data tables in parameterized tests is that it forces you to gather all input and output variables in a single place. Not only that, but unlike other solutions for parameterized tests (examples were shown with JUnit in chapter 3), data tables include both the names and the values of test parameters.

Adding a new scenario is literally a single line change. Adding a new output or input parameter is as easy as adding a new column. Figure 5.4 provides a visual overview of how this might work for listing 5.3.

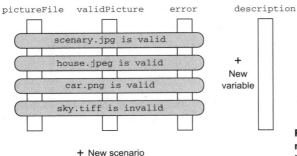

Figure 5.4 Adding a new test scenario means adding a new line in the where: block. Adding a new parameter means adding a new column in the where: block.

The ease of maintenance of Spock data tables is so addicting that once you integrate data tables in your complex tests, you'll understand that the only reason parameterized tests are considered difficult and boring is because of inefficient test tools.

The beauty of this format is that data tables can be used for any parameterized test, no matter the complexity involved. If you can isolate the input and output variables, the Spock test is a simple process of writing down the requirements in the source code. In some enterprise projects I've worked on, extracting the input/output parameters from the specifications was a more time-consuming job than writing the unit test itself.

The extensibility of a Spock data table is best illustrated with a semi-real example, as shown in the next listing.

Listing 5.7   Capturing business needs in data tables

```
def "Discount estimation for the eshop"() {
    [...rest of code redacted for brevity..]

    where: "some of the possible scenarios are"
price | isVip | points | order | discount | special || finalDiscount
50    | false | 0      | 50    | 0        | false   || 0
100   | false | 0      | 300   | 0        | false   || 10
500   | false | 0      | 0     | 0        | true    || 50
50    | true  | 0      | 50    | 0        | false   || 15
50    | true  | 0      | 50    | 25       | false   || 25
50    | true  | 0      | 50    | 5        | false   || 15
50    | true  | 0      | 50    | 5        | true    || 50
50    | false | 0      | 100   | 0        | false   || 0
50    | false | 0      | 75    | 10       | false   || 10
50    | false | 5000   | 50    | 0        | false   || 75
50    | false | 3000   | 50    | 0        | false   || 0
50    | true  | 8000   | 50    | 3        | false   || 75
}
```

Six parameters affect final discount

Business scenarios, one for each line, which are readable by business analysis

The unit test code isn't important. The data table contains the business requirements from the e-shop example that was mentioned in chapter 1. A user selects multiple products by adding them to an electronic basket. The basket then calculates the final discount of each product, which depends on the following:

- The price of the product
- The discount of the product
- Whether the customer has bonus/loyalty points
- The status of the customer (for example, silver, gold, platinum)
- The price of the total order (the rest of the products)
- Any special deals that are active

The production code of the e-shop may comprise multiple Java classes with deep hierarchies and complex setups. With Spock, you can directly map the business needs in a single data table.

Now imagine that you've finished writing this Spock test, and it passes correctly. You can show that data table to your business analyst and ask whether all cases are covered. If another scenario is needed, you can add it on the spot, run the test again, and verify the correctness of the system.

In another situation, your business analyst might not be sure about the current implementation status of the system[3] and might ask what happens in a specific scenario that's not yet covered by the unit test. To answer the question, you don't even need to look at the production code. Again, you add a new line/scenario in the Spock data table, run the unit test on the spot, and if it passes, you can answer that the requested feature is already implemented.

In less common situations, a new business requirement (or refactoring process) might add another input variable into the system. For example, in the preceding e-shop scenario, the business decides that coupon codes will be given away that further affect the discount of a product. Rather than hunting down multiple unit test methods (as in the naive approach of listing 5.2), you can add a new column in the data table and have all test cases covered in one step.

Even though Spock offers several forms of the where: block that will be shown in the rest of the chapter, I like the data table format for its readability and extensibility.

5.2.4 *Exploring the lifecycle of the where: block*

It's important to understand that the where: block in a parameterized test "spawns" multiple test runs (as many of its lines). A single test method that contains a where: block with three scenarios will be run by Spock as three individual methods, as shown in Figure 5.5. All scenarios of the where: block are tested individually, so any change in state (either in the class under test or its collaborators) will reset in the next run.

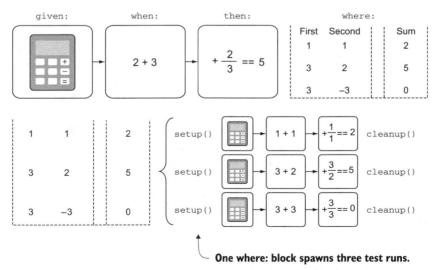

One where: block spawns three test runs.

Figure 5.5   Spock will treat and run each scenario in the where: block of a parameterized test as if it were a separate test method.

---

[3] A common case in legacy projects.

To illustrate this individuality of data tables, look at the following listing.

Listing 5.8   Lifecycle of parameterized tests

```
class LifecycleDataSpec extends spock.lang.Specification{

    def setup() {
            println "Setup prepares next run"
    }

    def "Trivial adder test"() {
            given: "an adder"
            Adder adder = new Adder()
            println "Given: block runs"

            when: "the add method is called for two numbers"
            int result = adder.add(first,second)
            println "When: block runs for first = $first and second =
                        $second"

            then: "the result should be the sum of them"
            result == sum
            println "Then: block is evaluated for sum = $sum"

            where: "some scenarios are"
            first   |second || sum
            1       | 1     || 2
            3       | 2     || 5
            3       | -3    || 0
    }

    def cleanup()
    {
            println "Cleanup releases resources of last run\n"
    }

}
```

The when: and then: blocks are executed once for each scenario.

Single test method runs multiple times.

Data table with three scenarios, centralized input and output parameters

Because this unit test has three scenarios in the where: block, the given-when-then blocks will be executed three times as well. Also, all lifecycle methods explained in chapter 4 are fully honored by parameterized tests. Both setup() and cleanup() will be run as many times as the scenarios of the where: block.

If you run the unit test shown in listing 5.8, you'll get the following output:

```
Setup prepares next run
Given: block runs
When: block runs for first = 1 and second = 1
Then: block is evaluated for sum = 2
Cleanup releases resources of last run

Setup prepares next run
Given: block runs
When: block runs for first = 3 and second = 2
```

```
Then: block is evaluated for sum = 5
Cleanup releases resources of last run

Setup prepares next run
Given: block runs
When: block runs for first = 3 and second = -3
Then: block is evaluated for sum = 0
Cleanup releases resources of last run
```

It should be clear that each scenario of the where: block acts as if it were a test method on its own. This enforces the isolation of all test scenarios, which is what you'd expect in a well-written unit test.

5.2.5 Using the @Unroll annotation for reporting individual test runs

In the previous section, you saw the behavior of Spock in parameterized tests when the when: block contains multiple scenarios. Spock correctly treats each scenario as an independent run.

Unfortunately, for compatibility reasons,[4] Spock still presents to the testing environment the collection of parameterized scenarios as a single test. For example, in Eclipse the parameterized test of listing 5.8 produces the output shown in figure 5.6.

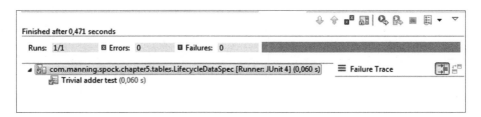

Figure 5.6 **By default, parameterized tests with multiple scenarios are shown as one test in Eclipse. The trivial adder test is shown only once, even though the source code defines three scenarios.**

This behavior might not be a big issue when all your tests succeed. You still gain the advantage of using a full sentence as the name of the test in the same way as with non-parameterized Spock tests.

Now assume that out of the three scenarios in listing 5.8, the second scenario is a failure (whereas the other two scenarios pass correctly). For illustration purposes, I modify the data table as follows:

```
where: "some scenarios are"
first  |second   || sum
1      | 1       || 2
3      | 2       || 7
3      | -3      || 0
```

---

[4] With older IDEs and tools that aren't smart when it comes to JUnit runners.

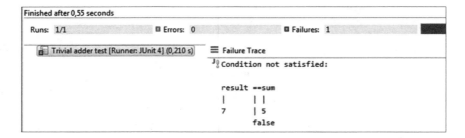

Figure 5.7   When one scenario out of many fails, it's not clear which is the failed one. You have to look at the failure trace, note the parameters, and go back to the source code to find the problematic line in the `where:` **block.**

The second scenario is obviously wrong, because 3 plus 2 isn't equal to 7. The other two scenarios are still correct. Running the modified unit test in Eclipse shows the output in figure 5.7.

Eclipse still shows the parameterized test in a single run. You can see that the test has failed, but you don't know which of the scenarios is the problematic one. You have to look at the failure trace to understand what's gone wrong.

This isn't helpful when your unit test contains a lot of scenarios, as in the example in listing 5.8. Being able to detect the failed scenario(s) as fast as possible is crucial.

To accommodate this issue, Spock offers the `@Unroll` annotation, which makes multiple parameterized scenarios appear as multiple test runs. The annotation can be added on the Groovy class (Spock specification) or on the test method itself, as shown in the next listing. In the former case, its effect will be applied to all test methods.

Listing 5.9   Unrolling parameterized scenarios

```
@Unroll                                        ◀── Marking the test method so
def "Trivial adder test"() {                       that multiple scenarios
    given: "an adder"                              appear as multiple runs
    Adder adder = new Adder()

    when: "the add method is called for two numbers"
    int result = adder.add(first,second)

    then: "the result should be the sum of them"
    result ==sum

    where: "some scenarios are"
    first  |second   || sum
    1      | 1       || 2
    3      | 2       || 5          Scenarios that will appear as separate
    3      | -3      || 0          unit tests, one for each line
}
```

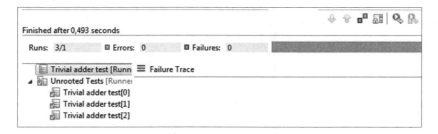

Figure 5.8 By marking a parameterized test with `@Unroll`, Eclipse now shows each run as an individual test.

With the `@Unroll` annotation active, running this unit test in Eclipse "unrolls" the test scenarios and presents them to the test runner as individual tests, as shown in figure 5.8.

The `@Unroll` annotation is even more useful when a test has failed, because you can see exactly which run was the problem. In large enterprise projects with parameterized tests that might contain a lot of scenarios, the `@Unroll` annotation becomes an essential tool if you want to quickly locate which scenarios have failed. Figure 5.9 shows the same failure as before, but this time you can clearly see which scenario has failed.

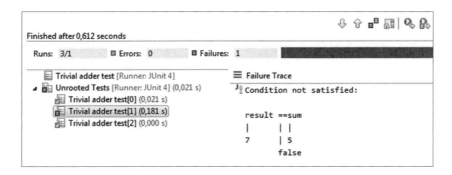

Figure 5.9 Locating failed scenarios with `@Unroll` is far easier than without it. The failed scenario is shown instantly as a failed test.

Remember that you still get the individual failure state for each scenario if you click it. Also note that the `@Unroll` annotation can be placed on the class level (the whole Spock specification) and will apply to all test methods inside the class.

5.2.6 *Documenting parameterized tests*

As you've seen in the previous section, the `@Unroll` annotation is handy when it comes to parameterized tests because it forces all test scenarios in a single test method to be reported as individual test runs. If you think that this feature isn't groundbreaking and should be the default, I agree with you.[5]

But Spock has another trick. With a little more effort, you can format the name shown for each scenario. The most logical things to include are the test parameters, as shown in the following listing.

Listing 5.10   Printing parameters of each scenario

```
@Unroll("Adder test #first, #second and  #sum (alt2)")
def "Trivial adder test (alt2)"() {
    given: "an adder"
    Adder adder = new Adder()

    when: "the add method is called for two numbers"
    int result = adder.add(first,second)

    then: "the result should be the sum of them"
    result ==sum

    where: "some scenarios are"
    first    |second    || sum
    1        | 1        || 2
    3        | 2        || 5
    3        | -3       || 0
}
```

◄— **Using parameter names with @Unroll so they're shown in the final run—alternative syntax**

◄— **Parameters that will be interpolated in the test description**

The `@Unroll` annotation accepts a string argument, in which you can put any English sentence. Variables marked with # will be replaced[6] with their current values when each scenario runs. The final result of this evaluation will override the name of the unit test, as shown in figure 5.10.

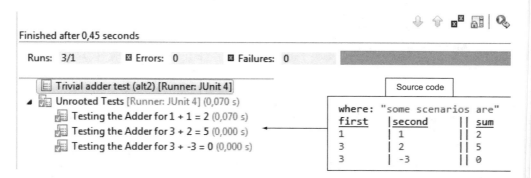

Figure 5.10   The parameter values for each scenario can be printed as part of the test name.

---

[5] After all, JUnit does this as well.

[6] The reasons that the # symbol is used instead of $ are purely technical and aren't relevant unless you're interested in Groovy and Spock internals.

I consider this feature one of the big highlights of Spock. I challenge you to find a test framework that accomplishes this visibility of test parameters with a simple technique. If you're feeling lazy, you can even embed the parameters directly in the test method name,[7] as shown in the following listing.

Listing 5.11 Parameter rendering on the test method

```
@Unroll
def "Testing the Adder for #first + #second = #sum "{    ◀──  Parameters inside the
    given: "an adder"                                         method name instead of
    Adder adder = new Adder()                                 using the unroll string

[...rest of code is same as listing 5.10...]
}
```

The result in Eclipse is the same as with listing 5.10, so pick any approach you like (but as always, if you work in a team, agree beforehand on the best practice).

5.2.7 Using expressions and statements in data tables

All the data tables I've shown you so far contain scalar values. Nothing is stopping you from using custom classes, collections, object factories, or any other Groovy expression that results in something that can be used as an input or output parameter. Take a look at the next listing (created strictly for demonstration purposes).

Listing 5.12 Custom expressions in data tables

```
@Unroll
def "Testing the Adder for #first + #second = #sum "() {
    given: "an adder"
    Adder adder = new Adder()                                       Full statement is
                                                                    used directly as
    expect: "that it calculates the sum of two numbers"            a parameter in
    adder.add(first,second)==sum                                   data table.

    where: "some scenarios are"
    first                                   |second             || sum
    2+3                                     | 10-2              || new
                                             Integer(13).intValue()  ◀──
    MyInteger.FIVE.getNumber()
                                            | MyInteger.NINE.getNumber() || 14
    IntegerFactory.createFrom("two")  | (7-2)*2                || 12
    [1,2,3].get(1)                          | 3                 ||
                                             IntegerFactory.createFrom("five")
    new Integer(5).intValue()               | new String("cat").size() ||
                                             MyInteger.EIGHT.getNumber()
    ["hello","world"].size()                | 5                 ||
                                             IntegerFactory.createFrom("seven")
}
```

Enumeration can be used as a parameter. → `MyInteger.FIVE.getNumber()`

An ObjectFactory that creates dynamic parameters → `IntegerFactory.createFrom("two")`

---

[7] Take that, TestNG !

The `MyInteger` class is a simple enumeration that contains the first 10 integers. The `IntegerFactory` class is a trivial factory that converts strings to integers. The details of the code aren't important; what you need to take away from this example is the flexibility of data tables. If you run this example, Spock will evaluate everything and present you with the final result, as shown in figure 5.11.

Figure 5.11   Spock will evaluate all expressions and statements so that they can be used as standard parameters. All statements from listing 5.12 finally resolve to integers.

I try to avoid this technique because I think it damages the readability of the test. I prefer to keep values in data tables simple. Using too many expressions in your data tables is a sign that you need to convert the tabular data into data pipes, as explained in the next section.

5.3   *Using data pipes for calculating input/output parameters*

Data tables should be your bread and butter when writing Spock parameterized tests. They shine when all input and output parameters are known in advance and thus can be embedded directly in the source code.

But sometimes the test parameters are computed on the spot or come from an external source (typically a file, as you'll see later in this chapter). For those cases, using data pipes is a better option. Data pipes are a lower-level construct of Spock parameterized tests that can be used when you want to dynamically create/read test parameters.[8]

As a first example, let's rewrite the first data table code of listing 5.1, using data pipes this time. The result is shown in the next listing.

Listing 5.13   Trivial example of data pipes

```
def "Valid images are PNG and JPEG files only"() {
    given: "an image extension checker"
    ImageNameValidator validator = new ImageNameValidator()

    expect: "that only valid filenames are accepted"
    validator.isValidImageExtension(pictureFile) == validPicture

    where: "sample image names are"
    pictureFile  << ["scenery.jpg","house.jpeg", "car.png ","sky.tiff"
                                           ,"dance_bunny.gif" ]
    validPicture << [ true, true, false, false, false]
}
```

Relationship of input and output parameters

All values of input parameter are inside a collection.

All values of output parameter are inside a collection.

---

[8]   Data tables can be seen as an abstraction over data pipes.

The code accomplishes the same thing as listing 5.1. But this time the tabular format is "rotated" 90 degrees. Each line of the `where:` block contains a parameter, and the scenarios of the test are the imaginary columns. The key point here is the use of the left-shift operator symbol (`<<`). In the context of the `where:` block, it means, "For the first scenario, pick the first value in the list for the input and output parameter; for the second scenario, pick the second value in the list, and so on."

In this example, I pass both input and output parameters in a list. But the left-shift operator can work on several other things, such as iterables, iterations, enumerations, other collections, and even strings. You'll examine the most common cases in the next sections.

5.3.1   Dynamically generated parameters

If you compared listing 5.13 to listing 5.2, you'd be right to say that there's no real advantage to using data pipes. That's because in that particular scenario, all parameters are known in advance and can be embedded directly in their full form. The power of data pipes becomes evident with computed data.

In the next listing, let's consider a different example, in which using a data table would be impractical because of the sheer size of input and output parameters.

Listing 5.14   Using Groovy ranges as data generators

```
def "Multiplying #first and #second is always a negative number"() {
    given: "a calculator"
    Calculator calc = new Calculator()

    expect: "that multiplying a positive and negative number is also
                        negative"
    calc.multiply(first,second) < 0                              ◀── No output parameter

    where: "some scenarios are"
    first << (20..80)
    second << (-65..-5)
}
```

This will expand to 60 positive numbers. ──▶ (points to `first << (20..80)`)

This will expand to 60 negative numbers. ──▶ (points to `second << (-65..-5)`)

The (*M..N*) notation is a Groovy range. It's similar to a list that will contain all values, starting from *M* and ending in *N*. Thus the (`20..80`) notation indicates a range of all integers from 20 to 80. Groovy expands the ranges and Spock picks each value in turn, resulting in a parameterized test with 60 scenarios. You can see the scenarios in detail if you run the unit test, as shown in figure 5.12.

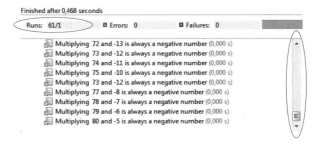

Finished after 0,468 seconds

Runs: 61/1   ⊠ Errors: 0   ⊠ Failures: 0

- Multiplying 72 and -13 is always a negative number (0,000 s)
- Multiplying 73 and -12 is always a negative number (0,000 s)
- Multiplying 74 and -11 is always a negative number (0,000 s)
- Multiplying 75 and -10 is always a negative number (0,000 s)
- Multiplying 73 and -12 is always a negative number (0,000 s)
- Multiplying 77 and -8 is always a negative number (0,000 s)
- Multiplying 78 and -7 is always a negative number (0,000 s)
- Multiplying 79 and -6 is always a negative number (0,000 s)
- Multiplying 80 and -5 is always a negative number (0,000 s)

Figure 5.12   Using ranges to automatically generate 60 scenarios instead of creating a data table with 60 lines.

Creating a data table with 120 values would make the unit test unreadable. By using data pipes and Groovy ranges, you've created 60 scenarios on the spot, while the source code only contains two statements (the ranges).

For a more realistic example, assume that you want to write an additional unit test for the `ImageValidator` class that ensures that all JPEG images are considered valid regardless of capitalization (anywhere in the name or the extension). Again, embedding all possible combinations in a data table would be time-consuming and error-prone.

You can calculate several possible variations with some Groovy magic, as shown in the following listing.

Listing 5.15   Using Groovy combinations

```
@Unroll("Checking image name #pictureFile")
def "All kinds of JPEG file are accepted"() {
    given: "an image extension checker"
    ImageNameValidator validator = new ImageNameValidator()

    expect: "that all jpeg filenames are accepted regardless of case"
    validator.isValidImageExtension(pictureFile)

    where: "sample image names are"
    pictureFile <<
    GroovyCollections.combinations([["sample.","Sample.","SAMPLE."],
        ['j', 'J'], ['p', 'P'],['e','E',''],['g','G']])*.join()
}
```

join() creates a string from each variation.

"combinations ()" creates a collection of all variations.

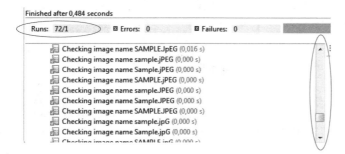

Finished after 0,484 seconds

Runs: 72/1   Errors: 0   Failures: 0

- Checking image name SAMPLE.JpEG (0,016 s)
- Checking image name sample.jPEG (0,000 s)
- Checking image name Sample.jPEG (0,000 s)
- Checking image name SAMPLE.jPEG (0,000 s)
- Checking image name sample.JPEG (0,000 s)
- Checking image name Sample.JPEG (0,000 s)
- Checking image name SAMPLE.JPEG (0,000 s)
- Checking image name sample.jpG (0,000 s)
- Checking image name Sample.jpG (0,000 s)
- Checking image name SAMPLE.jpG (0,000 s)

Figure 5.13   Creating 72 unit test runs from a single Groovy statement

The `where:` block contains a single statement. If you run the unit test, you'll see that this statement creates 72 scenarios (from 3 × 2 × 2 × 3 × 2 strings), as shown in figure 5.13.

The code works as follows: The `combinations()` method takes the variations of the word *sample*, the letters J, P, E, and G, and creates a new collection that contains all possible variations as collections themselves. The input parameter is a string. To convert each individual collection to a string, I call the `join()` method, which automatically creates a single string from a collection of strings. Because I want to do this with all collections, I use the star-dot Groovy operator (`*.`), which applies the `join()` method to all of them.

If your head is spinning at this point, don't worry! It took me a while to write this statement, and as you gain more Groovy expertise, you'll be able to write Groovy one-liners as well. The example is supposed to impress you, but don't be distracted by the core lesson here, which is the flexibility of Spock data pipes.

5.3.2 *Parameters that stay constant*

In all examples of parameterized tests I've shown you so far, the parameters are different for each scenario. But at times, one or more parameters are constant. Spock allows you to use direct assignments if you want to indicate that a parameter is the same for each scenario. Instead of the left-shift operator, you use the standard assignment operator, as shown in the following listing.

Listing 5.16   Constant parameters in Spock tests

```
def "Multipling #first and #second is always a negative number"() {
    given: "a calculator"
    Calculator calc = new Calculator()

    expect: "that multiplying a positive and negative number results in a
                          negative number"
    calc.multiply(first,second) < 0

    where: "some scenarios are"
    first << [20,34,44,67]
    second = -1
}
```

This parameter is always the same for each scenario. → (points to `second = -1`)

This parameter is different for each scenario. → (points to `first << [20,34,44,67]`)

The scenarios used for listing 5.16 are [20, -1], then [34, -1], [44, -1], and finally [67,-1]. I admit that the example isn't enticing. I needed to show it to you as a stepping stone to the true use of the assignment operator in the where: block—derived variables.

5.3.3 *Parameters that depend on other parameters*

You've seen how the assignment operator is used for constant variables in listing 5.16. What's not evident from the listing is that you can also refer to other variables in the definition of a variable.

In the next listing, the second parameter of the test is based on the first.

Listing 5.17   Derived parameters in Spock tests

```
def "Multipling #first and #second is always a negative number (alt)"() {
    given: "a calculator"
    Calculator calc = new Calculator()

    expect: "that multiplying a positive and negative number results in a
                          negative number"
    calc.multiply(first,second) < 0

    where: "some scenarios are"
    first << [20,34,44,67]
    second = first * -1
}
```

This parameter depends on another one; "second" is the first with minus sign. → (points to `second = first * -1`)

This parameter is explicitly defined; "first" is an integer. → (points to `first << [20,34,44,67]`)

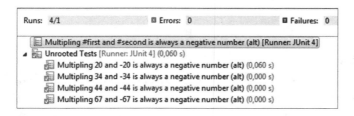

Figure 5.14   Derived values are recalculated for each test run. Here the second parameter is always the negative representation of the first one.

Running this test shows how the second parameter is recalculated for each scenario according to the value of the first, as shown in figure 5.14.

This technique allows you to have variables that are dynamically generated based on the context of the current scenario.

5.4   *Using dedicated data generators*

All the previous examples of data pipes use lists (Groovy ranges also act as lists) to hold the parameters for each test iteration. Grouping parameters in a list is the more readable option in my opinion, but Spock can also iterate on the following:

- Strings (each iteration will fetch a character).
- Maps (each iteration will pick a key).
- Enumerations.
- Arrays.
- RegEx matchers.
- Iterators.
- Iterables.

This list isn't exhaustive. Everything that Groovy can iterate on can be used as a data generator. Chapter 2 even includes a Groovy Expando as an example of an iterator. Iterables and iterators are interfaces, which means that you can implement your own classes for the greatest control of how Spock uses parameters. Even though custom implementations can handle complex transformations of test data when required, I consider them a last-resort solution because they're not always as readable as simpler data tables. The solutions offered by Spock are compared in figure 5.15.

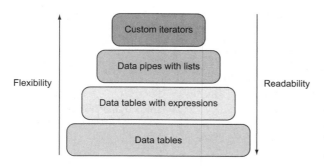

Figure 5.15   All solutions shown for parameterized Spock tests. Data tables are limited, but readable by even nontechnical people. All other techniques sacrifice readability for more expressive power.

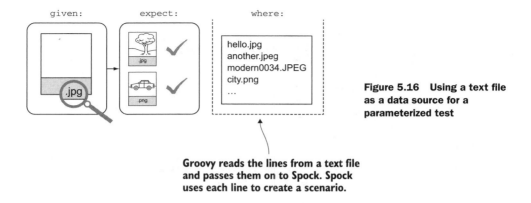

Figure 5.16   Using a text file as a data source for a parameterized test

Groovy reads the lines from a text file and passes them on to Spock. Spock uses each line to create a scenario.

If you need to create a custom iterator for obtaining business data, you should always ask yourself whether the transformation of the data belongs in the business class that you're trying to test, or whether it's part of the iterator.

Before trying custom iterators, you should spend some time determining whether you can use existing classes in your application that already return data in the format that you expect. As an example, assume you have a text file that holds image names that your program can accept, as shown in figure 5.16.

The content of the file validImageNames.txt is as follows:

```
hello.jpg
another.jpeg
modern0034.JPEG
city.Png
city_004.PnG
landscape.JPG
```

To read this file, you don't need a custom iterator. The Groovy File class already contains a readLines() method that returns a list of all lines in a file. The respective Spock test is shown in the following listing.

Listing 5.18   Using existing data generators

```
@Unroll("Checking image name #pictureFile")
def "Valid images are PNG and JPEG files"() {
    given: "an image extension checker"
    ImageNameValidator validator = new ImageNameValidator()

    expect: "that all filenames are accepted"
    validator.isValidImageExtension(pictureFile)

    where: "sample image names are"
    pictureFile  << new
                    File("src/test/resources/validImageNames.txt")
                        .readLines()
}
```

Gets a list of all lines of the file

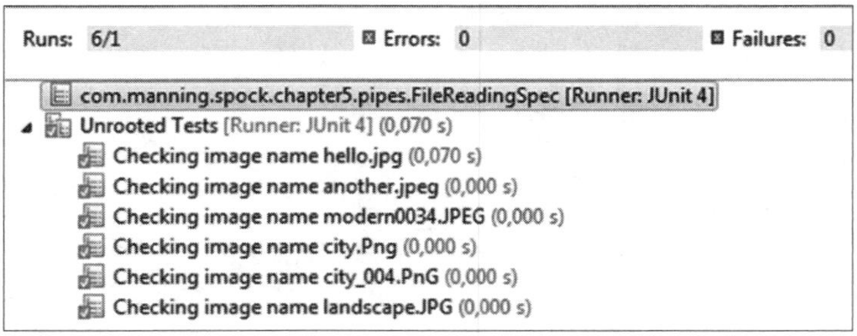

Figure 5.17   Reading test values from a file by using Groovy code

Here Groovy opens the file, reads its lines in a list, and passes them to Spock. Spock fetches the lines one by one to create all the scenarios of the test. Running the test produces the output shown in figure 5.17.

Before resorting to custom iterators, always see whether you can obtain data with your existing application code or GDK/JDK facilities.[9] Always keep in mind the excellent facilities of Groovy for XML and JSON reading (these were covered in chapter 2).

5.4.1 Writing a custom data generator

You show the unit test with the valid image names to your business analyst in order to explain what's supported by the system. The analyst is impressed, and as a new task, you get the following file named invalidImageNames.txt:

```
#Found by QA
starsystem.tiff
galaxy.tif

#Reported by client

    bunny04.gif
    looper.GIF
    dolly_take.mov
    afar.xpm
```

The file can't be used as is in a unit test. It contains comments that start with the # sign, it has empty lines, and it even has tabs in front of some image names.

You want to write a Spock test that checks this file and confirms the rejection of the image names (they're all invalid). It's obvious that the Groovy `File` class can't help you in this case; the file has to be processed before it's used in the Spock test.[10]

---

[9] Or even classes from Guava, Apache commons, CSV reading libraries, and so on.

[10] In this simple example, you could clear the file contents manually. In a larger file, this isn't practical or even possible.

To solve this new challenge, you should first create a custom data iterator, as shown in the next listing.

Listing 5.19 Java iterator that processes invalidImageNames.txt

```java
public class InvalidNamesGen implements Iterator<String>{        ◄─┐  Class will return
                                                                  │  strings (lines).
    private List<String> invalidNames;
    private int counter =0;

    public InvalidNamesGen() {
            invalidNames = new ArrayList<>();
            parse();
    }

    private void parse() {
                [...code that reads the file and discards
                 empty lines, tabs and comments not shown for brevity...]
    }

    @Override
    public boolean hasNext() {                    ◄─┐  Generate values while lines
            return counter < invalidNames.size();  │  are present in the file.
    }

    @Override
    public String next() {                        ◄─┐  Get the next line
            String result = invalidNames.get(counter); │  from the file.
            counter++;
            return result;
    }

    @Override
    public void remove() {          ◄─┐  No need to implement
    }                                 │  this for this example
}
```

There's nothing Spock-specific about this class on its own. It's a standard Java iterator that reads the file and can be used to obtain string values. You can use this iterator directly in Spock, as shown in the next listing.

Listing 5.20 Using Java iterators in Spock

```groovy
@Unroll("Checking image name #pictureFile")
def "Valid images are PNG and JPEG files"() {
    given: "an image extension checker"
    ImageNameValidator validator = new ImageNameValidator()

    expect: "that all filenames are rejected"
    !validator.isValidImageExtension(pictureFile)          ◄─┐  This time you expect
                                                             │  invalid images.
    where: "sample image names are"
    pictureFile << new InvalidNamesGen()
}
```

Instruct Spock to read strings from the custom class. ─►

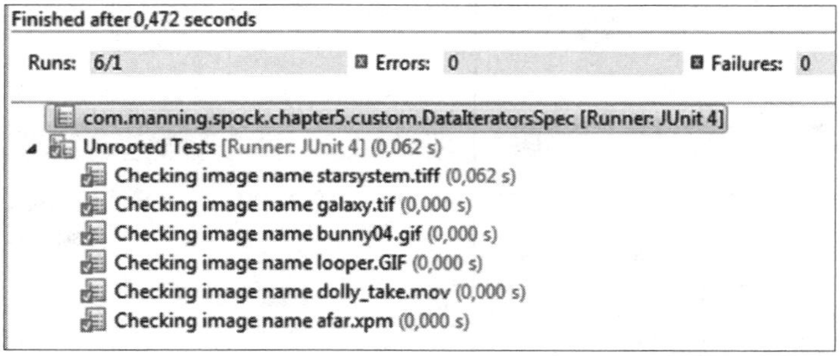

Figure 5.18   Using a Java iterator in a Spock unit test allows for more fine-grained file reading.

If you run this test, you'll see that the file is correctly cleaned up and processed, as shown in figure 5.18. Empty lines, comments, and tabs are completely ignored, and only the image names are used in each test scenario.

Happy with the result, you show the new test to your business analyst (thinking that you're finished). Apparently, you must face one last challenge.

> **Writing custom data generators in Groovy**
>
> In this section and the next, I use Java to implement a custom data generator because I assume that you're more familiar with Java. It's possible to write data generators in Groovy. This would be the preferred method when you know your way around Groovy, because you can include the generator inside the same source file as the Spock test (instead of having two separate files, one in Java for the iterator and one in Groovy for the Spock test).

5.4.2   *Using multivalued data iterators*

Your business analyst examines the two Spock tests (the one for valid images, and the one for invalid images) and decides that two files aren't needed. The analyst combines the two files into one, called imageNames.txt, with the following content:

```
#Found by QA
starsystem.tiff fail
galaxy.tif fail

desktop.png pass
europe.jpg pass
modern0034.JPEG pass
city.Png pass
city_004.PnG pass

#Reported by client
  bunny04.gif fail
              looper.GIF fail
  dolly_take.mov fail
  afar.xpm fail
```

This file is similar to the other two, with one important difference. It contains the word *pass/fail* in the same line as the image name.[11] At first glance, it seems that you need to write a test similar to listing 5.13, but using two custom iterators, as follows:

```
where: "sample image names are"
    pictureFile  << new CustomIterator1()
    validPicture << new CustomIterator2()
```

The first iterator is responsible for reading the image names as before, and the second iterator reads the pass/fail flag and converts it to a Boolean. This solution would certainly work, but having two custom iterators isn't practical. They would both share similar code (both need to ignore empty lines), and keeping them in sync if the file format changed would be a big challenge.

Hopefully, with Spock tests you don't need extra custom iterators for each parameter. Spock supports multivalue iterators (powered by Groovy multivalued assignments[12]), so you can obtain all your input/output parameters from a single iterator. For illustration purposes, our example uses a custom iterator to fetch two variables, but the same technique can work with any number of parameters. The iterator is shown in the next listing.

Listing 5.21 Java multivalued iterator

```
public class MultiVarReader implements Iterator<Object[]>{      ◄─┐ Class will return
                                                                  │ multiple values.
    private List<String> fileNames;
    private List<Boolean> validFlag;
    private int counter =0;

    public MultiVarReader() {
            fileNames = new ArrayList<>();
            validFlag = new ArrayList<>();
            parse();
    }

    private void parse() {
            [...code that reads the file and discards
            empty lines, tabs and comments not shown for brevity...]
    }

    @Override
    public boolean hasNext() {                          ◄─┐ Generate values while
            return counter< fileNames.size();              │ lines are present.
    }

    @Override
    public Object[] next() {                  ◄─┐ First parameter is the file, and second
            Object[] result = new Object[2];      │ parameter is the pass/fail result.
```

---

[11] In reality, this file would be a large XLS file with multiple columns that contained both important and unrelated data.

[12] You can find more details about Groovy multivalue assignments at htttp://www.groovy-lang.org/semantics .html#_multiple_assignment.

```
        result[0] = fileNames.get(counter);
        result[1] = validFlag.get(counter);
        counter++;
        return result;
    }

    @Override
    public void remove() {        ◀───┐ No need to
    }                                  │ implement this
}
```

Here the defined iterator returns two objects. The first object is the image name, and the second object is a Boolean that's `true` if the image should be considered valid, and `false` if the image name should be rejected. Notice again that there's nothing Spock-specific about this class. It's a normal Java class.

The Spock test that uses this multivalue iterator is shown in the following listing.

Listing 5.22 Using multivalued iterators in Spock

```
@Unroll("Checking image name #pictureFile with result=#result")
def "Valid images are PNG and JPEG files only 2"() {
    given: "an image extension checker"
    ImageNameValidator validator = new ImageNameValidator()

    expect: "that all filenames are categorized correctly"
    validator.isValidImageExtension(pictureFile) == result   ◀── Result is now an
                                                                 output parameter.
    where: "sample image names are"
    [pictureFile,result] << new MultiVarReader()
}
```

The iterator reads both parameters at once. ───▶ `[pictureFile,result]`

In the Spock test, the left-shift operator is used as before, but this time the left side is a list of parameters instead of a single parameter. Spock reads the respective values from the data generator and places them in the parameters in the order they're mentioned. The first value that comes out of the data generator is placed in the first parameter (the image name, in this case), and the second value from the generator (the Boolean flag, in this case) is placed in the second parameter. Running the test produces the output in figure 5.19.

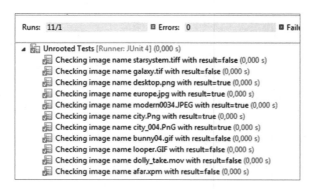

Figure 5.19 Multivalued iterators. For each test run, Spock reads both the input (image filename) and the output parameter (result of validity) from the data file.

This capability of the left-shift operator to handle multivalues isn't restricted to data generators (although that's where it's most useful). You can perform multivalue parameter assignments by using plain data pipes, as shown in the following listing.

Listing 5.23 Using multivalued assignments in Spock

Two parameters will be used in this Spock test pictureFile and result.

```
@Unroll("Checking harcoded image name #pictureFile with #result")
def "Valid images are PNG and JPEG files only"() {
    given: "an image extension checker"
    ImageNameValidator validator = new ImageNameValidator()

    expect: "that all filenames are categorized correctly"
    validator.isValidImageExtension(pictureFile) == result

    where: "sample image names are"
    [pictureFile,result] << [["sample.jpg",true],
                             ["bunny.gif",false]]
}
```

Multivalue assignment: the first parameter is pictureFile, and the second is result.

The right side of the assignment contains a list of all scenarios (which are lists). For each scenario, Spock again picks the first element and places it in the first variable of the left list. The second element from the scenario is placed in the second parameter, and so on.

5.5 *Working with third-party data generators*

With the current breadth of Java/Groovy input libraries that handle text, JSON, XML, CSV, and other structured data, writing custom iterators that can handle your specific business case is easy.

If you've already invested in JUnit tools that generate random data or construct data according to your needs, adapting them for your Spock tests should be easy. If they already implement the iterator interface, you can use them directly, or you can wrap them in your own data generator.

If your application is using a lot of data generators, you might also find the Spock genesis library (https://github.com/Bijnagte/spock-genesis) useful. It can be thought of as a meta-generator library because it allows you to do the following:

- Lazily create input data
- Compose existing generators into new ones
- Filter existing generators using predicates/closures
- Randomize or order the output for other generators

Always remember that your data generators can be written in both Java and Groovy. If you find a library in Java that suits your needs, you can integrate it directly in Spock.

A perfect example of this approach is the jFairy data generator library (https://github.com/Codearte/jfairy). The library is written in Java, but it can easily be used in Spock. Its own unit tests are implemented in Spock.

5.6   *Summary*

- Parameterized tests are tests that share the same test logic but have multiple input and output parameters.

- Spock supports parameterized tests via the `where:` block, which defines the individual scenarios.

- The simplest use of the `where:` block is with data tables; you directly embed all parameters inside the source code.

- Data tables are readable because they collect in a single place the names and values of all parameters.

- Each scenario in the `where:` block has its own lifecycle. A parameterized test with *N* scenarios will spawn *N* runs.

- The `@Unroll` annotation can be used to report individual runs of each scenario in its own test.

- In conjunction with the `@Unroll` annotation, it's possible to change the name of each test method to include the input and output parameters. This makes reporting clear, and pinpointing a failed test is easy.

- You can use statements and Groovy expressions in data tables. You should be careful not to harm the readability of the test.

- A more advanced form of parameterized tests is data pipes. These allow the automatic calculation of input/output parameters when embedding them directly in the source code isn't practical (either because of their size or their complexity).

- Data pipes can get data from a collection, Groovy ranges, strings, and even regular expression matchers. Anything that's iterable in Groovy can be used as a data generator.

- Test parameters can depend on other test parameters. In addition, defining a test parameter as a constant is easy.

- Existing libraries/classes can be easily wrapped in a data generator or used directly as an iterator.

- Spock can assign multiple variables at once for each scenario. This is also possible in plain Groovy. Data generators aren't limited to generating data for a single value. Multivalued data generators can be used to handle all input/output parameters of a scenario in a single step.

- Data generators can be implemented in both Java and/or Groovy.

Mocking and stubbing

This chapter starts with a quick reminder of the theory behind mocks and stubs (the terminology used by Spock). If you've never used them before in your unit tests, feel free to consult other external sources to complete your knowledge.[1] You may have already seen them as *test doubles* or *fake collaborators*, so if you know the theory, you can skip ahead to section 6.2 in order to see the implementation of Spock for fake objects.

Fake collaborators are a way to isolate a single class with your exact input and output specification so that you can examine it under a well-controlled environment. I briefly hinted about the mocking/stubbing capabilities of Spock in chapter

---

[1] A good start is the book *Effective Unit Testing* by Lasse Koskela (Manning, 2013)—chapter 3 in particular.

3 and promised to show you much more when the time comes (now!). Unlike JUnit, Spock has native support for mocks, and there's no need to add an external library to use this technique. The syntax for mocking and stubbing is much simpler than other mocking frameworks.

6.1   *Using fake collaborators*

Let's say you have a Java class in your application that shuts down a nuclear reactor when radiation levels from a sensor pass a critical threshold. You want to write a unit test for that class. It wouldn't be realistic to bombard the real sensor with radiation just to see your unit test work. It's also not realistic to shut down the nuclear reactor whenever the unit test runs.

For a more run-of-the-mill example, assume that your Java class sends a reminder email to a customer whenever an invoice isn't settled on time. Re-creating a delayed payment in the unit test would be difficult, and sending a real email each time the unit test runs would also be unrealistic.

For cases like this, you need to employ fake collaborators in your unit test. You need to fake the way your class gets the current sensor values as well as the communication with the nuclear reactor, and you also need to fake the delayed payment and the email server. A *fake collaborator* is a special class that replaces a real class in order to make its behavior deterministic (preprogrammed). No technical limitation ties fake classes to unit tests. But unit tests are much more flexible if they employ the power of fake classes (which is the running theme of this chapter).

A visual way to describe a fake object is shown in figure 6.1. The core of each circle is a class, and the arcs around it are its methods.[2]

6.1.1   *Using fake collaborators to isolate a class in unit tests*

If a bug shows up in a real system (or in an integration test), it's not immediately clear which class or classes are responsible for it. In a unit test that contains only a real class (as in figure 6.1), you can preprogram its collaborators with "correct" and "expected" answers. Thus, it's easy to focus the unit test on how this single class works and make sure that it contains no bugs (at least on its own).

These fake collaborators aren't real classes because

- They implement only the methods needed for the unit test and nothing else.
- When they make requests to the real class, the request parameters are preprogrammed and known in advance.
- When they answer requests from the real class, their answers are also preprogrammed.

The point to remember is that only the programmer knows the existence of the fake classes. From the point of view of the real class, everything is running normally. The real class thinks that it runs on a live system (because the fake classes still implement

---

[2] See https://docs.oracle.com/javase/tutorial/java/concepts/object.html for this drawing style.

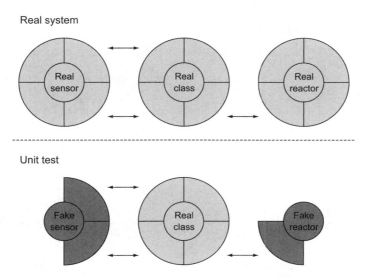

Figure 6.1   By using fake classes, you can define your own sensor values and replace the real nuclear reactor with a fake one. You can safely mimic any possible situation you want without affecting the real hardware.

the agreed-upon interfaces) without understanding that the whole stage is a single unit test.

For the rest of this chapter, I use the terms *stub* and *mock* for this type of fake class because this is the terminology used by Spock.

6.1.2   *Faking classes in Spock: mocks and stubs*

Mocks and stubs are a further subdivision of fake objects. Here are the definitions I first introduced in chapter 3:

- A *stub* is a fake class that comes with preprogrammed return values. It's injected into the class under test so that you have absolute control over what's being tested as input. In figure 6.1, the fake sensor is a stub so that you can re-create any radiation levels you want.
- A *mock* is a fake class that can be examined after the test is finished for its inter-actions with the class under test (for example, you can ask it whether a method was called or how many times it was called). In figure 6.1, the fake reactor class is a mock so that you can ask whether its shutdown() method was called after the unit test has ended.

In practice, because mocks can also be stubbed, you can think of them as a superset of stubs (which cannot be used for verification of interactions). In theory, you could write all your Spock tests using only mocks. For readability, it's best to decide in advance which type of fake object you're creating.

Unit testing and filmmaking analogy

If you still have trouble understanding the difference between mocks and stubs, imagine that instead of a programmer, you're a film director. You want to shoot a scene (create a unit test). First you set up the actors, camera, and sound that will create the illusion of the scene (you prepare stubs and mocks). You let the camera roll (run the unit test) and check the camera screen for the result (examine the test result).

Stubs are your sound technician, your lighting experts, and your camera man. You give them instructions before each scene, as you preprogram your stubs. They're essential for filming your scene, as stubs are essential for the correct functionality of your class under test. But they don't appear in the recorded scene, as stubs are never used for test verification.

Mocks are your actors. You also give them a script before the scene for their dialogue, in the same way that you prepare your mocks (for their interaction with the class under test). After filming is finished, you check their onscreen performance as you check the interactions of your mocks.

Under dire circumstances, you can force an actor to hold the boom microphone or the camera (use a mock in place of a stub), but you can never create an actor out of a technician on the spot (you can't use a stub for interaction verification).

6.1.3 *Knowing when to use mocks and stubs*

Knowing how to mock classes isn't enough for effective unit tests. You also need to know which classes to mock out of all the collaborators. In a large enterprise project, your class under test might interface with several other classes. You should ask yourself which classes need mocking and which classes can use their real implementation.[3]

I've seen both sides of the spectrum. Some developers don't use mocking at all, making all unit tests run as integration tests. I've also seen excessive mocking of classes that don't need it. The former situation isn't desirable because all tests will be slow and complex. The latter situation has its own problems as well. Upgrading badly designed mocked tests is difficult when the production code changes because of unforeseen business requirements.

As a general rule of thumb, you should mock/stub all collaborator classes that do the following:

- Make the unit test nondeterministic.
- Have severe side effects.
- Make the test depend on the computation environment.
- Make the test slow.
- Need to exhibit strange behavior typically not found on a real system.

The first case is obvious. If you're writing a unit test for a game that uses electronic dice, you can't possibly use the real dice class in your unit test. Instead, you mock it to make it return a particular number that fits your scenario.

---

[3] And which should be spies in some rare cases. Spies are explained in chapter 8.

The second case was demonstrated in chapter 3. If you have code that charges credit cards, prints documents, launches missiles, or shuts down nuclear reactors, you must mock it so that nothing bad happens when a unit test runs.

The third case is about creating reliable tests that always have the same behavior when they run either on the build server or a development workstation. Code that reads environment variables, reads external setting files, or asks for user input should be mocked with the variables used in that specific scenario.

In large enterprise projects, tests can be slow. A common speed-up technique is to mock out code that reads files, communicates with a database, or contacts an external network service. This makes the test CPU-bound instead of I/O-bound so tests run at the maximum capacity of the processor.

Finally, you need to stub objects when you want to create a specific behavior that's hard to reproduce with the real class. Common cases are emulating a full hard disk or a complete failure in the network.

The corollary of the preceding list is that if you have a collaborator class that doesn't depend on external services or the environment, doesn't perform I/O operations, and is fast in its responses, then you can use it as is in a unit test (with its real implementation).

> **The class under test is always a real class**
>
> I'm always baffled by questions in Stack Overflow and other forums and mailing lists indicating that people have difficulties with mocking because they try to mock the class under test instead of its collaborators. Some advanced unit tests need this (I'll show you spies in chapter 8), but this technique is only for extreme corner cases of legacy code. In vanilla unit tests, the class under test is always a real class. Mocks are used for its collaborators only. Even then, not all collaborators need to be mocked.

6.1.4 *Exploring a sample application for an electronic shop system*

The running example for this chapter is an expanded version of the e-shop system that you saw in chapter 4. Figure 6.2 shows a high-level overview of the system under test.

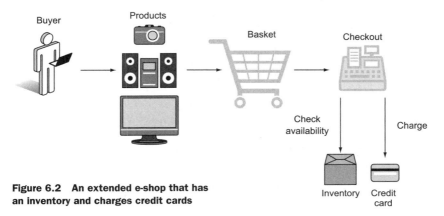

Figure 6.2 An extended e-shop that has an inventory and charges credit cards

In this e-shop, the client can browse product pages and add them to an electronic basket as before. But when the client checks out, two additional actions are performed. First, the inventory is checked to verify that the products are indeed ready for dispatching. Second, the credit card of the client is charged using an external preexisting service (which is the responsibility of another company).

The Java skeleton for this e-shop is shown in the following listing, and it's similar to the one introduced in chapter 4.

Listing 6.1   Java skeleton code for the e-shop

```java
public class Product {                                    Simple holder class
    private String name;                                  for a product
    private int price;
    private int weight;
    [...getters and setters..]

}
public class WarehouseInventory {                         Contains stocked products—
                                                          we'll stub this
    public int isProductAvailable(String productName)
    {
            [...code redacted for brevity..]
    }

    public boolean isProductAvailable(String productName,int count)
    {
            [...code redacted for brevity..]
    }

    public boolean isEmpty()                              Quick check of
    {                                                     product availability
            [...code redacted for brevity..]
    }


}
public class Basket {                                     Class under test

    public void addProduct(Product product) {             Triggered
            addProduct(product, 1);                        from the UI
    }

    public void addProduct(Product product, int times) {
            [...code redacted for brevity..]
    }

    public int getProductTypesCount() {
            [...code redacted for brevity..]
    }

    public void setWarehouseInventory(WarehouseInventory
                    warehouseInventory) {
            [...code redacted for brevity..]
    }

    public boolean canShipCompletely() {                  Method that needs
            [...code redacted for brevity..]              to be tested
    }

}
```

Checks whether a product is stocked → (points to `public boolean isProductAvailable(String productName,int count)`)

Setter injection → (points to `public void setWarehouseInventory(...)`)

Just by looking at figure 6.2, you can already guess which class you'll stub and which class you'll mock. The inventory class will be stubbed (so you can define the stock levels of various products, regardless of the real warehouse), and the credit card system will be mocked (so you don't charge real credit cards when a unit test runs).

I'll use this sample application throughout the chapter for increasingly complex examples of Spock unit tests that contain mocks and stubs.

6.2 Controlling input to the class under test with stubs

Now that you know the theory behind mocks and stubs and the system that you'll test, you're ready to see how to use them in your Spock tests. Let's start with stubs, which are simpler. You stub all collaborator classes that are used by your class under test but aren't otherwise tested. Either they have their own unit tests or they're external libraries and frameworks that are assumed to work correctly.

In general, your class under test makes requests to your stubs. You need to tell Spock what to do when any of the stubbed methods are called. By default, Spock won't complain if a method is called that wasn't explicitly stubbed.

Therefore, creating a stub is a two-step process:

1 Showing Spock which class won't use its real implementation and instead will be stubbed
2 Declaring what will happen when any of the stubbed methods are called by the class under test (what the return values will be)

6.2.1 Basic stubbing of return values

The first thing you want to test is the `canShipCompletely()` method of the basket from listing 6.1. This method returns `true` when all products selected by the customer are available in the warehouse, and `false` in any other case. You'll stub the warehouse inventory so that you can emulate both cases: the product is in stock and the product isn't currently available.

The warehouse inventory is a concrete class that's used by the basket class during checkout. Imagine that this class is part of an external system that you don't have any control over. You don't want your unit tests to be based on the real inventory of this e-shop. You need a way to trick the inventory to contain what you want for each business scenario that you test. The following listing shows an example of stubbing the warehouse inventory.

Listing 6.2 Creating a simple stub with Spock

```
def "If warehouse is empty nothing can be shipped"() {
    given: "a basket and a TV"
    Product tv = new Product(name:"bravia",price:1200,weight:18)
    Basket basket = new Basket()

    and:"an empty warehouse"
    WarehouseInventory inventory = Stub(WarehouseInventory)     ◄──┐ Creates
                                                                   Spock stub
```

Injects the stub into the class under test →

```
        inventory.isEmpty() >> true
        basket.setWarehouseInventory(inventory)

    when: "user checks out the tv"
    basket.addProduct tv

    then: "order cannot be shipped"
    !basket.canShipCompletely()
}
```

Instructs the stub to return true when isEmpty() is called

Calls the stub behind the scenes

The most important lines from listing 6.2 are the following:

```
WarehouseInventory inventory = Stub(WarehouseInventory)
inventory.isEmpty() >> true
```

The first line creates a Spock stub that looks and "acts" as the class WarehouseInventory, but all methods that are called on this stub are intercepted automatically by Spock and never reach the real implementation.

The second line uses the right-shift operator. This special Spock operator (remember that Groovy allows for operator overloading, unlike Java) hardwires the isEmpty() method to return true regardless of the real implementation of the original class. When the basket is asked to respond about the shipping status of the order it calls (behind the scenes), the stubbed method gets a negative result from the inventory.

To stub a method for specific arguments, you can use the right-shift operator directly on the method call you want to emulate, as shown in the next listing.

Listing 6.3 Stubbing specific arguments

```
def "If warehouse has the product on stock everything is fine"() {
    given: "a basket and a TV"
    Product tv = new Product(name:"bravia",price:1200,weight:18)
    Basket basket = new Basket()

    and:"a warehouse with enough stock"
    WarehouseInventory inventory = Stub(WarehouseInventory)
    inventory.isProductAvailable("bravia",1) >> true
    inventory.isEmpty() >> false
    basket.setWarehouseInventory(inventory)

    when: "user checks out the tv"
    basket.addProduct tv

    then: "order can be shipped right away"
    basket.canShipCompletely()
}
```

Creating a Spock stub

Instructing the warehouse to respond with false →

Instructing the stub to return true when specific arguments are used

Here you change the inventory to emulate the happy scenario in which the product exists in the warehouse. It's also possible to differentiate method calls according to their arguments and stub them with different return results. This is demonstrated in the following listing.

Listing 6.4   Argument-based stub differentiation

```
def "If warehouse does not have all products, order cannot be shipped"() {
    given: "a basket, a TV and a camera"
    Product tv = new Product(name:"bravia",price:1200,weight:18)
    Product camera = new Product(name:"panasonic",price:350,weight:2)
    Basket basket = new Basket()

    and:"a warehouse with partial availability"
    WarehouseInventory inventory = Stub(WarehouseInventory)
    inventory.isProductAvailable("bravia",1) >> true
    inventory.isProductAvailable("panasonic",1) >> false
    inventory.isEmpty() >> false
    basket.setWarehouseInventory(inventory)

    when: "user checks out both products"
    basket.addProduct tv
    basket.addProduct camera

    then: "order cannot be shipped right away"
    !basket.canShipCompletely()
}
```

Different stub results depending on the argument

Finally, you can group all stubbing instructions in a single code block in a similar way to the with() method shown in chapter 4. The following code listing behaves in exactly the same way as listing 6.4; only the syntax differs. You should decide for yourself which of the two you prefer.

Listing 6.5   Grouping all stubbed methods

```
def "If warehouse does not have all products, order cannot be shipped
                            (alt)"() {
    given: "a basket, a TV and a camera"
    Product tv = new Product(name:"bravia",price:1200,weight:18)
    Product camera = new Product(name:"panasonic",price:350,weight:2)
    Basket basket = new Basket()

    and:"a warehouse with partial availability"
    WarehouseInventory inventory = Stub(WarehouseInventory) {
            isProductAvailable("bravia",1) >> true
            isProductAvailable("panasonic",1) >> false
            isEmpty() >> false
    }
    basket.warehouseInventory = inventory

    when: "user checks out both products"
    basket.addProduct tv
    basket.addProduct camera

    then: "order cannot be shipped right away"
    !basket.canShipCompletely()
}
```

Compact way of stubbing methods

Setter injection using Groovy style

Notice that in all the preceding code listings, the real code of warehouse inventory never runs. The Spock unit tests shown can run on their own, regardless of the status of the real inventory. As long as the signature of the warehouse class stays the same (that is, the method definitions), these unit tests will continue to run correctly, even if new methods are added to the original class. Now you know how you can stub classes in Spock!

6.2.2 *Matching arguments leniently when a stubbed method is called*

The previous section showed how to stub methods by using the exact arguments you expect to be called. This works for trivial tests, but for bigger tests, this precision isn't always needed. For example, if I wanted to create a unit test that involved 10 different products, I'd have to stub 10 different calls for the same method.

Spock offers a more practical solution in the form of argument matchers when you don't want so much detail. The character Spock uses is the underscore (_), and in general it plays the role of "I don't care what goes in here," depending on the context (as you'll see throughout this chapter). The following listing shows the use of the underscore as an argument matcher.

Listing 6.6   Using argument matchers in stubs

```
def "If warehouse has both products everything is fine"() {
    given: "a basket, a TV and a camera"
    Product tv = new Product(name:"bravia",price:1200,weight:18)
    Product camera = new Product(name:"panasonic",price:350,weight:2)
    Basket basket = new Basket()

    and:"a warehouse with enough stock"
    WarehouseInventory inventory = Stub(WarehouseInventory)
    inventory.isProductAvailable(_, 1) >> true          ◄──┐ Stubbing a method call
    basket.setWarehouseInventory(inventory)                 │ regardless of the value
                                                            │ of an argument
    when: "user checks out the tv and the camera"
    basket.addProduct tv
    basket.addProduct camera

    then: "order can be shipped right away"
    basket.canShipCompletely()
```

Here I've stubbed the inventory method only once, and I know that it can be called for all products I ask for, regardless of their names.[4] I've chosen this approach because in this particular test I'm not interested in examining the correctness of the warehouse (the focus of the test is still the basket class).

---

[4] Unlike Mockito, Spock supports partial matching of arguments, where some have specific values and some don't. Mockito requires that all arguments use matchers if any matcher is used at all.

It's also possible to use matchers for all arguments of a method, resulting in powerful stubbing combinations. The following listing shows an example.

Listing 6.7   Ignoring all arguments of a stubbed method when returning a response

```
def "If warehouse is fully stocked stock everything is fine"() {
    given: "a basket, a TV and a camera"
    Product tv = new Product(name:"bravia",price:1200,weight:18)
    Product camera = new Product(name:"panasonic",price:350,weight:2)
    Basket basket = new Basket()

    and:"a warehouse with limitless stock"
    WarehouseInventory inventory = Stub(WarehouseInventory)
    inventory.isProductAvailable( _, _) >> true          ◄─┐ Stubbing a method for
    basket.setWarehouseInventory(inventory)                │ all its possible arguments

    when: "user checks out multiple products"
    basket.addProduct tv,33                              ┐ Both these calls
    basket.addProduct camera,12                          │ will be matched.

    then: "order can be shipped right away"
    basket.canShipCompletely()
```

Here I've instructed my warehouse to answer that the product is always in stock, regardless of the product. I don't care if the class under test asks for a TV or a camera; it will always be in stock.

Stubbing a method regardless of its arguments is a powerful technique that can be helpful in large unit tests in which the stub is a secondary dependency that's outside the focus of the test. Dispatchers, delegates, facades, decorators, and other design patterns are perfect candidates for this kind of stubbing, as often they get in the way of the class under test.

6.2.3   Using sequential stubs with different responses for each method call

Listing 6.5 showed how to differentiate the stub response based on the argument. This is one dimension of different responses. The other dimension is to stub different responses depending on the number of times a method is called.

This is accomplished with the unsigned right-shift operator (>>>), which was introduced in chapter 3. An example is shown in the next listing.

Listing 6.8   Stubbing subsequent method calls

```
def "Inventory is always checked in the last possible moment"() {
    given: "a basket and a TV"
    Product tv = new Product(name:"bravia",price:1200,weight:18)
    Basket basket = new Basket()
                                                      ┐ First call will return
                                                      │ true, and second
    and:"a warehouse with fluctuating stock levels"   │ will return false.
    WarehouseInventory inventory = Stub(WarehouseInventory)
    inventory.isProductAvailable( "bravia", _) >>> true >> false   ◄─
```

```
    inventory.isEmpty() >>> [false, true]                Spock can also iterate
    basket.setWarehouseInventory(inventory)              on a collection for
                                                         ordered responses.
    when: "user checks out the tv"
    basket.addProduct tv

    then: "order can be shipped right away"
    basket.canShipCompletely()                           The inventory stub is
                                                         called for the first time
    when: "user wants another TV"                        behind the scenes.
    basket.addProduct tv

    then: "order can no longer be shipped"
    !basket.canShipCompletely()
}
```

The inventory stub is called a second time.

The unsigned shift operator signifies to Spock that the expression following it will be used as a response for each subsequent call of the exact same method. Multiple answers can be chained together by using the normal shift operator, >>. In this listing this happens with the isProductAvailableMethod(). The first time it will return true and the second time it will return false to a query for a TV.

An alternative syntax (and the one I prefer) is to use a collection after the unsigned shift operator. Each item of the collection will be used in turn as a response when the stubbed method is called. As with parameterized tests, remember that Groovy has a more general idea of "iterable" things than Java, so you don't have to use a list as shown in listing 6.8.

6.2.4   *Throwing exceptions when a stubbed method is called*

I said in the introduction of this chapter that stubs are essential if you want to emulate a hard-to-reproduce situation or a corner case that doesn't typically happen with production code. For large-scale applications, when the code that handles error conditions can easily outweigh the code for happy-path scenarios, it's essential to create unit tests that trigger those error conditions.

In the most common case, the error conditions come in the form of Java exceptions. These can be easily emulated, as shown in the following listing.

Listing 6.9   Instructing stubs to throw exceptions

```
def "A problematic inventory means nothing can be shipped"() {
    given: "a basket and a TV"
    Product tv = new Product(name:"bravia",price:1200,weight:18)
    Basket basket = new Basket()

    and:"a warehouse with serious issues"
    WarehouseInventory inventory = Stub(WarehouseInventory)
    inventory.isProductAvailable( "bravia", _) >> { throw new        Stub is instructed to
        RuntimeException("critical error") }                        throw an exception
    basket.setWarehouseInventory(inventory)
```

```
when: "user checks out the tv"
basket.addProduct tv

then: "order cannot be shipped"
!basket.canShipCompletely()
}
```

Ensures that the basket class
can recover from the exception

The basket class calls the warehouse class, and if anything goes wrong (even if an exception is thrown), the canShipCompletely() method recovers by returning false (while leaving the basket class in a valid state). To verify this capability of the basket class, you need to instruct the warehouse to throw an exception when the stubbed method is called.

You still use the right-shift operator (>>) for stubbing, but instead of returning a standard value as in the previous examples, you can place any Java code inside the brackets (which in reality is a Groovy closure, as you know if you paid attention in chapter 2).

Inside the brackets, you can put any code with Java statements, so a useful capability is to throw an exception. The beauty of Spock[5] is that throwing exceptions isn't something extraordinary that requires special syntax. Instead, you're offered a generic way to do anything when a stubbed method is called, and throwing an exception is one possibility of many.

The great power of using Groovy closures in Spock stubs is revealed fully in the next section.

> ### Closures—the Swiss army knife of Groovy
>
> I briefly talked about closures in chapter 2. In their simplest form, you can think of them as anonymous Java functions with greater flexibility. If you've already worked with Java 8 and lambda expressions, Groovy closures will be familiar.

6.2.5 *Using dynamic stubs that check arguments when responding*

The previous section showed how to throw an exception in a stub by using a Groovy closure. I consider Groovy closures a powerful feature, even in the presence of Java 8, because the way Groovy closures are used in Spock is refreshing. In other mocking frameworks, such as Mockito, you need to learn separate syntax semantics for argument catchers, exception throwing, and dynamic responses. In Spock, all these are unified under Groovy closures.

Before I show any code, I'll repeat the suggestion in chapter 2. If you don't feel comfortable with Groovy closures (or Java 8 lambda expressions), feel free to skip this section and come back later. Closures can also be used with mocks, as you'll see later in this chapter.

---

[5] Thanks to Groovy's way of handling all exceptions as unchecked.

To make this example more interesting, I'll add another dependency to the basket class. This time, it will be an interface (instead of a concrete class), as shown here:

```
public interface ShippingCalculator {
   int findShippingCostFor(Product product, int times);
}
```

This interface is responsible for shipping charges. It accepts a product and the number of times it was added in the basket, and returns the shipping costs (in whatever currency the e-shop uses). The basket class is also augmented with a findTotalCost() method that calls the shipping calculator behind the scenes in order to add shipping charges to the product value. You want to test this new method of the basket class.

As a business scenario, you choose a simple shipping strategy. For each product, you add 10 dollars to the final cost for each time it's added to the basket, regardless of product type.[6] A naive way of stubbing the shipping calculator would be the following:

```
ShippingCalculator shippingCalculator = Stub(ShippingCalculator)
shippingCalculator.findShippingCostFor(tv, 2) >> 20
shippingCalculator.findShippingCostFor(camera, 2) >> 20
shippingCalculator.findShippingCostFor(hifi, 1) >> 10
shippingCalculator.findShippingCostFor(laptop, 3) >> 30
```

Here you instruct the shipping module with specific responses according to the arguments of the called method. This code isn't readable and clearly suffers from verbosity. Writing unit tests for a large number of products will also be difficult (imagine a unit test that adds 100 products from an external source).

With the power of closures, Spock allows you to capture a simple pricing strategy with a single line of code! The following listing demonstrates this technique and shows that Spock can stub both interfaces and concrete classes in an agnostic way.

Listing 6.10 Stubs that respond according to arguments

```
def "Basket handles shipping charges according to product count"() {
    given: "a basket and several products"
    Product tv = new Product(name:"bravia",price:1200,weight:18)
    Product camera = new Product(name:"panasonic",price:350,weight:2)
    Product hifi = new Product(name:"jvc",price:600,weight:5)
    Product laptop = new Product(name:"toshiba",price:800,weight:10)
    Basket basket = new Basket()

    and: "a fully stocked warehouse"                        ⟵ Stubbing a
    WarehouseInventory inventory = Stub(WarehouseInventory)   concrete class
    inventory.isProductAvailable( _ , _) >> true
    basket.setWarehouseInventory(inventory)

    and: "a shipping calculator that charges 10 dollars for each product"
    ShippingCalculator shippingCalculator = Stub(ShippingCalculator)
```

Stubbing a Java interface ⟶

---

[6] Not really sustainable for a true shop, but it's sufficient for illustration purposes.

Using a Groovy closure for a dynamic response

```
shippingCalculator.findShippingCostFor( _, _) >> { Product product, int
                    count ->  10 * count}
basket.setShippingCalculator(shippingCalculator)
```

```
when: "user checks out several products in different quantities"
basket.addProduct tv, 2
basket.addProduct camera, 2        Adding different
basket.addProduct hifi             quantities to the basket
basket.addProduct laptop, 3
```

Verifying that shipping charges are included

```
then: "cost is correctly calculated"
basket.findTotalCost() == 2 * tv.price + 2 * camera.price + hifi.price
                    + 3 * laptop.price + basket.getProductCount() * 10
}
```

Using the Groovy closure, you've instrumented the shipping calculator stub with your selected pricing strategy in a single line of code. With that one line, the shipping calculator can respond to 1, 2, or 100 products added to the basket. Its behavior is no longer statically defined, but it can understand its arguments.

For an even smarter stub, assume that the e-shop also sells downloadable goods. For these, the shipping cost should obviously be zero. Again, a naive way to cater to this case would be to instruct your stub with specific products to return 0—for example:

```
shippingCalculator.findShippingCostFor(ebook, _) >> 0
```

Doing this wouldn't be scalable because if a unit test examines 10 different downloadable goods, you'll have to manually stub the response 10 times. Remember that the interface for the shipping calculator also gives you access to the product, as well as the number of times it was added to the basket. Therefore, you can modify the Groovy closure to look at both arguments, as shown in the next listing.

Listing 6.11 A smart stub that looks at both its arguments

```
def "Downloadable goods do not have shipping cost"() {
    given: "a basket and several products"
    Product tv = new Product(name:"bravia",price:1200,weight:18)
    Product camera = new Product(name:"panasonic",price:350,weight:2)
    Product hifi = new Product(name:"jvc",price:600,weight:5)
    Product laptop = new Product(name:"toshiba",price:800,weight:10)
    Product ebook = new Product(name:"learning exposure",price:30,weight:0)
    Product suite = new Product(name:"adobe essentials",price:200,weight:0)
    Basket basket = new Basket()

    and: "a fully stocked warehouse"
    WarehouseInventory inventory = Stub(WarehouseInventory)
    inventory.isProductAvailable( _ , _) >> true
    basket.setWarehouseInventory(inventory)
```

Stubbing a Java interface

```
    and: "a shipping calculator that charges 10 dollars for each physical
                    product"
    ShippingCalculator shippingCalculator = Stub(ShippingCalculator)
```

```
        shippingCalculator.findShippingCostFor( _, _ ) >> { Product product, int
                      count ->  product.weight==0 ? 0 :10 * count}  ◄──┐   Groovy closure
        basket.setShippingCalculator(shippingCalculator)                │   that uses both
                                                                        │   arguments
        when: "user checks out several products in different quantities"
        basket.addProduct tv,2
        basket.addProduct camera,2
        basket.addProduct hifi
        basket.addProduct laptop
        basket.addProduct ebook
        basket.addProduct suite,3
```

60 is shipping charges for the physical goods only.

```
        then: "cost is correctly calculated"
        basket.findTotalCost() == 2 * tv.price + 2 * camera.price + hifi.price
                + laptop.price  + ebook.price + 3 * suite.price+ 60
    }
```

With a single Groovy code line, you've managed to instruct the shipping calculator to use a different behavior for downloadable and physical products. If the product has zero weight, shipping costs are free. In any other case, the standard charge of 10 dollars/euros is returned.

Using Groovy closures for argument matching is a technique that can be easily abused. Use it only when it adds to the scalability and readability of your Spock test. In simple tests, you might get away with direct stubbing of all argument combinations if their number is manageable.

6.2.6 *Returning stubs from the responses of other stubs*

Before leaving stubs and diving into mocks, it's worth demonstrating that Spock supports *recursive stubbing*. By this, I mean that it's possible to have stubs return stubs as responses, which themselves return stubs, and so on, until you get to values.

In well-designed code (which correctly uses dependency injection), this technique is not usually needed. It becomes handy for legacy code and incorrectly designed enterprise code bases. To mimic legacy code, let's assume that this is your basket class:

```
public class EnterprisyBasket{

    public EnterprisyBasket(ServiceLocator serviceLocator)
    {
    setWarehouseInventory(serviceLocator.getWarehouseInventory());
    }
    [...rest of implementation here...]
}
```

Here the basket class isn't injected directly with its dependencies but instead gets a ServiceLocator object that acts as an intermediary to the services needed. Here's its code:

```
public interface ServiceLocator {
    WarehouseInventory getWarehouseInventory();
    [... other services here...]
}
```

Spock can easily deal with this situation, as shown in the next listing.

Listing 6.12   Stubbing responses with other stubs

```
def "If warehouse is empty nothing can be shipped"() {
    given: "a TV"
    Product tv = new Product(name:"bravia",price:1200,weight:18)

    and:"an empty warehouse"
    WarehouseInventory inventory = Stub(WarehouseInventory)
    inventory.isEmpty() >> true
    ServiceLocator serviceLocator = Stub(ServiceLocator)
    serviceLocator.getWarehouseInventory() >> inventory

    and: "a basket"
    EnterprisyBasket basket = new EnterprisyBasket(serviceLocator)

    when: "user checks out the tv"
    basket.addProduct tv

    then: "order cannot be shipped"
    !basket.canShipCompletely()
}
```

Stub that will be used by the class under test ◄— (points to `WarehouseInventory inventory = Stub(WarehouseInventory)`)

Stubbing of intermediary class ◄— (points to `ServiceLocator serviceLocator = Stub(ServiceLocator)`)

Instructing a stub to return another stub —► (points to `serviceLocator.getWarehouseInventory() >> inventory`)

Using the parent stub in the class under test —► (points to `EnterprisyBasket basket = new EnterprisyBasket(serviceLocator)`)

This listing uses only two levels of stubs, but it's possible to use more if your legacy code requires it.

6.3   *Mocks: verifying values returned from the class under test*

Stubs are great when your class under test already has methods that allow you to understand whether everything works as expected (such as the canShipCompletely() method of the basket class). But most of the time, the only way to understand what happened during the unit test is to have a "log" of what methods were called along with their arguments and their responses.

Mocks are the answer to this need. By mocking a collaborator of the class under test, you not only can preprogram it with canned responses, but also can query it (after the unit test has finished) about all its interactions.

Spock has a huge range of options when it comes to mocks

Spock supports many features when it comes to mocking. Some are more useful than others, some apply only to extreme cases, and some are so confusing that I avoid them on purpose. This chapter shows the features I find useful (I've left out about 10% of Spock features). You can always consult the official Spock website as a reference.

6.3.1   *All capabilities of stubs exist in mocks as well*

The first thing to get out of the way is that mocks are a superset of stubs. All code listings I've shown you so far will work even if you use a mock. As an example, here's listing 6.2 written with a mock this time. Apart from a single line, the rest of the code is exactly the same.

Listing 6.13   Stubbing mocks

```
def "If warehouse is empty nothing can be shipped"() {
    given: "a basket and a TV"
    Product tv = new Product(name:"bravia",price:1200,weight:18)
    Basket basket = new Basket()

    and:"an empty warehouse"
    WarehouseInventory inventory = Mock(WarehouseInventory)
    inventory.isEmpty() >> true
    basket.setWarehouseInventory(inventory)

    when: "user checks out the tv"
    basket.addProduct tv

    then: "order cannot be shipped"
    !basket.canShipCompletely()
}
```

Inject the mock into the class under test.

Create a mock.

Instruct the mock to return true when isEmpty() is called.

This method calls the mock behind the scenes.

In Spock, you use stubs when you want to denote that the fake class you're going to use will come with only preprogrammed behavior and its interactions won't be verified. Of the two listings, the semantically correct is 6.2 (with the stub) because the warehouse inventory is never queried at the end of the unit test for its interactions with the basket class.

Spock enforces this convention, so although mocks will work in the place of stubs, the opposite doesn't apply. Attempting to use a stub in place of a mock will throw an error when Spock runs the unit test.

6.3.2   *Simple mocking—examining whether a method was called*

Let's add another collaborator class in the electronic basket example. In the following listing, you'll add the capability to charge credit cards.

Listing 6.14   Java skeleton for credit card charging

```
public class Customer {
    private String name;
    private boolean vip = false;
    private String creditCard;
    [...getters and setters here...]
}
public enum CreditCardResult {

    OK, INVALID_CARD, NOT_ENOUGH_FUNDS;
```

Simple object for customer

Credit card number

Possible results from charging a credit card

```
                 }
                 public interface CreditCardProcessor {
```
Interface provided by an external system

Charging method
```
                     CreditCardResult sale(int amount, Customer customer);

                     void shutdown();
```
Must be called after each charge
```
                 }
                 public class BillableBasket extends Basket{

                     private CreditCardProcessor creditCardProcessor;
```
Setter injection
```
                     public void setCreditCardProcessor(CreditCardProcessor
                             creditCardProcessor) {
                         this.creditCardProcessor = creditCardProcessor;
                     }

                     public void checkout(Customer customer)
                     {
```
Triggers credit card injection
```
                         [...code redacted..]
                     }

                 }
```

The credit card system is implemented by an external library (imagine that you don't even have the source code). Reading its API documentation, you see a big warning: its developers explain that the shutdown() method must be called whenever a credit card charge happens.[7]

Your job is to write a unit test that verifies the call of this method by the basket class without charging a credit card. You could get away with a stub if the credit card processor had a method named shutdownWasCalled()! But it doesn't.

You can use a mock instead of a pure stub, as shown in the following listing.

> **Listing 6.15   Verification of a mocked method**

```
def "credit card connection is always closed down"() {
    given: "a basket, a customer and a TV"
    Product tv = new Product(name:"bravia",price:1200,weight:18)
    BillableBasket basket = new BillableBasket()
    Customer customer = new
        Customer(name:"John",vip:false, creditCard:"testCard")
```
Creating a mock from an interface
```
    and: "a credit card service"
    CreditCardProcessor creditCardSevice = Mock(CreditCardProcessor)
    basket.setCreditCardProcessor(creditCardSevice)
```
Injecting the mock into the class under test
```
    when: "user checks out the tv"
    basket.addProduct tv
```
This method calls the mock behind the scenes.
```
    basket.checkout(customer)

    then: "connection is always closed at the end"
    1 * creditCardSevice.shutdown()
```
Verifying called method
```
}
```

---

[7]   Otherwise, the world will explode.

The important code line of this listing is the last one. Unlike all previous Spock tests, it doesn't contain a standard assert statement (checked according to Groovy truth). This line is special Spock syntax and comes in this format:

```
N * mockObject.method(arguments)
```

When Spock sees this line, it makes the test pass only if that method on the mock has been called *N* times with the arguments provided (which can also be argument matchers, as with stubs).

The last line in the listing means, "After this test is finished, I expect that the number of times the `shutdown()` method was called is once." The test will pass if this sentence is `true` and will fail in any other case.

Assume that with that unit test in place, a developer introduces a bug in the basket class that calls the `shutdown()` method two times. Spock will instantly fail the test with the error message shown in figure 6.3.

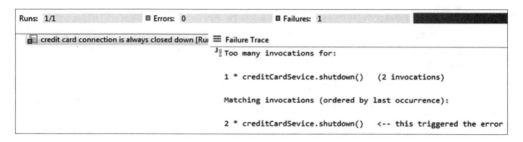

Figure 6.3   Spock fails the test when the mocked method is called twice.

Spock knows the exact invocations of all mocks because during the test, it has replaced the classes with its own proxies that record everything.

6.3.3   *Verifying order of interactions*

With the mock for the credit card processor in place, you can ensure that the credit card service is shut down after the transaction (and without charging a real credit card). But listing 6.13 misses the sequence of calls. How do you know that the `shutdown()` method is called at the end, and not before the credit card charge step (which would be an obvious bug)? Listing 6.13 doesn't cover this scenario.

Your first impulse, to check the order of calls that happen with the credit card service, would be to write something like this:

```
then: "credit card is charged and CC service is closed down"
1 * creditCardSevice.sale(1200,customer)
1 * creditCardSevice.shutdown()
```

This won't work as expected. Spock doesn't pay any attention to the order of verifications inside a specific then: block. The preceding unit test will always pass, regardless of the exact sequence of events (if both of them are correct on their own).

The correct unit test needs to exploit the fact that multiple then: blocks are checked in order by Spock,[8] as shown in the following listing.

Listing 6.16   Verification of a specific order of mocked methods

Creation of a mock from an interface →

```
def "credit card connection is closed down in the end"() {
    given: "a basket, a customer and a TV"
    Product tv = new Product(name:"bravia",price:1200,weight:18)
    BillableBasket basket = new BillableBasket()
    Customer customer = new
        Customer(name:"John",vip:false, creditCard:"testCard")

    and: "a credit card service"
    CreditCardProcessor creditCardSevice = Mock(CreditCardProcessor
    basket.setCreditCardProcessor(creditCardSevice)

    when: "user checks out the tv"
    basket.addProduct tv
    basket.checkout(customer)

    then: "credit card is charged and"          First this verification
    1 * creditCardSevice.sale( _, _)            will be checked.

    then: "the credit card service is closed down"   This will only be checked if
    1 * creditCardSevice.shutdown()                  the first verification passes.
}
```

Notice that in this test, you want to focus on the order of events and nothing else, so you've used unconditional argument matchers for the arguments of the sale() method because you don't care about them in this test. (Usually, there should be another unit test focusing on them.)

6.3.4   *Verifying number of method calls of the mocked class*

If you already have significant experience with other mocking frameworks,[9] you should have noticed something strange in listings 6.13 and 6.14. In listing 6.14, you're clearly noting to Spock that you expect the sale() method to be called. But listing 6.13 mentions nothing about the sale() method. How does the test in listing 6.13 pass?

It turns out that mocks and stubs created by Spock are lenient by default. The test will fail only if the behavior of the mocks is contained in the then: block against your explicit instructions. Calling a method of a mock that was never mentioned has no negative effect. Not calling a stubbed/mocked method also doesn't affect the unit test.

---

[8]   This was also shown in chapter 4.
[9]   And have been paying close attention to the code listings.

When you call a mocked method that doesn't have explicit stubbing instructions, Spock will return default values (`false` for Boolean variables, 0 for numbers, and `null` for objects). If you want to make sure that a method isn't called in a mock, you have to declare it in the `then:` block as well. Pay close attention to the last statement of the following code listing.

Listing 6.17   Explicit declaration of interactions

```
def "Warehouse is queried for each product"() {
    given: "a basket, a TV and a camera"
        Product tv = new Product(name:"bravia",price:1200,weight:18)
        Product camera = new Product(name:"panasonic",price:350,weight:2)
        Basket basket = new Basket()

        and: "a warehouse with limitless stock"
        WarehouseInventory inventory = Mock(WarehouseInventory)
        basket.setWarehouseInventory(inventory)

    when: "user checks out both products"
    basket.addProduct tv
    basket.addProduct camera
    boolean readyToShip = basket.canShipCompletely()

    then: "order can be shipped"
    readyToShip
    2 * inventory.isProductAvailable( _ , _) >> true
    0 * inventory.preload(_ , _)
}
```

Creating a mock/stub → (points to the `and:` "a warehouse with limitless stock" line)

Stubbing a mocked method → (points to the `2 * inventory.isProductAvailable` line)

Mocks are only checks in the when: block.

Verifying that a method was never called

There are three important points to notice in listing 6.17 that relate to the three lines in the `then:` block.

Starting from the bottom, you want to make sure that the basket only queries the warehouse, but never tampers with the stock levels. Therefore, the code explicitly states that you expect zero invocations for the method that fills the inventory.

The middle line verifies that the method of product availability is called twice (because the test deals with two products). Because you want the basket to think that the warehouse is full, you also stub the method to return `true` both times. Thus the code in this line is both a mock expectation and a predefined stubbed response:[10]

```
2 * inventory.isProductAvailable( _ , _) >> true
```

This line says to Spock, "After this test is finished, I expect that the method `isProductAvailable()` was called twice. I don't care about the arguments. But when it's called, please return `true` to the class that called it."

The last thing to notice is that unlike previous code listings, the `canShip-Completely()` method is called in the `when:` block, and only its result is checked in

---

[10] This is a big difference from Mockito. In Mockito, you can separately stub a mock and verify it in another statement. In Spock, you do both things at the same time.

the then: block. The reason for this is that Spock records the interactions of mocks in the when: block (which should always contain the trigger code). When using mocks (or stubs), the then: block must contain only verifications.

6.3.5 Verifying noninteractions for multiple mocked classes

Now you know how to verify individual methods for any number of invocations. But sometimes you want to cast a wider net, and control invocations at the class level instead of the method level. The underscore character is flexible regarding its position inside a verification statement. Consider the following listing.

Listing 6.18 Verifying interactions for all methods of a class

```
def "Warehouse is queried for each product - strict"() {
    given: "a basket, a TV and a camera"
    Product tv = new Product(name:"bravia",price:1200,weight:18)
    Product camera = new Product(name:"panasonic",price:350,weight:2)
    Basket basket = new Basket()

    and: "a warehouse with limitless stock"
    WarehouseInventory inventory = Mock(WarehouseInventory)
    basket.setWarehouseInventory(inventory)

    when: "user checks out both products"
    basket.addProduct tv
    basket.addProduct camera
    boolean readyToShip = basket.canShipCompletely()

    then: "order can be shipped"
    readyToShip
    2 * inventory.isProductAvailable(_,_) >> true
    1 * inventory.isEmpty() >> false
    0 * inventory._
}
```

Setting expectations for all other methods of the class → lines `2 * ... >> true`, `1 * ... >> false`, `0 * inventory._`

Setting expectations for specific methods → lines `2 * inventory.isProductAvailable(_,_) >> true`, `1 * inventory.isEmpty() >> false`

Here you've written a strict unit test because it assumes that regardless of the number of methods that exist in the inventory class, the basket class should call only isProductAvailable() and isEmpty() and nothing else. Therefore, the last verification line uses the underscore as a method matcher:

```
0 * inventory._
```

This line means, "I expect zero invocations for all other methods of the inventory class." Be careful when using this technique because it means that you know exactly the interface between the class under test and the mock. If a new method is added in the mock (in the production code) that's used by the class under test, this Spock test will instantly fail.

If you have multiple mocks, you can write even stricter tests by placing the underscore as a class name, as shown in the next listing.

Listing 6.19 Verifying noninteractions for all mocks

```
def "Only warehouse is queried when checking shipping status"() {
    given: "a basket, a TV and a camera"
    Product tv = new Product(name:"bravia",price:1200,weight:18)
    Product camera = new Product(name:"panasonic",price:350,weight:2)
    Basket basket = new Basket()

    and: "a warehouse with limitless stock"
    WarehouseInventory inventory = Mock(WarehouseInventory)
    basket.setWarehouseInventory(inventory)
    ShippingCalculator shippingCalculator = Mock(ShippingCalculator)
    basket.setShippingCalculator(shippingCalculator)

    when: "user checks out both products"
    basket.addProduct tv
    basket.addProduct camera
    boolean readyToShip = basket.canShipCompletely()

    then: "order can be shipped"
    readyToShip
    2 * inventory.isProductAvailable( _ , _) >> true
    _ * inventory.isEmpty() >> false
    0 * _
}
```

Underscore matches number of invocations. → (points to `_ * inventory.isEmpty()` line)

Underscore matches arguments. → (points to `2 * inventory.isProductAvailable( _ , _)` line)

Underscore matches mocked classes. → (points to `0 * _` line)

In this code listing, the basket class is injected with two mocks (one for shipping costs and one for the inventory). After running the test, you want to verify that only two specific methods were called on the inventory and that nothing was called for the shipping cost service. Instead of manually declaring all other methods with zero cardinality one by one, you use the underscore character in the class part of the verification. In Spock, the line

```
0 * _
```

means, "I expect zero invocations for all other methods of all other classes when the test runs." Also notice that you don't care how many times the isEmpty() method is called, and you use the underscore operator in the cardinality:

```
_ * inventory.isEmpty() >> false
```

This line means, "I expect the isEmpty() method to be called any number of times, and when it does, it should return false."

The many faces of the underscore character

As you may have noticed by now, the underscore character is a special matcher for Spock tests. In the basic form of a mock verification, N * class.method(argument), the underscore can be used to match arguments (listings 6.16, 6.17), methods (listing 6.18), classes, and even the cardinality N (listing 6.19). For all these cases, you don't care about the respective part of the verification.

6.3.6 *Verifying types of arguments when a mocked method is called*

I've shown how to verify specific arguments in mock invocations and how to say to Spock that you don't care about arguments (the underscore character). But between these two extremes, you can verify several other attributes of arguments. One of the most useful verifications is to make sure that the argument passed isn't `null`. This can be described naturally in Spock, as shown in the next listing.

Listing 6.20   Verifying that arguments aren't `null` when a mocked method is called

```
def "Warehouse is queried for each product - null "() {
    given: "a basket, a TV and a camera"
    Product tv = new Product(name:"bravia",price:1200,weight:18)
    Product camera = new Product(name:"panasonic",price:350,weight:2)
    Basket basket = new Basket()

    and: "a warehouse with limitless stock"
    WarehouseInventory inventory = Mock(WarehouseInventory)      ◀─── Creating a
    basket.setWarehouseInventory(inventory)                            Spock mock

    when: "user checks out both products"
    basket.addProduct tv
    basket.addProduct camera
    boolean readyToShip = basket.canShipCompletely()

    then: "order can be shipped"
    readyToShip                                                         Verifying that the first
    2 * inventory.isProductAvailable(!null ,1) >> true    ◀──────────   argument isn't null
}
```

In this listing, you want to make sure that whatever argument is passed to the inventory isn't `null` (because the arguments should be names of products). For the second argument, where you know exactly what will be used, you directly put in the value:

```
2 * inventory.isProductAvailable(!null ,1) >> true
```

This line means, "I expect that the method `isProductAvailable()` will be called twice. The first argument can be anything apart from `null`, and the second argument will always be `1`. When that happens, the method will return `true`."

In unit tests with complex class hierarchies, you can verify the type of arguments as well. The following listing illustrates this (for this trivial example, verifying the type of arguments is probably overkill).

Listing 6.21   Verifying the type of arguments

```
def "Warehouse is queried for each product - type "() {
    given: "a basket, a TV and a camera"
    Product tv = new Product(name:"bravia",price:1200,weight:18)
    Product camera = new Product(name:"panasonic",price:350,weight:2)
    Basket basket = new Basket()
```

```
          and: "a warehouse with limitless stock"
          WarehouseInventory inventory = Mock(WarehouseInventory)        ◀─┐  Creating a
          basket.setWarehouseInventory(inventory)                           │  Spock mock

          when: "user checks out both products"
          basket.addProduct tv
          basket.addProduct camera                                          Verifying that the first
          boolean readyToShip = basket.canShipCompletely()                  argument is always a
                                                                            string and the second
          then: "order can be shipped"                                      always an integer
          readyToShip
          2 * inventory.isProductAvailable(_ as String ,_ as Integer) >> true  ◀──
    }
```

Again you use the magic underscore character, this time combined with the as keyword. Notice that a null argument will also fail the verification so the as/underscore
combination includes the null check.

6.3.7   *Verifying arguments of method calls from mocked classes*

Using the underscore character as an argument in your mock verifications means that
you don't care about the argument at all. But what happens if your unit test is focused
on the arguments and you do care?

   In that case, my advice is to declare exactly what you expect. You've already seen
that with scalar values, you use them directly as arguments. The same thing happens
with full objects, as shown in the next listing.

Listing 6.22   Verifying exact arguments of a mocked method

```
def "vip status is correctly passed to credit card - simple"() {
    given: "a basket, a customer and a TV"
    Product tv = new Product(name:"bravia",price:1200,weight:18)
    Product camera = new Product(name:"panasonic",price:350,weight:2)
    BillableBasket basket = new BillableBasket()
    Customer customer = new
            Customer(name:"John",vip:false,creditCard:"testCard")

    and: "a credit card service"
    CreditCardProcessor creditCardSevice = Mock(CreditCardProcessor)
    basket.setCreditCardProcessor(creditCardSevice)

    when: "user checks out two products"
    basket.addProduct tv
    basket.addProduct camera
    basket.checkout(customer)

    then: "credit card is charged"
    1 * creditCardSevice.sale(1550, customer)
}
```

Creating a Spock mock [points to: CreditCardProcessor creditCardSevice = Mock(CreditCardProcessor)]

Verifying that the second argument is equal to a specific object instance [points to: 1 * creditCardSevice.sale(1550, customer)]

As you can see in this listing, there's no special syntax for objects:

```
1 * creditCardSevice.sale(1550, customer)
```

This line means, "When the test ends, I expect the `sale()` method to be called exactly once. Its first argument should be the number `1500`, and its second argument should be the `customer` instance."

If you want to verify part of an object instance and not the whole instance, you can use Groovy closures in a similar way to stubs (as was shown in listing 6.8). The same syntax applies to mocks, as the following listing shows.

Listing 6.23   Verifying part of an object instance used as a mock argument

```
def "vip status is correctly passed to credit card - vip"() {
    given: "a basket, a customer and a TV"
    Product tv = new Product(name:"bravia",price:1200,weight:18)
    Product camera = new Product(name:"panasonic",price:350,weight:2)
    BillableBasket basket = new BillableBasket()
    Customer customer = new
            Customer(name:"John",vip:false,creditCard:"testCard")

    and: "a credit card service"
    CreditCardProcessor creditCardSevice = Mock(CreditCardProcessor)
    basket.setCreditCardProcessor(creditCardSevice)

    when: "user checks out two products"
    basket.addProduct tv
    basket.addProduct camera
    basket.checkout(customer)

    then: "credit card is charged"
    1 * creditCardSevice.sale(1550, { client -> client.vip == false})
}
```

Creating a Spock mock → (annotation pointing to `CreditCardProcessor creditCardSevice = Mock(CreditCardProcessor)`)

Verifying that the second has a field called vip with the value false → (annotation pointing to `1 * creditCardSevice.sale(1550, { client -> client.vip == false})`)

The last verification line in this listing checks only the `vip` field of the customer object. The other two fields (`name` and `creditCard`) can be anything, and the test will still pass. With the power of Groovy closures, you can check a mocked argument against any expression you can think of.

Listing 6.24   Using full Groovy closures for argument verification

```
def "vip status is correctly passed to credit card - full"() {
    given: "a basket, a customer and a TV"
    Product tv = new Product(name:"bravia",price:1200,weight:18)
    Product camera = new Product(name:"panasonic",price:350,weight:2)
    BillableBasket basket = new BillableBasket()
    Customer customer = new
            Customer(name:"John",vip:false,creditCard:"testCard")

    and: "a credit card service"
    CreditCardProcessor creditCardSevice = Mock(CreditCardProcessor)
    basket.setCreditCardProcessor(creditCardSevice)

    when: "user checks out two products"
    basket.addProduct tv
```

Creation of a Spock mock → (annotation pointing to `CreditCardProcessor creditCardSevice = Mock(CreditCardProcessor)`)

Custom expression for both mocked arguments →

```
basket.addProduct camera
basket.checkout(customer)

then: "credit card is charged"
1 * creditCardSevice.sale({amount -> amount ==
        basket.findOrderPrice()}, { client -> client.vip == false})
}
```

This listing uses two closures, one for each argument of the sale() method. As before, the second closure checks a single field of an object (the vip field from the customer class). The first closure makes its own calculation with a completely external method, the findOrderPrice():

```
1 * creditCardSevice.sale({amount -> amount ==
    basket.findOrderPrice()}, { client -> client.vip == false})
```

The whole line means, "When this unit test is complete, I expect the sale method to be called exactly once. It should have two arguments. The first argument should be equal to the result of basket.findOrderPrice(). The second argument should be an object instance with a vip field. The value of the vip field should be false."

If any facts of this sentence don't stand, the Spock test will fail. All of them must be correct for a successful test.

6.4   *Putting it all together: credit card charging in two steps*

All the examples shown so far illustrate various features of mocks and stubs. I'll close this chapter with a bigger example that combines most of the techniques shown so far and is closer to what you'd write in a production application.

If you look back at listing 6.14, you'll see that the basket class also contains the fullCheckout() method. This method does the following:

1   Checks the credit card of the customer. If the card is invalid or doesn't have enough funds, the method stops there.
2   If the credit card is OK, the price for the products is reserved from the credit card. (This is called an *authorization event* in credit card terminology.)
3   The inventory is checked. If the products are in stock and can be shipped, the amount from the card that was previously reserved is now transferred to the account of the e-shop. (This is called a *capturing event* in credit card terminology.)

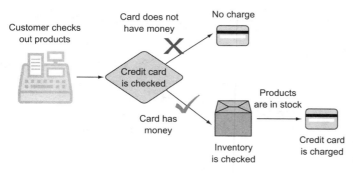

In listing 6.12, you can see these two methods (for authorization and capturing) in the credit card processor class. Figure 6.4 is a diagram of what you want to test.

Figure 6.4   Business requirements for credit card charging

As a starting point, the first scenario that you'll test is the case where the card doesn't have enough money. The Spock test is shown in the next listing.

Listing 6.25 Using mocks and stubs in the same test

```
def "card has no funds"() {
    given: "a basket, a customer and some products"
    Product tv = new Product(name:"bravia",price:1200,weight:18)
    Product camera = new Product(name:"panasonic",price:350,weight:2)
    BillableBasket basket = new BillableBasket()
    Customer customer = new
            Customer(name:"John",vip:false,creditCard:"testCard")

    and: "a credit card service"
    CreditCardProcessor creditCardSevice = Mock(CreditCardProcessor)
    basket.setCreditCardProcessor(creditCardSevice)

    and: "a fully stocked warehouse"
    WarehouseInventory inventory = Stub(WarehouseInventory) {
            isProductAvailable(_,_) >> true
            isEmpty() >> false
    }
    basket.setWarehouseInventory(inventory)

    when: "user checks out two products"
    basket.addProduct tv
    basket.addProduct camera
    boolean charged = basket.fullCheckout(customer)

    then: "nothing is charged if credit card does not have enough money"
    1 * creditCardSevice.authorize(1550, customer) >>
                    CreditCardResult.NOT_ENOUGH_FUNDS
    !charged
    0 * _

}
```

Create a Spock mock.

Stub the inventory to be full.

Trigger the tested action.

Mock the credit card to be invalid.

Verify that nothing was charged.

The resulting code doesn't have any surprises. Because you directly mock the credit card processor to assume that the card doesn't have enough money, the charging process stops.

Things get more interesting if you want to write a unit test for the full scenario, where the card has money. The complicated part here is the two-step process between the authorize and capture steps. The reason for this is that the response from the first is a special token (assume that in this example it's a single string). Then when the basket calls the capture step, it must pass the same token to the credit card processor. This way, the credit card processor can link the two events together and distinguish multiple capture events.

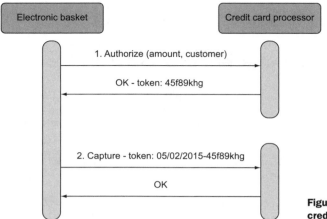

Figure 6.5   Two steps of charging a credit card with the same token

To further complicate things, assume also that the credit card processor wants the current date prepended to the token for logistical reasons. Figure 6.5 shows a sample conversation between the basket class and the credit card processor.

The respective unit test is shown next.

Listing 6.26   Verifying a sequence of events with interconnected method calls

```
def "happy path for credit card sale"() {
    given: "a basket, a customer and some products"
    Product tv = new Product(name:"bravia",price:1200,weight:18)
    Product camera = new Product(name:"panasonic",price:350,weight:2)
    BillableBasket basket = new BillableBasket()
    Customer customer = new
            Customer(name:"John",vip:false,creditCard:"testCard")

    and: "a credit card that has enough funds"
    CreditCardProcessor creditCardSevice = Mock(CreditCardProcessor)
    basket.setCreditCardProcessor(creditCardSevice)
    CreditCardResult sampleResult = CreditCardResult.OK
    sampleResult.setToken("sample");

    and: "a warehouse"
    WarehouseInventory inventory = Mock(WarehouseInventory)
    basket.setWarehouseInventory(inventory)

    when: "user checks out two products"
    basket.addProduct tv
    basket.addProduct camera
    boolean charged = basket.fullCheckout(customer)

    then: "credit card is checked"
    1 * creditCardSevice.authorize(1550, customer) >>  sampleResult
```

Mock the credit card service.

Create a sample credit card token.

Mock the warehouse.

Trigger the tested action.

Pass the sample token to the basket class.

Group interactions using with() →

```
        then: "inventory is checked"
        with(inventory)  {
            2 * isProductAvailable(!null , 1) >> true
            _ * isEmpty() >> false
        }
```

Verify that the inventory is queried twice (once for each product). ◄

Verify that the previous token is reused by the basket class. ↳

```
        then: "credit card is charged"
        1 * creditCardSevice.capture({myToken -> myToken.endsWith("sample")},
                        customer) >> CreditCardResult.OK
        charged
        0 * _
    }
```

◄ **Ensure that no other method from mocks was called.**

◄ **Verify that the credit card was charged.**

This listing demonstrates several key points. First, this time the warehouse inventory is a mock instead of a stub because you want to verify the correct calling of its methods. You also want to verify that it gets non-`null` arguments.

Mocks and stubs support the `with()` Spock method that was introduced in chapter 4. You've used it to group the two interactions of the warehouse inventory.

To verify that the basket class honors the token given back by the credit card processor, you create your own dummy token (named `sample`) and pass it to the basket when the authorization step happens. You can then verify that the token handed to the capture event is the same. Because the basket also prepends the token with the date (which is obviously different each time the test runs), you have to use the `ends-With()` method in the Groovy closure that matches the token.

> ### Mocks and stubs are relevant only to the scenario being tested
>
> If you look at listing 6.25, you'll see that the warehouse is a stub. But in listing 6.26, it's a mock. It's therefore possible to create stubs of a specific class in one unit test, and mocks of the same class in another unit test, depending on your business needs. Also, it's possible to have Spock tests that use only stubs, tests that use only mocks, and tests that use both depending on the case (as you'll see if you look back at the examples of this chapter). Use whatever you need according to the situation.

And there you have it! You've tested two credit card scenarios without charging a real credit card and without calling the real credit card service, which might be slow to initialize. As an exercise,[11] feel free to create more unit tests to cover these scenarios:

- The card becomes invalid between the authorize and capture steps.
- The authorize step succeeds, but the inventory doesn't have the products in stock.

---

[11] A possible solution can be found in the source code of the book at GitHub.

6.5   *Architecture considerations for effective mocking/stubbing*

This chapter closes with some theory that isn't strictly specific to Spock, but is essential to effective unit tests that contain mocks and stubs.

6.5.1   *Designing testable code that allows painless mocking*

If after reading the examples in this chapter, you get the feeling that I was always lucky that collaborator classes were so easily mocked and stubbed, you're half correct. One of the prerequisites of easy mocking is to have written your source code in a testable manner. By that I mean

- Code that's injected with its dependencies (inversion of control)
- No static classes/global state
- No static fields
- No singletons
- No complex constructors
- No service locators and hidden dependencies

Spock (and any other testing framework, for that matter) can't help you if the production code isn't in a usable state. It helps to follow the test-driven-development paradigm when you create Spock tests.

Also note that for Java production code, Spock can't mock static methods and/or private methods on its own. This is done by design.[12] Even though this might seem like a limitation, you should see it as a motivation for writing testable code. For more information, consult *Test Driven* by Lasse Koskela (Manning, 2007). The book talks about JUnit, but the advice it gives on testable Java code also applies to Spock.

If you really, really want to mock static/private methods, you need to use a framework such as PowerMock (https://code.google.com/p/powermock/). You might already have experience with it because Mockito also doesn't support mocking of private methods and needs PowerMock for this purpose. I don't like the PowerMock solution (it uses a custom class loader and bytecode manipulation) and would use it only as a last resort. Spock can be used together[13] with PowerMock via the PowerMockRule JUnit rule (https://code.google.com/p/powermock/wiki/PowerMockRule).

6.5.2   *Understanding lenient vs. strict mocks*

The underscore character is powerful in Spock, and as you've seen, it can be used on a wide range of elements, from single arguments to full classes. But as with all things in software engineering, a trade-off exists between strict tests (which explicitly specify all interactions and arguments) and lenient tests (which rely heavily on the underscore character and the default stubbing behavior of Spock).

---

[12] Mockito also does not support mocking of static/private methods.
[13] See https://github.com/kriegaex/Spock_PowerMock for an example.

Strict tests catch subtle bugs, but in the long run are hard to maintain, because even the slightest change in external interfaces or business requirements will make them break. Even adding a single method to a class that's used in a mock will instantly break any test that uses the 0 * _ line as a last statement.

On the other hand, lenient tests won't break often, but may miss some hard-to-reproduce bugs that occur because of corner cases and strange combinations of arguments.

My advice is to use strict tests for the mission-critical parts of your application and lenient tests for everything else. Following the Pareto principle, about 20% of your tests should be strict and the rest (80%) should be lenient. As always, this suggestion should only be a starting point for your own application and business needs.

6.6 Summary

- Fake classes can be used in unit tests instead of real classes. They're needed in several cases, such as when the real implementations are slow or have severe side effects.
- Spock supports two kinds of fake classes: mocks and stubs. Stubs are fake classes with preprogrammed behavior. Mocks are fake classes with preprogrammed behavior that can also be queried at the end of the test for their interactions.
- Spock can mock/stub both Java interfaces and concrete Java classes.
- Canned responses in stubs are programmed with the right-shift operator: >>.
- Preprogrammed responses can be differentiated according to the argument method or the number of times a method was called.
- The unsigned right-shift operator (>>>) can be used to stub sequential calls of the same method with the same arguments.
- The underscore character acts as a universal matcher in Spock when you don't care about the exact content of a call. It can be used to match arguments, methods, classes, or even the number of times a method was called.
- By using Groovy closures, a stub can be instructed to throw exceptions, run custom statements, or perform any other side effects.
- Groovy closures can also be used in stubs to create dynamic responses according to the argument passed to the stubbed method.
- It's possible to mix the underscore operator, fixed arguments, and Groovy closures in the same stubbed method call.
- Stubs/mocks can return other stubs/mocks. Recursive stub creation is possible if legacy production code requires it.
- In Spock, mocks are a superset of stubs, but for readability, you should use mocks only when you want to verify the interaction with the class under test. For fake objects that are used only for their responses, you should use stubs.

- By default, the order of mock verifications inside a `then:` block doesn't matter. You should use multiple `then:` blocks if you care about the order of verifications. Each `then:` block will be evaluated in turn.

- It's possible to verify the number of times a method was called. Using zero as cardinality means that you expect that a method was never called. Using the underscore character means that you don't care how many times it was called.

- You can verify arguments of a mocked method to ensure that they weren't `null`, or that they had a specific type.

- You can use Groovy closures as argument catchers to perform further validations on specific arguments of mocked methods.

- As with JUnit/Mockito, Spock is more easily applied to Java code that's designed to be testable in the first place.

- With Java classes, Spock can't mock private methods and static methods/objects. You should refactor your Java code first before writing Spock tests, or use PowerMock if you're desperate.

- Care must be exercised with the underscore character. It can result in lenient tests that let subtle bugs slip through.

Part 3

Spock in the Enterprise

The last part of the book examines Spock in the context of a large enterprise application. Enterprise applications sometimes have unique requirements in terms of their complexity and the breadth of features they must offer. Spock is ready for the Enterprise, as it comes with several features that come in handy in large and complicated unit tests.

Chapter 7 examines the use of Spock in the full testing lifecycle of an enterprise application. Spock can cover trivial plain unit tests, larger integration tests, and even functional tests. Several examples (mostly with Spring) show that Spock allows you to reuse your favorite Java testing tools with zero additional effort. At the same time, Spock can employ Groovy testing libraries, which may be more appropriate in your specific application.

Chapter 8 builds upon the knowledge of all previous chapters by describing corner cases that need special attention in your Enterprise Spock tests. It describes several additional Spock annotations that enable/disable the running of a test in a static or dynamic way and then shows you how to refactor large Spock tests with helper methods. The chapter finishes with a demonstration of Spock spies, a feature that I explicitly advise you not to use.

Integration and functional testing with Spock

This chapter covers

- Understanding the categories of unit tests in an enterprise application
- Writing integration tests for the Spring framework
- Testing REST endpoints with Spock
- Performing web-based tests with Spock and Geb
- Using Spock as part of the build process

At this point in the book, you probably want to start writing Spock tests for your own application. If you're a single developer or your application is fairly small and self-contained (for example, a standalone utility), then the previous chapters have covered the most important Spock features you'll need. If, on the other hand, you're part of a bigger team that works in large enterprise applications with an existing build infrastructure (automatic builds, test environments, code quality, and so on), you might be wondering how Spock fits the existing paradigm and practices already used in your organization.

In this chapter, you'll see how Spock can be used for the full testing lifecycle of an enterprise application that includes multiple layers of testing procedures running either automatically (after each code change) or on demand as part of a release. Spock is suitable for both *integration* tests (which cover multiple classes/modules and don't focus on a single class) and *functional* tests (which cover end-to-end functionality and view the whole system as a single entity instead of individual classes). Like the previous chapter, this one briefly covers the theory behind these types of tests.

Last but not least, a popular requirement for enterprise testing is examining web applications. You'll see how Spock can be used in conjunction with Geb (www.gebish.org), another Groovy library that makes web testing easy.

7.1   *Unit tests vs. integration tests vs. functional tests*

Let's start with a brief review of the types of tests useful to an enterprise application. This knowledge isn't specific to Spock, so if you already know the theory,[1] feel free to skip ahead to the Spock implementation.

Each time you want to create a new unit test, you have to decide on its scope. An automated test can focus on a single class, multiple classes, a single module, or even the whole system. The breadth of the tested area will affect several factors of your unit test, from the time it takes to complete (the more you're trying to test, the bigger the unit test execution) to the readability and effort it takes to write it (a unit test that needs to set up several modules needs more preparation).

At one end of the spectrum, you have "pure" unit tests that focus on a single class. These are easy to write, run quickly, and depend only on the production code. At the opposite end are functional tests (also called *acceptance tests*) that examine the system as a whole, emulating user behavior and even interacting with the graphical user interface (GUI). A functional test sends a request to the system and expects a response without any other knowledge of the inner workings of the system.

In the middle of these extremes, tests can examine either a code module or a code service. These are the integration tests (because they examine how individually tested classes integrate into modules). Figure 7.1 shows the scope examined by these categories of tests.

The example in this figure is the e-shop application mentioned multiple times in the previous chapters. The image shows the following test types:

- *Unit tests* always examine a single class. All other classes are mocked/stubbed so that they don't interfere with the result of the test. A unit test, for example, would verify that the basket class correctly calculates the weight of products it contains.
- *Integration tests* focus on multiple classes. Mocks/stubs are rarely used, as you're interested in both the code and the way communication happens between modules. An integration test, for example, would verify the communication between the warehouse inventory (which is backed by a database) and the products

---

[1] For more information, see *Test Driven* by Lasse Koskela (Manning, 2007).

Functional test

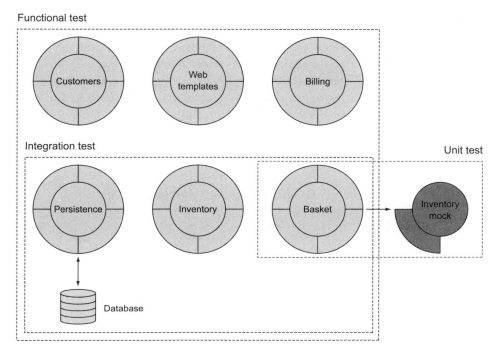

Figure 7.1   Unit tests focus on a single class, integration tests cover multiple modules, and functional tests cover end-to-end testing from the web interface to the database.

contained in the basket. When the customer attempts to check out, the basket will show which products are in stock and which aren't (after querying the inventory, which queries the database).

- *Functional tests* assume that the whole system is a black box. They test end-to-end interactions starting from the user interface (or the network API), and pass through the whole system. Functional testing usually requires a clone or duplicate of the real system. A functional test, for example, would be an automated test that opens a browser on its own, selects products by emulating the clicking of buttons on the web pages, checks out, enters a credit card, and expects to "see" onscreen a tracking number of the order shipped.

The distinction between these three categories isn't always clear. After all, concepts such as *module* may mean different things to different people. Don't get consumed by terminology.

7.1.1   *Characteristics of the test categories*

A well-tested application needs tests from all three categories. I sometimes imagine that a well-designed software product is like a well-designed car. If you're a car manufacturer, you need to test the individual screws, bolts, and frames of a car (unit tests);

test how these are assembled (integration tests); and in the end, perform tests on the final product by driving it in a controlled environment[2] (functional tests).

It would be unrealistic to release a car without making sure that all screws are correctly assembled, and it would also be foolish to release a car without testing it as a whole on the road. I'm still puzzled when I see software organizations that either have only functional tests or only integration tests, and at the same time don't understand why more bugs than expected are found in production.

The challenge of these three categories of tests is that they have different requirements and need different accommodations in the software lifecycle of a project. Table 7.1 briefly outlines the differences among them.

Table 7.1   Test categories in an enterprise application must be handled differently.

	Unit test	Integration test	Functional test
Scope of test	A single Java class	A single module or multiple classes	The whole system
Focus of test	Correctness of Java class	Class communication, transactions, logging, security, and more	End-to-end user experience
Result depends on	Java code	Java code, filesystem, network, DB, other systems	Java code, filesystem, network, DB, other systems, GUI, API endpoints
Stability	Very stable	May break from environment changes	Very brittle (a trivial GUI change may break it)
Failed test means	A regression	Either a regression or an environment change	A regression, an environment change, a GUI change
Effort required to set up	Minimal	Medium (may need external systems)	High (needs a running replica system)
Effort required to fix	Minimal	Medium (multiple classes may have bugs)	Medium/high (bug can be in any layer of the application)
Tools required	A test framework	Test framework, a container, a DB, and external services	Specialized and sometimes proprietary external tools, a staging system
Mocking/stubbing	Used when needed	Rarely used if ever	Rarely used if ever
Time to run a single test	Milliseconds	Seconds	Seconds or minutes
Time to run all tests of that type	Five minutes max	Can be hours	Can be hours

---

[2]   Or perform crash tests with dummies, which is much more fun.

Table 7.1   Test categories in an enterprise application must be handled differently.

	Unit test	Integration test	Functional test
Tests are run	After every commit automatically	Automatically at various scheduled intervals	Automatically/manually before a release
People involved	Developers	Developers, architects	Developers, architects, testers, analysts, customer

Table 7.1 is intended as a rough guide and is geared toward large enterprise projects.[3] Your project might be different, but the general principles still apply. You can write pure unit tests with Spock with no additional external library. But if you need to write a test that launches a web browser and starts pressing buttons in an automated manner, Spock isn't enough on its own.

7.1.2   *The testing pyramid*

So far, all tests you've seen in the previous chapters are mainly unit tests (pure tests). You might be wondering why I devoted three whole chapters (chapters 4, 5, and 6) for basic unit tests and left only a single chapter for both integration and functional tests.

The reason is that although all three categories of tests are essential, pure unit tests have a larger weight. This is best illustrated by a testing pyramid[4] that shows the percentage of tests from each category that compose your whole testing suite, as shown in figure 7.2.

Pure unit tests are your first line of defense. They're the foundation that other tests build upon. It makes no sense to start creating complex integration tests if you're not sure about the quality of the individual Java classes that compose them.

Only after you have enough unit tests can you start writing integration tests. Integration tests should be focused on testing things that pure unit tests can't detect. Typical examples are transactions, security, and other cross-cutting concerns in your application. Integration tests are often used to ensure correct functionality between the prior code base and new modules added to a project.

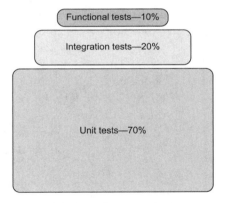

Figure 7.2   Breakdown of total test count for each test category in a large enterprise application: the testing pyramid

---

3   Think of a code base of 500K lines of code, a team of 20 people, a dedicated QA department, requirements that resemble a small book when printed—you get the picture.

4   See "Just Say No to More End-to-End Tests" by Mike Wacker on the Google Testing Blog for more details (http://googletesting.blogspot.co.uk/2015/04/just-say-no-to-more-end-to-end-tests.html).

Finally, when you're happy with the number of integration tests, it's time to create functional tests. These view the whole system as a black box and should be used as a way to catch serious runtime or graphical errors that slip through the rest of the tests.

> ## Common pitfalls with the pyramid of unit tests
>
> If you look back at the pyramid, you can imagine that any other shape is an antipattern. A project that has no unit tests is clearly missing the foundations of the pyramid.[a] A project that has too many functional tests is also problematic (the pyramid will fall under its own weight).
>
> ---
>
> [a] For more information on the test pyramid, see http://martinfowler.com/bliki/TestPyramid.html.

7.1.3   *Spock support for integration and functional testing*

Unfortunately, unlike pure unit tests (which can be covered using just Spock), integration tests require a different infrastructure depending on the Java framework you use. Given the number of Java frameworks present, covering all possible cases would be difficult.

This section covers integration testing with Spock and Spring (https://spring.io/) and gives you pointers for Java EE[5] and Guice (https://github.com/google/guice). I chose Spring because of its popularity at the time of this writing. This section also shows how to test back-end applications that use REST services (powered by HTTP/JSON). I assume that your application has a web interface and explain that you can use Spock and Geb together to automate the web browser for effective functional tests. Finally, I complete the puzzle by covering Maven configuration and some advice on the build server setup.

If you're writing an exotic Java application that doesn't match this profile, I apologize in advance. You need to do some research on your own. Either a Spock extension already exists for what you need or you can use Spock's compatibility with JUnit and attempt to use a tool from the JUnit world.

> ## The selection of examples in this chapter is indicative of Spock capabilities
>
> Covering integration testing for all kinds of Java applications in a single chapter would be impossible. I'd need a series of books for that. I know that everybody has a favorite testing tool or way to do integration testing, and I can't cover them all. This chapter covers mainly Spring applications because they seem to be more popular and Spock has built-in support for them. But I'll give you helpful pointers on what to do if your application isn't based on Spring. The main theme of the chapter is that in Spock you

---

[5]   Java EE can be tested with the help of Arquillian. See http://arquillian.org/.

(continued)

can use your favorite Java testing libraries and learn new tricks with Groovy-based testing utilities. The testing tools I show here are my personal selection. I tried to find simple examples that anybody can understand. All the examples are contrived. If you want to learn more about integration testing for Java applications in general, you should consult books that focus on the specific technology of your application.

7.1.4 Source code organization of the examples

Unlike other chapters, the source code for this chapter is organized into three distinct projects, as shown in figure 7.3.

Each project is a mini application on its own. Showing all source files in the book as code list-

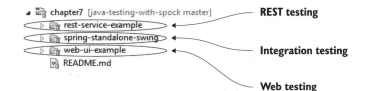

Figure 7.3 Source code contains three projects

ings would be unmanageable. Instead, I focus on only important classes, so feel free to consult the GitHub code at https://github.com/kkapelon/java-testing-with-spock/tree/master/chapter7 while reading the book. The projects were created strictly for illustration purposes, so take notice of the Spock tests instead of the "production" code.

7.2 Integration testing with Spock

In chapter 6, you saw various techniques used to mock collaborator classes so that only the class under test affects the outcome of the tests. In some cases, however, you don't want to mock collaborators but want to test multiple real classes together.

An integration test spans multiple Java classes (instead of just one) and examines the communication among them. Common scenarios that need integration tests are database mappings, security constraints, communication with external systems, and any other cases where testing is focused on a module rather than a single class.

7.2.1 Testing a Spring application

To start, you'll look at a standalone application powered by a Swing user interface that manages the warehouse inventory of an e-shop (see figure 7.4).

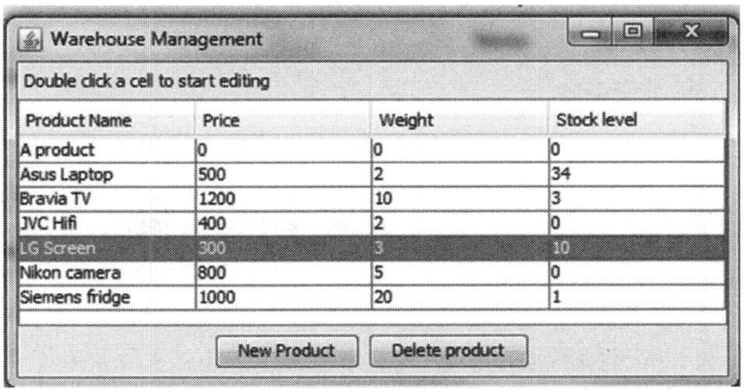

Figure 7.4 A simple database application with a Swing user interface

The application is based on the Spring framework and saves all its data in a JPA/Hibernate database, which in this case is an HSQLDB[6] file. The design of the application is straightforward. In the middle is the Spring dependency injection container, and all other classes revolve around it, as shown in figure 7.5.

The Spring context that binds all other classes is an XML file defined in src/main/resources/spring-context.xml. You want to write a Spock test that examines the Hibernate mappings for the `Product` class. To achieve that, you need to test the whole chain of database loading and saving. The following classes should be tested:

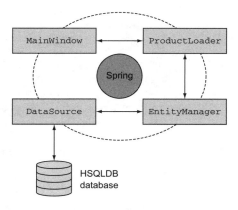

Figure 7.5   The Spring context initializes all Java classes.

- The `ProductLoader` class, which is the DAO
- The JPA entity manager that manages database mappings
- The `Datasource` that provides access to the real database.

The good news is that Spock already contains a Spring extension that instantly recognizes the `@ContextConfiguration`[7] annotation provided by the Spring test facilities, as shown in the following listing.

Listing 7.1   Access Spring context from a Spock test

```
@ContextConfiguration(locations = "classpath:spring-context.xml")    ◄── Marking the test with the Spring ContextConfiguration annotation
class RealDatabaseSpec extends spock.lang.Specification{

    @Autowired                                  ◄── Wiring a Spring bean as in normal production code
    ProductLoader productLoader

    @Sql("clear-db.sql")                        ◄── Spring facility to initialize a database
    def "Testing hibernate mapping of product class"() {
        given: "the creation of a new product"
        productLoader.createDefaultProduct()    ◄── Saves something to the database

        when: "we read back that product"
        List<Product> allProducts = productLoader.getAllProducts();   ◄── Reads back again from the database

        then: "it should be present in the db"
        allProducts.size() == 1                 ◄── Verifies database read

        and: "it should start with zero quantity"
        allProducts[0].getStock() ==0
    }
}
```

---

[6]   See the HyperSQL website at http://hsqldb.org/ for more information on HSQLDB.

[7]   And the @SpringApplicationConfiguration annotation from Spring Boot.

In this listing, you can see that all testing facilities and annotations are already offered by Spring. Spock automatically understands that this file uses a Spring context and allows you to obtain and use Spring beans (in this case, `ProductLoader`) as in normal Java code.

The important line here is the `@ContextConfiguration` annotation because it's used by Spock to understand that this is a Spring-based integration test. Notice also that you use the Spring `@Sql` annotation, which allows you to run an SQL file before the test runs. This is already offered by Spring and works as expected in the Spock test.

The resulting test is an integration test, because the real database is initialized, and a product is saved on it and then read back. Nothing is mocked here, so if your database is slow, this test will also run slowly.

> ### Options for Spring testing
>
> The Spring framework contains a gazillion options when it comes to testing. Explaining them all is outside the scope of this book. You should consult the official Spring documentation (https://spring.io/docs). This chapter presents some techniques that prove that Spock and Spring play well together.

A nice facility offered by Spring is the automatic rollback of database changes during a unit test, as shown in the following listing. This is an effective way to keep your unit tests completely independent from one another. Activating this behavior is (unsurprisingly) done by using standard Spring facilities that apply automatically, even in the case of a Spock test.

Listing 7.2 Rolling back database changes automatically

```
@ContextConfiguration(locations = "classpath:spring-context.xml")
@Transactional                                              ◄─── Making this test
class RealDatabaseSpec extends spock.lang.Specification{         honor transactions

    @Autowired
    ProductLoader productLoader

    @Rollback                                              ◄─── Database changes
    @Sql("clear-db.sql")                                        will be reverted once
    def "Testing hibernate mapping of product class"() {        the test finishes.
            [...code redacted for brevity...]
    }
}
```

The test code in this listing is exactly the same as in listing 7.1. I have only added two extra Spring annotations. The `@Transactional` annotation notifies Spring that this test will use database transactions. The `@Rollback` annotation instructs Spring to revert[8] all database changes performed inside the Spock feature method after the test finishes.

---

[8] The default behavior by Spring is to revert all transactions. I show the `@Rollback` annotation for emphasis only.

Even if your Spock test deletes or changes data in the database, these changes won't be persisted at the end of the test suite. Again, this capability is offered by Spring, and Spock is completely oblivious to it.

In summary, Spock support for Spring tests is as easy as marking a test with the Spring test annotations. If you've written JUnit tests by using `SpringJUnit4Class-Runner`, you'll feel right at home.

7.2.2 Narrowing down the Spring context inside Spock tests

If you've written Spring integration tests before, you should have noticed two serious flaws of the Spock tests shown in listings 7.1 and 7.2. Both tests use the same Spring context as the production code. The two flaws are as follows:

1 Tests use the same database as production code. This isn't desirable and sometimes not even possible because of security constraints.
2 The Spring context initializes all Java classes even though not all of them are used in the Spock test.

For example, in the Swing application, the Spock test also creates the `Swing` class for the GUI even though you never test the GUI. The Spock tests shown in listings 7.1 and 7.2 might not run easily in a headless machine (and build servers are typically headless machines).

The recommended way to solve these issues is to use a different Spring context for the tests. The production context contains all classes of the application, and the test context contains a reduced set of the classes tested. A second XML file is created, as shown in figure 7.6.

With the reduced context, you're free to redefine the beans that are active during the Spock test. Two common techniques are replacing the real database with a memory-based one and removing beans that aren't needed for the test. If you look at the contents of the reduced-text context file, you'll see that I've removed the GUI class and replaced the file-based datasource with an in-memory H2 DB[9] with the following line:

```
<jdbc:embedded-database id="dataSource" type="H2"/>
```

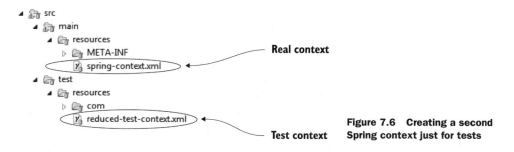

Figure 7.6 Creating a second Spring context just for tests

---

[9] You can find more information about the H2 database at www.h2database.com/html/main.html.

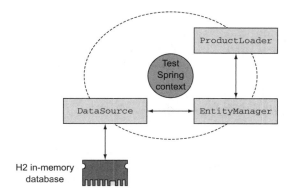

H2 in-memory
database

**Figure 7.7   Spring context for tests uses an
in-memory database and no GUI classes.**

The in-memory database is much faster than a real database, but it works for only small datasets (you can't easily use it as a clone of a real database). Because unit tests use specific datasets (small in size) and also need to run fast, an in-memory database is a good candidate for DB testing.

The context for the Spock test is now simplified, as shown in figure 7.7.

To run the test, you inform Spring of the alternative context file. Spock automatically picks up the change, as shown in the following listing.

Listing 7.3   Using a reduced Spring context for unit testing

```
@ContextConfiguration(locations = "classpath:reduced-test-context.xml")   ◄─┐
@Transactional                                                              │
class DummyDatabaseSpec extends spock.lang.Specification{          Defining an
                                                                   alternative
                                                                   Spring context
    @Autowired
    ProductLoader productLoader

    def "Testing hibernate mapping of product class - mem db"() {
            given: "the creation of a new product"
            productLoader.createDefaultProduct()

    when: "we read back that product"
    List<Product> allProducts = productLoader.getAllProducts();   ◄─┐

    then: "it should be present in the db"               Data is fetched from
    allProducts.size() == 1                                an in-memory
                                                           database, making
    and: "it should start with zero quantity"             the test fast.
    allProducts[0].stock ==0
    }
}
```

Data is written to an in-memory database. (points to `productLoader.createDefaultProduct()`)

You can find the reduced Spring context at GitHub.[10] Because this test runs with an in-memory database, it's much faster than the original test shown in listing 7.2. Also

---

[10] https://github.com/kkapelon/java-testing-with-spock/blob/master/chapter7/spring-standalone-swing/
src/test/resources/reduced-test-context.xml

you removed the GUI class from the context, so this unit test can run in any Unix/Linux system in a shell environment (the typical case for build servers).

You need to examine your own application and decide what you'll discard/replace in the test context. A good starting point is to remove all beans that aren't used in your tests.

7.2.3 Directly accessing the database with Groovy SQL

At this point, you've seen that a Spock test has access to Spring beans without any special configuration,[11] and that you can use common Spring features as testing aids.

The additional advantage of Spock tests is that you also have all Groovy tools and libraries at your disposal. I introduced you to some essential Groovy facilities back in chapter 2, but you should spend some extra time exploring the full Groovy documentation to see what's available to help you while writing Spock tests for your application needs.

A handy Groovy feature not mentioned in chapter 2 (because it's mainly a nice-to-have feature) is the Groovy SQL interface.[12] The Groovy SQL class is a thin abstraction over JDBC that allows you to access a database in a convenient way. You can think of it as a Spring JDBC template on steroids.

Let's assume that you want to verify that the DAO of the e-shop brings back all products in alphabetical order. You can initialize your database by using Groovy SQL, as shown in the next listing.

Listing 7.4 Using Groovy SQL to prepare the DB in a Spock test

```
@ContextConfiguration(locations = "classpath:reduced-test-context.xml")
class DummyDatabaseGroovySqlWriteSpec extends spock.lang.Specification{
    @Autowired
    DataSource dataSource                       ◄─── Getting the underlying
                                                     datasource from Spring
    @Autowired
    ProductLoader productLoader

    def "Testing ordering of products"() {
        given: "the creation of 3 new products"         Groovy SQL creation over
        Sql sql   = new Sql(dataSource)          ◄───── an existing datasource
        sql.execute("DELETE FROM PRODUCT")
        sql.execute("INSERT INTO PRODUCT (id,name,price, weight,stock)
                VALUES (1, 'samsung',400,1,45);")
        sql.execute("INSERT INTO PRODUCT (id,name,price, weight,stock)
                VALUES (2, 'bravia',1200,3,2);")
        sql.execute("INSERT INTO PRODUCT (id,name,price, weight,stock)
                VALUES (3, 'canon',500,5,23);")
```

Clears the DB → (points to `sql.execute("DELETE FROM PRODUCT")`)

Inserts data directly on the database → (points to the three INSERT statements)

---

[11] JUnit tests need the special SpringJUnit4ClassRunner in order to access Spring beans.

[12] The takeaway of this section is that you can easily use Groovy libraries to do what you want. Groovy SQL is used as an example. Details of the Groovy SQL interface are provided at http://docs.groovy-lang.org/latest/html/api/groovy/sql/Sql.html.

```
                    when: "we read back the products"
                    List<Product> allProducts = productLoader.getAllProducts();

                    then: "they should be ordered by name"
                    allProducts.size() == 3
                    allProducts[0].name =="bravia"
                    allProducts[1].name =="canon"
                    allProducts[2].name =="samsung"
```

Always a good practice ⟶
```
                    cleanup: "remove inserted data"
                    sql.execute("DELETE FROM PRODUCT")
                    sql.close()
```
◄── **Clean up so that other tests are unaffected.**

```
                }

            }
```

The Groovy SQL interface is a powerful feature. It supports all SQL statements you'd expect (schema creations/data writing/data querying), and explaining all its capabilities is beyond the scope of this book. It can be used both in production code and in Spock tests.

I tend to use it when I want to do something strange on the DB (perhaps re-create an error condition) that's normally not possible via the DAOs of the application. Be careful when using it in your Spock tests, because as you've seen in listing 7.4, it gets direct access to the database, so it acts outside the caches of JPA/Hibernate.

Despite these shortcomings, it's a natural Groovy way to access the DB, and you'll find its code compact and comfortable. The last example can be further improved by extracting the common SQL statement in its own string, as shown in the next listing.

Listing 7.5 Using Groovy SQL to prepare the DB in a Spock test—improved

```
def "Testing ordering of products - improved"() {
    given: "the creation of 3 new products"
    Sql sql  = new Sql(dataSource)
    sql.execute("DELETE FROM PRODUCT")
    String insertProduct = "INSERT INTO PRODUCT (id,name,price,
                  weight,stock) VALUES (?, ?,?,?,?);"
    sql.execute(insertProduct,[1, 'samsung',400,1,45])
    sql.execute(insertProduct,[2, 'bravia',1200,3,2])
    sql.execute(insertProduct,[3, 'canon',500,5,23])

    when: "we read back the products"
    List<Product> allProducts = productLoader.getAllProducts();

    then: "they should be ordered by name"
    allProducts.size() == 3
    allProducts[0].name =="bravia"
    allProducts[1].name =="canon"
    allProducts[2].name =="**sa**msung"

    cleanup: "remove inserted data"
    sql.execute("DELETE FROM PRODUCT")
    sql.close()
}
```

Creates Groovy SQL over an existing data source (arrow pointing to `Sql sql = new Sql(dataSource)`)

Defines a parameterized SQL statement (arrow pointing to `String insertProduct = ...`)

Runs the same SQL statement with different parameters (pointing to the three `sql.execute(insertProduct,...)` lines)

A final note regarding Groovy SQL is that if you use it in multiple test methods, it's best to make it a @Shared field so that it's created only once. Otherwise, performance of your unit tests will suffer.

7.2.4 *Integration testing with other containers (Java EE and Guice)*

The example application in the previous paragraph was based on the Spring container because the Spring framework is mature and popular among Java developers. If you're not using Spring, chances are that your application is based on Java EE. In that case, the respective facilities offered by Spring in integration tests can be replicated by using Arquillian, a test framework for Java EE applications that acts as a testing container and allows access to EJBs, CDI injection,[13] and other enterprise services.

Arquillian (http://arquillian.org/) natively supports JUnit tests, but for Spock tests, you need the Spock-Arquillian extension (https://github.com/arquillian/arquillian-testrunner-spock). The extension has its own repository and a different lifecycle than Spock releases. It works by creating a special runner that brings the Arquillian facilities inside the Spock test.

Apart from Spring, the core Spock distribution also includes support for the Guice dependency injection framework (https://github.com/google/guice). In a similar manner, it allows you to access Guice services/beans inside the Spock test.

If the dependency injection framework you use is something else (other than Spring, Guice, and Java CDI), and there isn't a Spock extension for that by the time you're reading this book, you have two choices:

- Manually initialize and inject your services in the Spock setupSpec() method.[14]
- Find a way to initialize the DI container programmatically inside the Spock test.

The first option isn't practical because you have to write a lot of boilerplate code that's usually not needed, going against the mentality of writing Spock tests in the first place (compact and readable tests).

The second way depends on the capabilities of the container you use and whether it supports declarative or programmatic configuration. As an example, assume that the Spock-Spring extension didn't exist. The Spring container can be still created programmatically, as shown in the next listing.

Listing 7.6 Manual Spring context creation

```
class ManualInjectionSpec extends spock.lang.Specification{
    def "Testing hibernate mapping of product class - mem db"() {
        given: "a product DAO"
        ApplicationContext ctx = new
        ClassPathXmlApplicationContext("reduced-test-context.xml");
        ProductLoader productLoader =
            ctx.getBean(ProductLoader.class)
```

Creates a Spring context from an XML file →

← *Manually initializes a Spring bean*

---

[13] The Java spec for dependency injection.

[14] You can find the code in ManualInjectionSpec in GitHub (the second test method).

Uses the Spring bean as before →

```
when: "we read products from the DB"
List<Product> allProducts = productLoader.getAllProducts();

then: "the db is empty"
allProducts.size() == 0
    }
}
```

This Spock test still has access to the Spring context because it creates one manually. Notice the lack of any extra annotations in this listing. If your dependency injection framework supports programmatic initialization, you can still write Spock integration tests without needing a special extension.

7.3 *Functional testing of REST services with Spock*

Moving up in the testing pyramid, you leave integration tests behind and reach functional tests. Functional tests, depicted in figure 7.8, view the whole system as a black box (in contrast with integration tests that deal with internal modules).

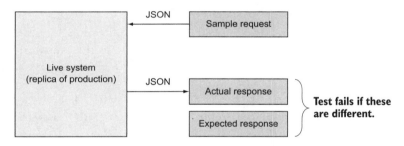

Figure 7.8 A functional test sends a request and expects a certain response.

For non-interactive systems (those with no user-visible component), functional testing involves the testing of the services they provide to the outside world. In practice, this usually means testing the HTTP/REST endpoints of the back-end modules.

REST services use JSON or XML for the transport format. These examples use JSON.

7.3.1 *Working with a simple REST service*

A REST service is based on HTTP and a predefined message format (typically JSON or XML) and is implementation-agnostic. Even though the application in this example is a Spring-based one, it doesn't matter to Spock. The application doesn't even have to be a Java one. You can use Spock if you want to test the REST service of a Python or Ruby application.

The example application is the REST API for the warehouse management example, as already discussed in the previous sections. Table 7.2 provides an overview of the endpoint and operations it supports (all responses are in JSON format).

Table 7.2 HTTP endpoints of example application

Endpoint	GET	POST	PUT	DELETE
/status	Returns a success message ("up and running")	-	-	
/products	Lists all products	Creates a default product	-	Deletes all products
/products/{id}	Returns a specific product	-	-	-
/products/{id}/name	-	-	Renames a product	-

Like all applications shown so far, this back-end application was created for illustration purposes. The application uses Spring MVC for the implementation, but this is completely irrelevant as far as functional tests are concerned. It could be implemented in any other framework or even programming language, as long as it accepts JSON messages over HTTP endpoints.

7.3.2 *Testing REST services by using Java libraries*

Writing a Spock test for REST services is straightforward. You can use any REST client library that you're already familiar with. Many are available in the Java world, and at least for Spock tests, you should choose the one that you feel is more readable and compact.[15]

As a starting example, I've selected the Spring RestTemplate.[16] The first test checks the /status endpoint (which returns a single string and not JSON), as shown in the next listing.

Listing 7.7 Testing REST services with Spock and Spring RestTemplate

```
def "Simple status checker"() {
    when: "a rest call is performed to the status page"        Creates a Spring REST client
    RestTemplate restTemplate = new RestTemplate()    ◀
    String status = restTemplate.getForObject("http://localhost:8080/rest-
        service-example/status", String.class)

    then: "the correct message is expected"
    status == "Up and Running"                        ◀   Examines the response
}                                                         of the REST call
```

Performs a GET call on the / status endpoint

The takeaway from this trivial example is that because of Groovy/Java compatibility, you can use any Java REST client library you already use in your JUnit tests. Spock can use it without any extra modifications. It's that simple!

---

[15] Such as RESTEasy (http://resteasy.jboss.org/), Jersey (https://jersey.java.net/), or Restlet (http://restlet.com/).

[16] See a tutorial on calling REST services from Spring at https://spring.io/guides/gs/consuming-rest/.

7.3.3 *Using the @Stepwise annotation to run tests in order*

Now you're ready to create additional tests for the business endpoints of your application. The next listing provides the whole Spock specification.

Listing 7.8 Running multiple test methods in order

```
@Stepwise                                              ◄─── Ensures that all methods
class SpringRestSpec extends Specification {                 run in the order shown
                                                             in the source file
    def "Simple status checker"() {
        when: "a rest call is performed to the status page"
        RestTemplate restTemplate = new RestTemplate()
        String status =
        restTemplate.getForObject("http://localhost:8080/rest-service-
                        example/status", String.class)

        then: "the correct message is expected"
        status == "Up and Running"
    }

    def "Cleaning all products"() {
        given: "a rest call is performed that deletes everything"
        RestTemplate restTemplate = new RestTemplate()
        restTemplate.delete("http://localhost:8080/rest-service-
                example/products")

        when: "a product list is requested"
        List<Product> products =
                restTemplate.getForObject("http://localhost:8080/rest-
                        service-example/products", List.class)

        then: "it should be empty"
        products.size() == 0
    }

    def "Creating a product"() {
        given: "a rest template"
        RestTemplate restTemplate = new RestTemplate()

        when: "a new product is created"
        Product product =
                restTemplate.postForObject("http://localhost:8080/rest-
                service-example/products","unused",Product.class)

        and: "product list is requested again"
        List<Product> products =
                restTemplate.getForObject("http://localhost:8080/rest-
                        service-example/products", List.class)

        then: "it should have default values"
        with(product)
        {
                name == "A product"
                stock == 0
```

Annotations (left margin):
- **Performs a DELETE call on the / products endpoint** → (points to `restTemplate.delete`)
- **Performs a GET call on the / products endpoint** → (points to `restTemplate.getForObject`)
- **Performs a POST call on the / products endpoint** → (points to `restTemplate.postForObject`)

Annotation (right margin):
- **Examines the JSON response** ◄─── (points to `with(product)`)

```
                price == 0
                weight == 0
        }

        and: "product list should contain it"
        products.size() == 1
    }
}
```

This listing includes test methods for the /products endpoint. The code should be familiar if you've ever worked with the Spring RestTemplate. There's nothing Spock-specific inside the test methods. All code segments are Java statements that would work the same way in a JUnit test.

You should pay special attention, however, to the @Stepwise annotation at the top of the class. This Spock annotation comes in handy and does two things:

- It makes sure that Spock will run all test methods in the order they're defined in the Specification class.
- During runtime, if any test method fails, those that come after it will be skipped.

The purpose of the @Stepwise annotation is to save you time when you have many functional tests. Although in theory all functional tests are independent, in practice this is rarely the case. For example, if the first test method fails (the one that checks the /status endpoint), the test environment is probably down, so there's no point in running any more tests.

The @Stepwise annotation saves you time because you're informed right away when something fails and can understand what the problem is more easily than when all tests fail. Figure 7.9 shows the runtime result with and without the @Stepwise annotation.

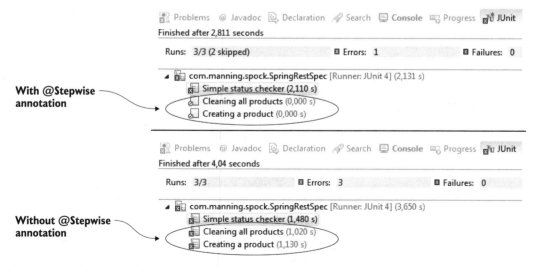

Figure 7.9   The @Stepwise **annotation skips subsequent test methods after a failure.**

With the `@Stepwise` annotation enabled, you can see in two seconds that the test environment is down, instead of waiting four seconds for all tests to run (and fail). In a real enterprise project with hundreds of functional tests that may take several minutes (or even hours), the `@Stepwise` annotation is a lifesaver, as it drastically cuts the time of developer feedback after a failed build. With the `@Stepwise` annotation, you also get a clear indication if a bug failed because another precondition (contained in a previous test method) also failed.

7.3.4 *Testing REST services using Groovy RESTClient*

As with integration tests, the advantage of using Spock is that you're not constrained to Java libraries; you can also use Groovy utilities. As an example, an alternative REST client can be used instead of the Spring RestTemplate.[17]

The following listing presents the same test as in listing 7.8, this time using the Groovy RESTClient.

Listing 7.9 Using Groovy RESTClient in a Spock test

```
@Stepwise                                              ◄── Makes sure that all
class GroovyRestClientSpec extends Specification {         methods run in order

    @Shared
    def client = new RESTClient("http://localhost:8080/rest-service-
                 example/")
    def "Simple status checker"() {        Creates a REST client
        when: "a rest call is performed to the status page"
        def response = client.get(path : "status")   ◄── Performs a GET
                                                          call on the /status
        then: "the correct message is expected"           endpoint
        with(response)
        {                                   Examines the text response
                data.text == "Up and Running"
                status == 200               ◄── Examines HTTP
        }                                       error code
    }

    def "Cleaning all products"() {
        given: "a rest call is performed that deletes everything"
        client.delete(path : "products")    Performs a DELETE call on
                                            the /products endpoint
        when: "a product list is requested"
        def response = client.get(path : "products")

        then: "it should be empty"
        with(response)
        {
                data.isEmpty()
                status == 200
```

---

[17] A Groovy library for consuming REST services is found at https://github.com/jgritman/httpbuilder/wiki/RESTClient.

```
            }
        }

    def "Creating a product"() {
        when: "a new product is created"
        def response = client.post(path : "products")    ◄──┐ Performs a POST call on
                                                              the /products endpoint
        and: "product list is requested again"
        def listResponse = client.get(path : "products")

        then: "it should have default values"
        with(response)
        {
            data.name == "A product"
            data.stock == 0
            data.price == 0
            status == 200
        }

        and: "product list should contain it"
        listResponse.data.size() == 1
    }
}
```

As you can see, the code is mostly the same. For each method call, you also check the HTTP error code, as it's easy to verify with the RESTClient. As an exercise, feel free to write a functional test for the other endpoints of the application (the calls for renaming an existing product). The Groovy RESTClient has many more facilities, not shown in listing 7.9, that might be helpful in your own application should you choose to use it.

7.4   *Functional testing of web applications with Spock*

The previous section covered functional tests for back-end Java applications that aren't interactive. This section shows you how to test front-end applications that sport a web interface accessible via the browser.

For these kinds of tests, you need a way to control the browser and replicate the actions (for example, fill forms or click buttons) that a human user typically performs. Spock doesn't have built-in support for this and instead collaborates with Geb, the Groovy browser automation library.

7.4.1   *Browser automation with Geb*

Geb is a library that provides a Groovy abstraction on top of the popular Selenium/WebDriver[18] framework for automating a browser. If you've worked with Selenium, you already know what Geb does. What Geb brings to the table is excellent integration[19]

---

[18] You can learn more about the Selenium suite of tools at www.seleniumhq.org/.
[19] Geb is written by Luke Daley, who is also a Spock committer.

with Spock and a jQuery-like language[20] for accessing web page content. If you already know jQuery (or any other similar CSS selector syntax), Geb will be familiar to you.

As a quick example, if you want to examine the text for the h2 header in a web page, Geb allows you to write the following:

```
$("h2").text()
```

If you want to click the button with an ID myButton, Geb offers you this:

```
$("#myButton").click()
```

With Geb, you reuse your knowledge of jQuery. If you're not familiar with jQuery, you need to examine its documentation, and especially the part for CSS selectors, in order to fully use Geb.

7.4.2 The example web application

The application you'll test with Spock and Geb is a simple web interface over the warehouse manager you've seen in the previous examples. Figure 7.10 shows a sample screen from this application.

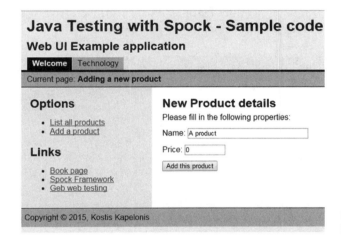

Figure 7.10   Web interface that will be used for Spock tests

The code uses Spring MVC, but in a similar manner to the REST tests, the implementation technology doesn't matter. Geb interacts with only the final web page and doesn't care about the underlying technology. You could write Spock/Geb tests for a PHP application, using the same CSS selectors.

---

[20] You can learn more about jQuery at https://jquery.com/.

Figure 7.11   Expected result for title page is the string "Spock/Geb Web example"

7.4.3   *Spock and Geb: a match made in heaven*

Let's start with a simple example of Spock and Geb together. As a first test, you'll verify the title of the first page of the application. Figure 7.11 shows the expected result.

The next listing provides the Geb specification that tests this.

Listing 7.10   Using Geb and Spock together

```
class HomePageSpec extends GebSpec {

    def "Trivial Geb test for homepage"() {
        when: "I go to homepage"
        Browser.drive {
            go "http://localhost:8080/web-ui-example/index.html"
        }

        then: "First page should load"
        title == "Spock/Geb Web example"
    }

}
```

Spock specification class that makes Geb facilities available

Orders the test browser to load a specific URL

Tests the title of the application

The most important thing to notice in listing 7.10 is that the test class extends the `GebSpec` class and not the Spock `Specification`, as shown in all examples so far. This is essential so that Geb methods and objects are available inside the Spock methods.

After this is done, you use the `Browser` object to load the first page of the application. Finally, you examine the `title` object. This object is an implicit one offered by Geb and always represents the HTML title of the current HTML page. It doesn't follow the jQuery pattern because it's not part of the content of the page.

> ## Will this test launch a browser?
>
> Remember that Geb is an abstraction over Selenium/WebDriver, so it supports whatever browser implementations are already there. In the source code of the book, the default browser is Firefox, so if you run this test, a new Firefox instance will be launched on your computer and you'll see it react automatically to the test definitions. You can use other browsers or even browser emulators (such as Phantom.js, http://phantom js.org/) as other options. Consult the Geb documentation on how to achieve this.

To see the jQuery syntax of Geb, let's modify the test to look at the page content in addition to the page title. You'll test an HTML header (h1) and also make sure that the first tab of the user interface is selected. Figure 7.12 shows the expected result.

Figure 7.12 HTML content that will be verified by the Geb test. You'll verify the h1 element and the "active" CSS class.

The updated Spock test verifies the `title` as before and reads the page content to make sure that the expected text is present on the page (see the following listing).

Listing 7.11 Using Geb to access page content

```
def "Trivial Geb test for homepage -header check"() {
    when: "I go to homepage"
    Browser.drive {
        go "http://localhost:8080/web-ui-example/index.html"
    }

    then: "First page should load"
    title == "Spock/Geb Web example"
    $("h1").text() == "Java Testing with Spock - Sample code"
    $(".active").text() == "Welcome"
}
```

Launches the first page of the application in the browser

Examines the title of the page

Examines the content of the h1 element

Examines the content of the element with the "active" CSS class

This listing demonstrates the jQuery-like style of Geb for accessing page content. The last two lines in the then: block will be examined by Geb against the HTML content found in the browser. The test will fail if the HTML content differs from the expected one.

7.4.4   Using Geb to interact with a web page

For a more useful example than simple page loading, let's see how to emulate user actions on a web page. The sample application contains a form, shown in figure 7.13, that allows the user to create a new product. An HTML form is used to define the name of the product and its price. After the user submits the form, a success message appears. You'll create a test that navigates to the form page, inputs the name of the product, submits the form, and verifies the success message (not shown in figure 7.13). The code is shown in the next listing.

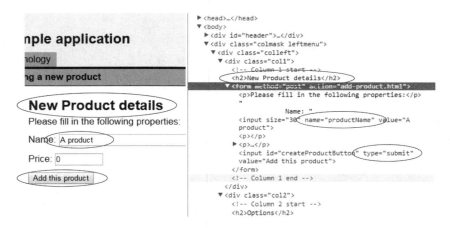

Figure 7.13   Details of an HTML form. You'll fill the input fields and submit it programmatically.

Listing 7.12   Using Geb to submit HTML forms

```
@Stepwise
class AddProductGebSpec extends GebSpec {

    def "Navigation to page"() {
        when: "I go to the new product page"
        Browser.drive {
            go "http://localhost:8080/web-ui-example/add-
                           product.html"
        }

        then: "the form should load"
        $(".col1").$("h2").text() == "New Product details"
    }
}
```

Ensures that test methods will run in order

Verifies that browser is in correct page

This Spock test has access to Geb facilities by extending GebSpec.

Navigates to the page with the HTML form

Enters text into an input field

Verifies the success message shown on page

Activates the form button

```
def "Creation of new product"() {
    when: "I fill in product details"
    $("input[name='productName']").value("Bravia TV")
    $("#createProductButton").click()

    then: "I should see a success message"
    $(".ok").text() == "You added new product named: Bravia TV."
}

}
```

This listing has several important points. First, you use the @Stepwise annotation again. The reason for this is that the test contains two methods. The first one navigates to the HTML form page, and the second submits the form. If the first fails for some reason (for example, the application isn't up), there's no point in running the second method. The @Stepwise annotation ensures that the form won't be submitted if its page can't be found.

Second, in order to verify the formed page, you use an HTML element chain:

```
$(".col1").$("h2").text() == "New Product details"
```

This line means, "Locate an element with the CSS class col1 and then search for a child that is a header of level 2. This header should contain the text *New product details*."

Next, the form is submitted with the following two lines:

```
$("input[name='productName']").value("Bravia TV")
$("#createProductButton").click()
```

The first line means, "Locate an HTML element of type input that has a name attribute with value productName. Then fill in the text *Bravia TV*." The second line says, "Find an element with ID createProductButton. Then click it (assuming that it's a button)."

Running the test launches the Firefox browser on your computer, and you'll see it perform these actions in real time. The final line in the then: block locates an element with CSS class ok and checks its text (in the example application, it's a span HTML element).

I hope that this example gives you an idea of the capabilities of Geb. I've barely scratched the surface of all the possible use cases. Check the official Geb documentation (http://www.gebish.org/manual/current/) for more details. Make sure not to miss the Page Objects pattern[21] for reducing[22] duplicated code among tests and the ability to get screenshots[23] while a test runs. The previous tests shown are contrived examples so that you get a feel for Geb's capabilities. In a real application, you'd organize all your Spock tests around pages to make them resilient to GUI changes.

---

[21] http://docs.seleniumhq.org/docs/06_test_design_considerations.jsp#page-object-design-pattern
[22] www.gebish.org/pages
[23] http://www.gebish.org/manual/current/

As an exercise, write Geb tests for the page of the application that lists existing products. Write a test that also fills in the price field of the form and then goes to the inventory page and verifies that the product is correctly inserted with the correct price.

As another exercise, modify your Geb tests to use Page objects instead of exposing HTML elements inside them.

7.5   *Running Spock tests as part of a build process*

So far, I've silently assumed that whenever I show you a Spock test, you run it manually and visually check the results in the IDE or the command-line shell. Although this is true for your day-to-day development schedule, a well-designed enterprise application employs a build server that automatically checks out code at various time intervals, compiles it, runs unit tests, and creates reports in a completely automated manner.

If you're not familiar with build servers, explaining them is outside of the scope of this book. As a suggestion, start by downloading Jenkins (https://jenkins-ci.org/) and then read both the theory[24] and practice[25] behind a sound build process.

For the rest of the chapter, I assume that you already have a build server in place for running JUnit tests and mention only what you need to do for Spock (spoiler: almost nothing, as Spock is JUnit-compatible).

7.5.1   *Splitting unit, integration, and functional tests*

If you look back at table 7.1, which lists the characteristics of unit, integration, and functional tests, it should be clear that they have different requirements.

For starters, functional (and sometimes integration) tests require a running replica of the system that's tested. Therefore, you know that functional tests must be treated differently than the rest of the tests.

Another big difference is the speed of tests. Unit tests (which depend only on Java code) are fast and give quick feedback. Integration and functional tests are much slower (especially when external systems and real databases are involved).

The speed of unit tests means that they can be executed automatically after every developer commit for quick feedback. Functional tests, on the other hand, may run less frequently (for example, once a day) and also require the setup of a test environment exclusive to them (which typically replicates the production environment).

These best practices aren't specific to Spock. They also apply to JUnit or TestNG. I mention them here so that before complaining that "Geb tests are really slow," you should understand that Geb tests must run in a different manner than simpler Spock tests.

---

[24] See "Continuous Delivery" by Jez Humble and David Farley on the Martin Fowler website (http://martin fowler.com/books/continuousDelivery.html).

[25] See *Jenkins: The Definitive Guide* by John Ferguson Smart (O'Reilly, 2011), www.wakaleo.com/books/jenkins-the-definitive-guide.

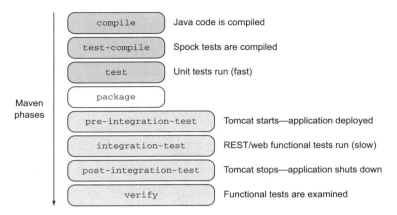

Figure 7.14   Tomcat is launched before functional tests and shuts down afterward.

In the sample code of the book, I use Maven and have chosen to launch the Tomcat application server before the functional tests run. Figure 7.14 shows the Maven lifecycle[26] for the examples of this chapter.

With this approach, you have a split between slow and fast tests. Running `mvn test` runs only the fast unit tests, and running `mvn verify` also runs the slow functional tests (after launching a Tomcat instance). This lifecycle is accomplished by using the Maven Failsafe plugin (https://maven.apache.org/surefire/maven-failsafe-plugin/) and the Tomcat plugin (http://tomcat.apache.org/maven-plugin.html), as shown in the following listing.

Listing 7.13   Running Spock functional tests on a Tomcat instance

```
[...rest of pom.xml....]
<build>
    <plugins>
    [...rest of build plugins....]
    <plugin>
        <groupId>org.apache.maven.plugins</groupId>
        <artifactId>maven-failsafe-plugin</artifactId>
        <version>2.18</version>
        <executions>
        <execution>
            <goals>
            <goal>integration-test</goal>
            <goal>verify</goal>
            </goals>
        </execution>
        </executions>
```

◄ **Instructs Failsafe plugin to run Spock tests in integration-test phase**

---

[26] You can learn more about the Maven lifecycle at the Apache Maven Project website (https://maven.apache.org/guides/introduction/introduction-to-the-lifecycle.html).

```
                <configuration>
                        <useFile>false</useFile>
                        <includes>
                        <include>**/*Spec.java</include>          ◀── Naming convention for
                        </includes>                                     Spock tests that will run
                </configuration>                                        as integration-test phase
        </plugin>
        <plugin>
                <groupId>org.apache.tomcat.maven</groupId>
                <artifactId>tomcat7-maven-plugin</artifactId>
                <version>2.2</version>
                <executions>
            <execution>
                <id>tomcat-run</id>
                <goals>
                <goal>run-war-only</goal>
                </goals>
                <phase>pre-integration-test</phase>               ◀── Starts Tomcat before
                <configuration>                                        Spock tests run
                <fork>true</fork>
                        </configuration>
                </execution>
                <execution>
                        <id>tomcat-shutdown</id>
                        <goals>
                        <goal>shutdown</goal>
                        </goals>
                        <phase>post-integration-test</phase>      ◀── Stops Tomcat after
                </execution>                                           Spock tests run
                </executions>
        </plugin>
        </plugins>
</build>
```

This technique works for small- to medium-size applications. For large-scale enterprise applications that need specialized test environments, you need to adapt your build system according to your business requirements in cooperation with the team responsible for provisioning.[27]

> ### Running both Spock and JUnit tests in the same Java project
>
> If it isn't clear by now, the Maven plugins (Surefire and Failsafe) will run both JUnit and Spock tests in a similar manner. No special configuration is needed if you have both kinds of tests. You can mix and match, and many configurations are possible. For example, you could have JUnit tests run as pure unit tests and use Spock only for web tests (with Geb). Consult the Maven documentation for the respective plugins and appendix A of this book for more information on the subject.

---

[27] I hear they're called "devops" these days.

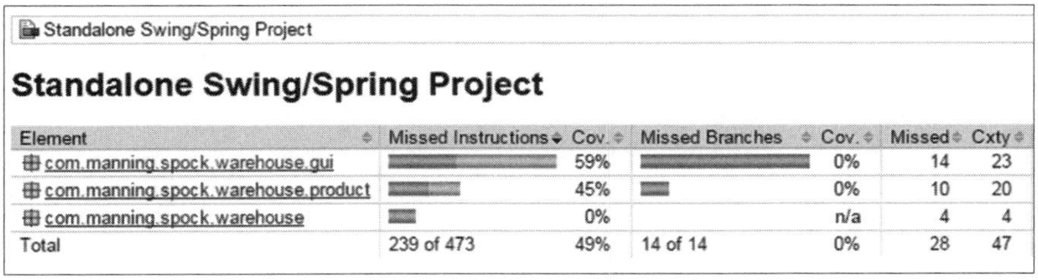

Element	Missed Instructions ⬦	Cov. ⬦	Missed Branches ⬦	Cov. ⬦	Missed ⬦	Cxty ⬦
⊞ com.manning.spock.warehouse.gui	▬▬▬▬▬▬	59%	▬▬▬▬▬▬	0%	14	23
⊞ com.manning.spock.warehouse.product	▬▬▬	45%	▬	0%	10	20
⊞ com.manning.spock.warehouse	▬	0%		n/a	4	4
Total	239 of 473	49%	14 of 14	0%	28	47

Standalone Swing/Spring Project

Standalone Swing/Spring Project

Figure 7.15 Code coverage by Spock tests

7.5.2 Getting code coverage from Spock tests

For some strange reason, when I introduce Spock to Java developers, even after I explain that it uses the JUnit runner, the first question they ask is how to obtain code coverage statistics with Spock.

The answer to this question is, "In the same way that you get coverage reports[28] for JUnit." There's nothing special about it. Figure 7.15 shows a sample JaCoCo report (www.eclemma.org/jacoco/) that was generated by Spock tests.

There's nothing Spock-specific about this report. I obtained it by adding JaCoCo in my pom.xml file and executing the `jacoco:report` goal with Maven as I would for Junit, as shown in the following listing.

Listing 7.14 Using JaCoCo with Spock

```
[...rest of build plugins here...]
<plugin>
    <groupId>org.jacoco</groupId>
    <artifactId>jacoco-maven-plugin</artifactId>
    <version>0.7.4.201502262128</version>
    <executions>
    <execution>
        <id>prepare-agent</id>
        <goals>
        <goal>prepare-agent</goal>
        </goals>
    </execution>
    </executions>
</plugin>
[...rest of pom.xml here...]
```

The same principle applies to any other tools that you have around JUnit. If they work fine with JUnit, they'll probably work with Spock as well. For a full-blown, code-quality reporting tool, you should also look at SonarQube (www.sonarqube.org) if you aren't already using it.

---

[28] Common coverage tools are Cobertura (http://cobertura.github.io/cobertura/) and Clover (www.atlassian .com/software/clover/).

Figure 7.16   Code coverage from SonarQube after Spock tests run

Using Spock with SonarQube requires exactly zero extra configuration (apart from the standard instructions[29]). An example of SonarQube results from a Spock test is shown in listing 7.16.

I hope that the level of compatibility between JUnit-enabled tools and Spock tests is clear to you now.

7.6   Summary

- Unit tests focus on a single class. Integration tests focus on a module. Functional tests focus on the whole application.
- Unit/integration/functional tests have different characteristics and constraints. They should be handled differently.
- According to the testing pyramid, as a rule of thumb, 70% of total tests should be pure unit tests, 20% should be slower integration tests, and 10% should be even slower functional tests.
- Spock supports both integration and functional tests (as well as pure unit tests, as already shown in the previous chapters).
- Spock will automatically load a Spring context if the `Specification` class is annotated with the Spring `ContextConfiguration` annotation.

---

[29] An excellent resource is *SonarQube in Action* by G. Ann Campbell and Patroklos P. Papapetrou (Manning, 2013), www.manning.com/papapetrou/.

- Inside a Spring-enabled Spock test, all normal test facilities from Spring are available (including transactions).

- A good practice is using a separate Spring context just for tests. It shouldn't contain classes unrelated to testing and it should replace slow services and databases with mocked ones or in-memory implementations, respectively.

- Groovy SQL can be used to directly access the database as an alternative to existing Java solutions.

- Spock supports Guice tests via a built-in extension. Spock also supports Arquillian tests via an external extension.

- Spock can test REST services by using the existing Java client REST libraries.

- An alternative to Java REST client libraries is the Groovy RESTClient library.

- The `Stepwise` annotation can be used in Spock tests with multiple test methods to ensure correct ordering of the method.

- All methods that come after a failed one will be skipped by Spock, allowing for faster developer feedback if the `Stepwise` annotation is used.

- Geb is a browser automation library that uses WebDriver/Selenium and offers a jQuery-like syntax for accessing page content.

- Spock and Geb can work together to create web-related functional tests.

- Geb facilities are possible if a test extends the `GebSpec` class instead of the standard Spock `Specification`.

- Geb can direct the browser, fill in forms, click buttons, and generally mimic a human user interacting with a browser.

- Spock unit/integration/functional tests should be handled differently inside the build process, mainly because of different time constraints.

- You can use the Maven failsafe and Tomcat plugins to run Spock functional tests with a live application.

- Running both JUnit and Spock tests is possible without any special configuration.

- Getting coverage reports from Spock tests is exactly the same as getting coverage reports from JUnit (using JaCoCo).

- Spock is compatible with the SonarQube quality dashboard out of the box.

Spock features for enterprise testing

This chapter covers

- Using Spock annotations that are helpful in enterprise testing
- Refactoring large Spock tests
- Testing legacy code with spy objects

One of the good qualities of a flexible software tool is the ability to adapt to any software situation, especially the corner cases that appear in large enterprise projects. Enterprise projects often come in large code bases (think millions of code lines), have an endless stream of requirements, and more often than not contain legacy modules that can't be changed for political or technical reasons.

Chapter 1 showed that Spock is a holistic testing solution that will cover your needs regardless of the size of the application and whether you work solo or as part of a large team. A bigger code base always amounts to extra complexity on all fronts (compilation, documentation, and delivery), and it's good to know that Spock has you covered even when your needs are off the beaten path.

This last chapter of the book shows you extra Spock features that are geared toward large enterprise projects. These techniques are in no way essential for Spock testing, as they solve specific problems that you might not encounter in your current project. Before employing any of the advice in this chapter, make sure that you indeed suffer from the specific problem being discussed. More importantly, the last section explains spy objects, a feature that I strongly advise you *not* to use, unless this is your last resort.

This chapter has three distinct parts, listed here in roughly the order I expect you to use them in your Spock tests:

1 Using Spock annotations for time-outs, exceptions, conditional test running, and so on
2 Refactoring of large then: blocks that contain assertions or interactions
3 Using spies as partial mocks (continuing fake objects from chapter 6)

Spies are a controversial feature (not just with Spock[1]), so make sure that you understand the implications of using them in your unit tests (and what that means for your Java production code). Use of spies implies that your Java code suffers from design problems, as you'll see in the last section.

8.1 Using additional Spock features for enterprise tests

Chapter 4 covered all Spock blocks in detail as well as the general structure of a Spock test. Spock offers several complementary features in the form of annotations that further enhance the expressiveness of your tests.

The Spock tests demonstrated here are based on the e-shop example introduced in chapter 6. They revolve around placing products in an electronic basket and paying via credit card.

8.1.1 Testing the (non)existence of exceptions: thrown() and notThrown()

In all Spock tests that I've shown you so far, the expected result is either a set of assertions or the verification of object interactions. But in some cases, the "expected" result is throwing an exception. If you're developing a library framework, for example, you have to decide what exceptions will be thrown to the calling code and verify this decision with a Spock test. The next listing demonstrates the capturing of an exception.

> **Listing 8.1   Expecting an exception in a Spock test**

```
def "Error conditions for unknown products"() {
    given: "a warehouse"
    WarehouseInventory inventory = new WarehouseInventory()

    when: "warehouse is queried for the wrong product"
    inventory.isProductAvailable("productThatDoesNotExist",1)

    then: "an exception should be thrown"
    thrown(IllegalArgumentException)
}
```

This test will pass only if
IllegalArgumentException is
thrown in the when: block.

---

[1]   Mockito's official documentation also has a huge warning against the usage of spies.

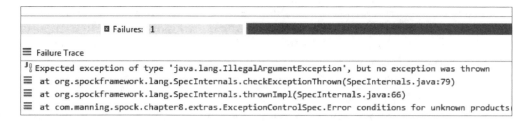

Figure 8.1   The test will fail if an exception isn't thrown in the `when:` **block.**

Here you design the `Warehouse` class so that it throws an exception when it can't find the name of a product. When this test runs, you explicitly tell Spock that the `when:` block will throw an exception. The test will fail if an exception isn't thrown, as shown in figure 8.1.

In this case, you use an existing exception as offered by Java, but the same syntax works with any kind of exception. (You could create a custom exception class called `ProductNotFoundException` instead.)

It's also possible to "capture" the exception thrown and perform further assertions in order to make the test stricter. The following listing provides an example of a message of an exception that's checked.

Listing 8.2   Detailed examination of an expected exception

```
def "Error conditions for unknown products - better"() {
    given: "a warehouse"
    WarehouseInventory inventory = new WarehouseInventory()

    when: "warehouse is queried for the wrong product"
    inventory.isProductAvailable("productThatDoesNotExist",1)

    then: "an exception should be thrown"
    IllegalArgumentException e = thrown()
    e.getMessage() == "Unknown product productThatDoesNotExist"
}
```

The test will pass only if the exception contains a specific message.

Keeps the exception thrown in the e variable

This listing further enhances the code of listing 8.1 by checking both the type of the exception and its message. Here you examine the built-in `message` property that's present in all Java exceptions, but again, you could examine any property of a custom-made exception instead (the last statement in listing 8.2 is a standard Groovy assertion).

Finally, it's possible to define in a Spock test that you don't expect an exception for an operation in the `when:` block, as the following listing shows. I admit that the semantics of this syntax are subtle, but the capability is there if you need it.

Listing 8.3 Explicit declaration that an exception shouldn't happen

```
def "Negative quantity is the same as 0"() {
    given: "a warehouse"
    WarehouseInventory inventory = new WarehouseInventory()
    and: "a product"
    Product tv = new Product(name:"bravia",price:1200,weight:18)

    when: "warehouse is loaded with a negative value"
    inventory.preload(tv,-5)

    then: "the stock is empty for that product"
    notThrown(IllegalArgumentException)
    !inventory.isProductAvailable(tv.getName(),1)
}
```

> **Clarifies the intention of testing normal operation without exception**

I believe that the notThrown() syntax is intended as a hint to the human reader of the test and not so much to the test framework itself.

8.1.2 Mapping Spock tests to your issue-tracking system: @Issue

In chapter 4, you saw the @Subject, @Title, and @Narrative annotations that serve as metadata for the Spock test. These annotations are particularly useful to nontechnical readers of the tests (for example, business analysts) and will show their value when reporting tools use them for extra documentation.

Any nontrivial enterprise application has a product backlog or issue tracker that serves as a central database of current bugs and future features. Spock comes with an @Issue annotation that allows you to mark a test method that solves a specific issue with the code, as shown in the following listing.

Listing 8.4 Marking a test method with the issue it solves

```
@Issue("JIRA-561")
def "Error conditions for unknown products"() {
    given: "a warehouse"
    WarehouseInventory inventory = new WarehouseInventory()

    when: "warehouse is queried for the wrong product"
    inventory.isProductAvailable("productThatDoesNotExist",1)

    then: "an exception should be thrown"
    thrown(IllegalArgumentException)
}
```

> **This test method verifies the fix that happened for JIRA issue 561.**

Notice that the annotation has a strictly informational role. At least at the time of writing, no automatic connection to any external system exists (in this example, to JIRA, available at www.atlassian.com/software/jira). In fact, the value inside the annotation is regarded as free text by Spock. The next listing shows another example using a full URL of a Redmine tracker (www.redmine.org).

Listing 8.5 Using the URL of an issue solved by a Spock test

```
@Issue("http://redmine.example.com/issues/2554")
def "Error conditions for unknown products - better"() {
    given: "a warehouse"
    WarehouseInventory inventory = new WarehouseInventory()
    when: "warehouse is queried for the wrong product"
    inventory.isProductAvailable("productThatDoesNotExist",1)

    then: "an exception should be thrown"
    IllegalArgumentException e = thrown()
    e.getMessage() == "Uknown product productThatDoesNotExist"
}
```

◄—— This test method verifies the fix that happened for Redmine issue 2554.

Finally, a common scenario is having multiple issue reports that stem from the same problem. Spock has you covered, and you can use multiple issues, as shown in the following listing.

Listing 8.6 Marking a Spock test with multiple issues

```
@Issue(["JIRA-453","JIRA-678","JIRA-3485"])
def "Negative quantity is the same as 0"() {
    given: "a warehouse"
    WarehouseInventory inventory = new WarehouseInventory()

    and: "a product"
    Product tv = new Product(name:"bravia",price:1200,weight:18)

    when: "warehouse is loaded with a negative value"
    inventory.preload(tv,-5)

    then: "the stock is empty for that product"
    notThrown(IllegalArgumentException)
    !inventory.isProductAvailable(tv.getName(),1)
}
```

◄—— This test method verifies the fix for three duplicate bugs.

The @Issue annotation is also handy when you practice test-driven development, as you can use it to mark Spock tests for product features before writing the production code.

8.1.3 *Failing tests that don't finish on time: @Timeout*

Chapter 7 covered integration and functional tests and how they differ from pure unit tests. A common characteristic of integration tests is their slow execution time because of real databases, web services, and external systems that are often used as part of the test.

Getting quick feedback from a failed unit test should be one of your primary goals when writing integration tests. The external systems used in integration tests can affect the execution time in a nondeterministic way, as their response time is affected by their current load or other environmental reasons.

Spock comes with an `@Timeout` annotation that unconditionally fails a test if its execution time passes the given threshold. The following listing shows an example.

Listing 8.7 Declaring a test time-out

```
@Timeout(5)                                                ◄─┐ This test should finish
def "credit card charge happy path"() {                     │ within five seconds.
    given: "a basket, a customer and a TV"
    Product tv = new Product(name:"bravia",price:1200,weight:18)
    BillableBasket basket = new BillableBasket()
    Customer customer = new
        Customer(name:"John",vip:false,creditCard:"testCard")

    and: "a credit card service"
    CreditCardProcessor creditCardSevice = new CreditCardProcessor()
    basket.setCreditCardProcessor(creditCardSevice)

    when: "user checks out the tv"
    basket.addProduct tv
    boolean success = basket.checkout(customer)            ◄─┐ This is a lengthy
                                                             │ operation that contacts
    then: "credit card is charged"                           │ the credit card service.
    success
}
```

The Credit-CardProcessor class is an external service. ──►

The reasoning behind the `@Timeout` annotation is that it helps you quickly isolate environmental problems in your integration tests. If a service is down, there's no point in waiting for the full time-out of your Java code (which could be 30 minutes, for example) before moving to the next unit test.

Using the `@Timeout` annotation, you can set your own bounds on the "expected" runtime of an integration test and have Spock automatically enforce it. The default unit is seconds, as shown in the previous listing, but you can override it with your own setting, as shown in the next listing.

Listing 8.8 Declaring a test time-out—custom unit

```
@Timeout(value = 5000, unit = TimeUnit.MILLISECONDS)       ◄─┐ Treats the defined
def "credit card charge happy path - alt "() {               │ value as milliseconds
    given: "a basket, a customer and a TV"
    Product tv = new Product(name:"bravia",price:1200,weight:18)
    BillableBasket basket = new BillableBasket()
    Customer customer = new
        Customer(name:"John",vip:false,creditCard:"testCard")

    and: "a credit card service"
    CreditCardProcessor creditCardSevice = new CreditCardProcessor()
    basket.setCreditCardProcessor(creditCardSevice)

    when: "user checks out the tv"
    basket.addProduct tv
    boolean success = basket.checkout(customer)

    then: "credit card is charged"
    success
}
```

The importance of the @Timeout annotation is evident in the case of multiple long tests that take a long time to finish. I've seen build jobs that typically take minutes but because of a misconfiguration can take hours if time-outs aren't used correctly.

8.1.4   *Ignoring certain Spock tests*

A large enterprise application can have thousands of unit tests. In an ideal world, all of them would be active at any given time. In real life, this is rarely the case.

Test environments that get migrated, features that wait to be implemented, and business requirements that aren't yet frozen are common reasons that force some tests to be skipped. Fortunately, Spock offers several ways to skip one or more tests deliberately so your tests don't fail while these restructurings and developments are taking place.

IGNORING A SINGLE TEST: @IGNORE

Spock allows you to knowingly skip one or more tests and even provides you with the ability to give a reason for skipping that test (see the next listing).

> **Listing 8.9   Ignoring a single test**

```
@Ignore("Until credit card server is migrated")      ◀── This test will be skipped
def "credit card charge happy path"() {                   when Spock runs it.
    given: "a basket, a customer and a TV"
    Product tv = new Product(name:"bravia",price:1200,weight:18)
    BillableBasket basket = new BillableBasket()
    Customer customer = new
            Customer(name:"John",vip:false,creditCard:"testCard")

    and: "a credit card service"
    CreditCardProcessor creditCardSevice = new CreditCardProcessor()
    basket.setCreditCardProcessor(creditCardSevice)

    when: "user checks out the tv"
    basket.addProduct tv
    boolean success = basket.checkout(customer)

    then: "credit card is charged"
    success

}
```

The primary purpose of skipping a test is so that the rest of your test suite is run successfully by your build server. An ignored test should always be a temporary situation because you're vulnerable to code changes that would normally expose a bug verified by that test.

The human-readable description inside the @Ignore annotation should give a hint about why this test is ignored (the value is free text, as far as Spock is concerned). More often than not, the original developer who marks a test as ignored doesn't always remove the @Ignore annotation, so it's essential to document inside the source code the reason why the test was skipped in the first place.

You can place @Ignore on a single test method or on a whole class if you want all its test methods to be skipped.

IGNORING ALL BUT ONE TEST: @IGNOREREST

If you're also lucky, and you want to ignore all but one test in a Spock specification, you can use the @IgnoreRest annotation. Assume that you have a set of integration tests that contact a credit card external service in a staging environment (it doesn't actually charge cards). The service is down for maintenance. To keep your tests running, you could ignore tests selectively, as shown in the following listing.

Listing 8.10 Ignoring all tests except one

```
class KeepOneSpec extends spock.lang.Specification{

    def "credit card charge - integration test"() {          ◄─── This test uses the real
            [...code redacted for brevity...]                        credit card service—it
                                                                     will be skipped.
    }

    @IgnoreRest
    def "credit card charge with mock"() {                    ◄─── This test uses only
            [...code redacted for brevity...]                        mocks and thus
                                                                     can run normally
    }

    def "credit card charge no charge - integration test"() {  ◄───
            [...code redacted for brevity...]

    }                                                          This test uses the real
                                                               credit card service—it
}                                                                     will be skipped.
```

Marking this test as the only one that will run ──► (points to @IgnoreRest)

Running the Spock test shown in this listing produces the output in figure 8.2.

Again, I admit that this Spock annotation is specialized, and you might never need to use it.

IGNORING SPOCK TESTS ACCORDING TO THE RUNTIME ENVIRONMENT: @IGNOREIF PART 1

The @Ignore annotations shown in the previous paragraph are completely static. A test is either skipped or not, and that decision is made during compile time.

Figure 8.2 Only the test marked with @IgnoreRest runs.

Spock offers a set of smarter `@Ignore` annotations that allow you to skip tests dynamically (by examining the runtime environment). As a first step, Spock allows a test to query the following:

- The current environment variables
- The JVM system properties
- The operating system

Spock then decides whether the test will run, depending on that result. An example of skipping tests is shown in the next listing.

Listing 8.11   Skipping Spock tests according to the environment

```
class SimpleConditionalSpec extends spock.lang.Specification{

    @IgnoreIf({ jvm.java9 })
    def "credit card charge happy path"() {
          [...code redacted for brevity...]

    }

    @IgnoreIf({ os.windows })
    def "credit card charge happy path - alt"() {
          [...code redacted for brevity...]

    }

    @IgnoreIf({ env.containsKey("SKIP_SPOCK_TESTS") })
    def "credit card charge happy path - alt 2"() {
          [...code redacted for brevity...]
    }

}
```

This test will be skipped on Java 9.

This test will be skipped if run on Windows.

This test will be skipped if the property **SKIP_SPOCK_TESTS** is defined.

Running this listing on my Windows system with JDK 7 and no extra JVM properties produces the output shown in figure 8.3.

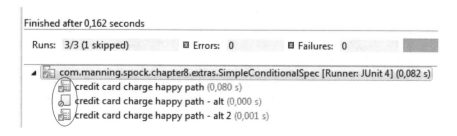

Finished after 0,162 seconds

Runs: 3/3 (1 skipped)   ⊠ Errors: 0   ⊠ Failures: 0

▲ com.manning.spock.chapter8.extras.SimpleConditionalSpec [Runner: JUnit 4] (0,082 s)
        credit card charge happy path (0,080 s)
        credit card charge happy path - alt (0,000 s)
        credit card charge happy path - alt 2 (0,001 s)

Figure 8.3   A test is skipped because the current OS is Windows.

I won't list all possible options supported by Spock. You can find the full details in its source code.[2] Ignoring tests depending on environment variables enables you to split your tests into separate categories/groups, which is a well-known technique. As an example, you could create "fast" and "slow" tests and set up your build server with two jobs for different feedback lifecycles.

IGNORING CERTAIN SPOCK TESTS WITH PRECONDITIONS: @IGNOREIF PART 2

To obtain the maximum possible flexibility from @IgnoreIf annotations, you need to define your own custom conditions. You can do this easily in Spock because the @IgnoreIf annotation accepts a full closure. The closure will be evaluated and the test will be skipped if the result is false.

The following listing shows a smarter Spock test that runs only if the CreditCard-Service is up and running.

Listing 8.12 Skipping a Spock test based on a dynamic precondition

```
@IgnoreIf({ !new CreditCardProcessor().online() })       ◄─── This test will run only
def "credit card charge happy path - alt"() {                 if the method online()
    given: "a basket, a customer and a TV"                     of the credit card
    Product tv = new Product(name:"bravia",price:1200,weight:18)  service returns true.
    BillableBasket basket = new BillableBasket()
    Customer customer = new
            Customer(name:"John",vip:false,creditCard:"testCard")

    and: "a credit card service"
    CreditCardProcessor creditCardSevice = new CreditCardProcessor()
    basket.setCreditCardProcessor(creditCardSevice)

    when: "user checks out the tv"
    basket.addProduct tv
    boolean success = basket.checkout(customer)      ◄─── This operation contacts
                                                          the credit card service.
    then: "credit card is charged"
    success
}
```

The Credit-CardProcessor class is an external service.

This listing assumes that the Java class representing the external credit card system has a built-in method called online() that performs a "ping" on the remote host. Spock runs this method, and if it gets a negative result, it skips the test (there's no point in running it if the service is down).

The contents of the closure passed as an argument in the @IgnoreIf annotation can be any custom code you write. If, for example, the built-in online() method wasn't present, you could create your own Java (or Groovy) class that performs an HTTP request (or something appropriate) to the external system and have that inside the closure.

---

[2] https://github.com/spockframework/spock/tree/master/spock-core/src/main/java/spock/util/environment

REVERSING THE BOOLEAN CONDITION OF IGNOREIF: @REQUIRES

If for some reason you find yourself always reverting the condition inside the `@IgnoreIf` annotation (as seen in listing 8.12, for example), you can instead use the `@Requires` annotation, as the following listing shows.

Listing 8.13   `Requires` is the opposite of `IgnoreIf`

```
@Requires({ new CreditCardProcessor().online() })                    ◀── This test will run only
def "credit card charge happy path"() {                                   if the method online()
    given: "a basket, a customer and a TV"                                of the credit card
    Product tv = new Product(name:"bravia",price:1200,weight:18)          service returns true.
    BillableBasket basket = new BillableBasket()
    Customer customer = new
            Customer(name:"John",vip:false,creditCard:"testCard")

    and: "a credit card service"
    CreditCardProcessor creditCardSevice = new CreditCardProcessor()
    basket.setCreditCardProcessor(creditCardSevice)

    when: "user checks out the tv"
    basket.addProduct tv
    boolean success = basket.checkout(customer)                       ◀── This operation contacts
                                                                          the credit card service.
    then: "credit card is charged"
    success

}
```

The CreditCardProcessor class is an external service. ──▶

The `@Requires` annotation has the same semantics as `@IgnoreIf` but with the reverse behavior. The test will be skipped by Spock if the code inside the closure does not evaluate to `true`. The option to use one or the other annotation comes as a personal preference.

8.1.5 *Automatic cleaning of resources: @AutoCleanup*

Chapter 4 showed you the `cleanup:` block as a way to release resources (for example, database connections) at the end of a Spock test regardless of its result. An alternative way to achieve the same thing is by using the `@AutoCleanup` annotation, as shown in the following listing.

Listing 8.14   Releasing resources with `AutoCleanup`

```
@AutoCleanup("shutdown")                                                           ◀──
private CreditCardProcessor creditCardSevice = new CreditCardProcessor()

def "credit card connection is closed down in the end"() {          The shutdown()
    given: "a basket, a customer and a TV"                           method of the
    Product tv = new Product(name:"bravia",price:1200,weight:18)     credit card service
    BillableBasket basket = new BillableBasket()                     will be called at the
    Customer customer = new                                          end of the tests.
            Customer(name:"John",vip:false,creditCard:"testCard")
```

```
        and: "a credit card service"
        basket.setCreditCardProcessor(creditCardSevice)

        when: "user checks out the tv"
        basket.addProduct tv
        boolean success = basket.checkout(customer)

        then: "credit card is charged"
        success
}
```

If you mark a resource with the `@AutoCleanup` annotation, Spock makes sure that the `close()` method will be called on that resource at the end of the test (even if the test fails). You can use the annotation on anything you consider a resource in your tests. Database connections, file handles, and external services are good candidates for the `@AutoCleanup` annotation.

You can override the method name that will be called by using it as an argument in the annotation, as done in listing 8.11. In that example, the `shutdown()` method will be called instead (Spock will call `close()` by default).

I prefer to use the `cleanup:` block and `cleanup()`/`cleanupSpec()` methods as explained in chapter 4 (especially when multiple resources must be released), but if you're a big fan of annotations, feel free to use `@AutoCleanup` instead.[3] As you might guess, `@AutoCleanup` works both with instance fields and objects marked with the `@Shared` annotation shown in chapter 4.

This concludes the additional Spock annotations,[4] and we can now move to refactoring of big Spock tests.

8.2 Handling large Spock tests

The projects in most examples so far are trivial projects designed as a learning material instead of production-quality applications. In the real world, enterprise projects come with huge code bases that directly affect the size of unit tests.

Even in the case of pure unit tests (non-integration tests), preparing the class under test and its collaborators is often a lengthy process with many statements and boilerplate code that's essential for the correct functionality of the Java code tested, but otherwise unrelated to the business feature being tested.

I've provided some hints for making clear the intention of Spock tests using Groovy `with()` and Spock `with()` methods, as seen in chapter 4. In this section, you'll take this grouping of statements one step further by completely refactoring the respective statements in their own methods.

---

[3] You can also ignore exceptions during cleanup if you use the annotation like `@AutoCleanup(quiet = true)`, but I don't endorse this practice unless you know what you're doing.

[4] Yes, I know that expecting exceptions does not happen via annotations. Thanks for catching it!

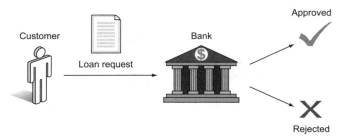

Figure 8.4   A customer requests a loan from a bank. The bank approves or rejects the loan.

The running example here is a loan-approval application, shown in figure 8.4. The Java classes that take part in the system are as follows:

- `Customer.java`
- `Loan.java`
- `CreditCard.java`
- `ContactDetails.java`
- `BankAccount.java`

You can find the full source code in the GitHub repository of the book,[5] but notice that most classes are only skeletons designed to demonstrate specific techniques in the Spock tests.

8.2.1   Using helper methods to improve code readability

Chapter 4 stressed the importance of the `when:` block and how critical it is to keep its code short and understandable. But in big enterprise projects, long code segments can appear in any Spock block, harming the readability of the test. As a starting example, let's see a unit test that has a long setup process, shown in the next listing.

> **Listing 8.15   A Spock test with long setup—*don't do this***

```
def "a bank customer with 3 credit cards is never given a loan"() {
    given: "a customer that wants to get a loan"
    Customer customer = new Customer(name:"John Doe")

    and: "his credit cards"
    BankAccount account1 = new BankAccount()
    account1.with {
            setNumber("234234")
            setHolder("John doe")
            balance=30
    }
    CreditCard card1 = new CreditCard("447978956666")
    card1.with{
            setHolder("John Doe")
```

A badly designed and: block. It contains too much code.

---

5 https://github.com/kkapelon/java-testing-with-spock/tree/master/chapter8/src/main/java/com/manning/spock/chapter8/loan

```
                    assign(account1)
    }
    customer.owns(card1)
    BankAccount account2 = new BankAccount()
    account2.with{
            setNumber("3435676")
            setHolder("John Doe")
            balance=30
    }
    CreditCard card2 = new CreditCard("4443543354")
    card2.with{
            setHolder("John Doe")
            assign(account2)
    }
    customer.owns(card2)
    BankAccount account3 = new BankAccount()
    account2.with{
            setNumber("45465")
            setHolder("John Doe")
            balance=30
    }
    CreditCard card3 = new CreditCard("444455556666")
    card3.with{
            setHolder("John Doe")
            assign(account3)
    }
    customer.owns(card3)

    when:"a loan is requested"          ◄──┐  A well-designed when:
    Loan loan = new Loan()                 │  block. Code is short.
    customer.requests(loan)

    then: "loan should not be approved"    ┐  A well-designed then:
    !loan.approved                       ◄─┘  block. Code is short.
}
```

At first glance, this unit test correctly follows the best practices outlined in chapter 4. All the blocks have human-readable descriptions, the when: block clearly shows what's being tested (a loan request), and the final result is also clear (either the loan is approved or it's rejected).

The setup of the test, however, is a gigantic piece of code that's neither clear nor directly relevant to the business case tested. The description of the block talks about credit cards but contains code that creates both credit cards and bank accounts (because apparently a credit card requires a valid bank account in place).

Even with the use of the with() method for grouping several statements that act on the same project, the setup code makes the test hard to read. It contains a lot of variables, and it's not immediately clear whether they affect the test. For example, does it matter that the account balance is $30 in each connected account? Does this affect the approval of the loan? You can't answer that question by reading the Spock test.

In such cases, a refactoring must take place so that the intention of the test becomes clear and concise. Large amounts of code should be extracted to helper methods, as shown in the next listing.

Listing 8.16   Spock test with helper methods

```
def "a bank customer with 3 credit cards is never given a loan -alt"() {
    given: "a customer that wants to get a loan"
    Customer customer = new Customer(name:"John Doe")

    and: "his credit cards"
    customer.owns(createSampleCreditCard("447978956666","John Doe"))
    customer.owns(createSampleCreditCard("4443543354","John Doe"))
    customer.owns(createSampleCreditCard("444455556666","John Doe"))

    when:"a loan is requested"
    Loan loan = new Loan()
    customer.requests(loan)

    then: "loan should not be approved"
    !loan.approved
}

private CreditCard createSampleCreditCard(String number, String holder)
{
    BankAccount account = new BankAccount()
    account.with{
        setNumber("45465")
        setHolder(holder)
        balance=30
    }
    CreditCard card = new CreditCard(number)
    card.with{
        setHolder(holder)
        assign(account)
    }
    return card
}
```

Setup code is now short and clear

A helper method that deals with credit card

The fact that each credit card needs a bank account is hidden in the helper method.

This helper method creates a credit card.

Here you extract the common code into a helper method. The helper method has the following positive effects:

- It reduces the amount of setup code.
- It clearly shows that the setup code is a set of sample credit cards.
- It hides the fact that a bank account is needed for creating a credit card (as this is unrelated to the approval of a loan).
- It shows by its arguments that the holder of the credit card must be the same as the customer who requests the loan.

The added advantage of helper methods is that you can share them across test methods or even across specifications (by creating an inheritance among Spock tests, for example). You should therefore design them so they can be reused by multiple tests.

Depending on your business case, you can further refine the helper methods you use to guide the reader of the test to what exactly is being tested. In a real-world project, you might modify the Spock test as shown in the following listing.

Listing 8.17 Using arguments that imply their importance in the test

```
def "a bank customer with 3 credit cards is never given a loan -alt 2"() {
    given: "a customer that wants to get a loan"
    String customerName ="doesNotMatter"
    Customer customer = new Customer(name:customerName)
```
◀── Enforces the same customer for the loan and credit cards

Makes it clear that credit card numbers are unused in loan approval
```
    and: "his credit cards"
    customer.owns(createSampleCreditCard("anything",customerName))
    customer.owns(createSampleCreditCard("whatever",customerName))
    customer.owns(createSampleCreditCard("notImportant",customerName))

    expect: "customer already has 3 cards"
    customer.getCards().size() == 3
```
◀── Explicitly verifies the result of the setup
```
    when:"a loan is requested"
    Loan loan = new Loan()
    customer.requests(loan)

    then: "therefore loan is not approved"
    !loan.approved
}
```

This improved listing makes minor adjustments to the arguments of the helper method. First, you use a single variable for the customer name. This guards against any spelling mistakes so you can be sure that all credit cards are assigned to the same customer (because as the description of the test says, the number of credit cards of the customer is indeed examined for loan approval).

Second, you replace the credit card numbers with dummy strings. This helps the reader of the test understand that the number of each credit card isn't used in loan approval.

As a final test, you add an `expect:` block (as demonstrated in chapter 4) that strengthens the readability of the setup code.

After all these changes, you can compare listings 8.15 with 8.17. In the first case, you have a huge amount of setup code that's hard to read, whereas in the second case, you can understand in seconds that the whole point of the setup code is to assign credit cards to the customer.

8.2.2 *Reusing assertions in the then: block*

Helper methods should be used in all Spock blocks when you feel that the size of the code gets out of hand. But because of technical limitations, the creation of helper methods for the `then:` block requires special handling.

Again, as a starting example of a questionable design, let's start with a big `then:` block, as shown in the next listing.

Listing 8.18   Spock test with dubious then: block

```
def "Normal approval for a loan"() {
    given: "a bank customer"
    Customer customer = new Customer(name:"John
        Doe",city:"London",address:"10 Bakers",phone:"32434")

    and: "his/her need to buy a house "
    Loan loan = new Loan(years:5, amount:200.000)

    when:"a loan is requested"
    customer.requests(loan)

    then: "loan is approved as is"
    loan.approved
    loan.amount == 200.000
    loan.years == 5
    loan.instalments == 60
    loan.getContactDetails().getPhone() == "32434"
    loan.getContactDetails().getAddress() == "10 Bakers"
    loan.getContactDetails().getCity() == "London"
    loan.getContactDetails().getName() == "John Doe"
    customer.activeLoans == 1
}
```

These checks are secondary.

These examine the loan approval.

Here the `then:` block contains multiple statements with different significance. First, you have some important checks that confirm that the loan is indeed approved. Then you have other checks that examine the details of the approved loan (and especially the fact that they match the customer who requests it). Finally, it's not clear whether the numbers and strings that take part in the `then:` block are arbitrary or depend on something else.[6]

As a first step to improve this test, you'll split the `then:` block into two parts and group similar statements, as shown in the following listing.

Listing 8.19   Improved Spock test with clear separation of checks

```
def "Normal approval for a loan - alt"() {
    given: "a bank customer"
    Customer customer = new Customer(name:"John
        Doe",city:"London",address:"10 Bakers",phone:"32434")

    and: "his/her need to buy a house "
    int sampleTimeSpan=5
    int sampleAmount = 200.000
```

Makes clear the connection between expected results

---

[6] In this simple example, it's obvious that the contact details of the loan are the same as the customer ones. In a real-world unit test, this isn't usually the case.

```
           Loan loan = new Loan(years:sampleTimeSpan, amount:sampleAmount)

           when:"a loan is requested"
           customer.requests(loan)

           then: "loan is approved as is"          ┌─── Grouping of primary
           with(loan)                          ◄───┘     loan checks
           {
                 approved
                 amount == sampleAmount
                 years == sampleTimeSpan             ┐  Makes clear the
                 installments == sampleTimeSpan * 12 ├─ expected result
           }                                      ◄──┘
           customer.activeLoans == 1

           and: "contact details are kept or record"  ◄─┐ Different block for
           with(loan.contactDetails)                     │ secondary checks
           {
                 getPhone() == "32434"
                 getAddress() == "10 Bakers"
                 getCity() == "London"
                 getName() == "John Doe"
           }
     }
```

The improved version of the test clearly splits the checks according to the business case. You've replaced the number 60, which was previously a magic number, with the full logic that installments are years times 12 (for monthly installments).

The code that checks loan details still has hardcoded values. You can further improve the code by using helper methods, as shown in the next listing.

Listing 8.20 Using helper methods for assertions

```
def "Normal approval for a loan - improved"() {
    given: "a bank customer"
    Customer customer = new Customer(name:"John
        Doe",city:"London",address:"10 Bakers",phone:"32434")

    and: "his/her need to buy a house "
    int sampleTimeSpan=5
    int sampleAmount = 200.000
    Loan loan = new Loan(years:sampleTimeSpan, amount:sampleAmount)

    when:"a loan is requested"
    customer.requests(loan)

    then: "loan is approved as is"
    loanApprovedAsRequested(customer,loan,sampleTimeSpan,sampleAmount)

    and: "contact details are kept or record"
    contactDetailsMatchCustomer(customer,loan)
}
```

Helper methods with descriptive names

```
private void loanApprovedAsRequested(Customer customer,Loan loan,int
          originalYears,int originalAmount)
{
    with(loan)
    {
        approved
        amount == originalAmount
        loan.years == originalYears
        loan.instalments == originalYears * 12
    }
    assert customer.activeLoans == 1
}


private void contactDetailsMatchCustomer(Customer customer,Loan loan )
{
    with(loan.contactDetails)
    {
        phone == customer.phone
        address == customer.address
        city == customer.city
        name== customer.name
    }
}
```

with() method works as expected in helper method.

assert keyword is needed in helper method.

Clear connection between loan and customer who requested it

This listing refactors the two separate blocks into their own helper methods. The important thing to note is the format of each helper method.

Your first impulse might be to design each helper method to return a Boolean if all its assertions pass, and have Spock check the result of that single Boolean. This doesn't work as expected.

The recommended approach, as shown in listing 8.20, is to have helper methods as void methods. Inside each helper method, you can put one of the following:

- A group of assertions with the Spock with() method
- A Groovy assert but with the assert keyword prepended

Notice this line:

```
assert customer.activeLoans == 1
```

Because this statement exists in a helper method and not directly in a then: block, it needs the assert keyword so Spock can understand that it's an assertion. If you miss the assert keyword, the statement will pass the test regardless of the result (which is a bad thing).

This listing also refactors the second helper method to validate loan details against its arguments instead of hardcoded values. This makes the helper method reusable in other test methods where the customer could have other values.

Spend some time comparing listing 8.20 with the starting example of listing 8.18 to see the gradual improvement in the clarity of the unit test.

8.2.3 Reusing interactions in the then: block

As you saw in the previous section, Spock needs some help to understand assertions in helper methods. A similar case happens with mocks and interactions.

The following listing shows an alternative Spock test, in which the loan class is mocked instead of using the real class.[7]

Listing 8.21 Spock tests with questionable `then:` block

```
def "Normal approval for a loan"() {
    given: "a bank customer"
    Customer customer = new Customer(name:"John
        Doe",city:"London",address:"10 Bakers",phone:"32434")

    and: "his/her need to buy a house "
    Loan loan = Mock(Loan)

    when:"a loan is requested"
    customer.requests(loan)

    then: "loan is approved as is"
    1 * loan.setApproved(true)
    0 * loan.setAmount(_)
    0 * loan.setYears(_)
    _ * loan.getYears() >> 5
    _ * loan.getAmount() >> 200.000
    _ * loan.getContactDetails() >> new ContactDetails()

}
```

Primary checks for the loan (annotation for the `1 * loan.setApproved(true)`, `0 * loan.setAmount(_)`, `0 * loan.setYears(_)` lines)

Stubbed methods needed for the correct functioning of the test (annotation for the `_ * loan.getYears() >> 5`, `_ * loan.getAmount() >> 200.000`, `_ * loan.getContactDetails() >> new ContactDetails()` lines)

The test in this listing contains multiple interaction checks in the `then:` block that have a different business purpose. The Loan class is used in this case both as a mock and as a stub. This fact is implied by the cardinalities in the interaction checks.

You can improve this test by making clear the business need behind each interaction check, as seen in the next listing.

Listing 8.22 Explicitly declaring helper methods with interactions

```
def "Normal approval for a loan - alt"() {
    given: "a bank customer"
    Customer customer = new Customer(name:"John
        Doe",city:"London",address:"10 Bakers",phone:"32434")

    and: "his/her need to buy a house "
    Loan loan = Mock(Loan)

    when:"a loan is requested"
    customer.requests(loan)
```

---

[7] In this example, mocking the loan class is overkill. I mock it for illustration purposes only to show you helper methods with mocks.

Helper methods named after the business check

```
    then: "loan request was indeed evaluated"
    interaction {
            loanDetailsWereExamined(loan)
    }

    and: "loan was approved as is"
    interaction {
            loanWasApprovedWithNoChanges(loan)
    }

}

private void loanWasApprovedWithNoChanges(Loan loan)
{
    1 * loan.setApproved(true)
    0 * loan.setAmount(_)
    0 * loan.setYears(_)
}

private void loanDetailsWereExamined(Loan loan)
{
    _ * loan.getYears() >> 5
    _ * loan.getAmount() >> 200.000
    _ * loan.getContactDetails() >> new ContactDetails()
}
```

Interaction blocks are needed for helper methods that contain mocks.

You've created two helper methods and added a then: block. The first helper method holds the primary checks (the approval of the loan with its original values). The other helper method is secondary, as it contains the stubbed methods of the loan object (which are essential for the test but not as important as the approval/rejection status of the loan).

The important thing to understand in this listing is that you wrap each helper method in an interaction block:

```
interaction {
        loanDetailsWereExamined(loan)
    }
```

This is needed so that Spock understands the special format of the N * class.method (N) interaction check, as shown in chapter 6. Spock automatically understands this format in statements found directly under the then: block, but for helper methods you need to explicitly tell Spock that statements inside the method are interaction checks.

Constructing a custom DSL for your testing needs

The Groovy language is perfect for creating your own domain-specific language (DSL) that matches your business requirements. Rather than using simple helper methods, you can take your Spock tests to the next level by creating a DSL that matches your business vocabulary. Creating a DSL with Groovy is outside the scope of this book, so feel free to consult chapter 19 of *Groovy in Action, Second Edition,* by Dierk Koenig et al. (Manning Publications, 2015) for more information on this topic.

Real object   Fake   Partial fake

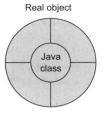
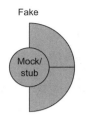

Figure 8.5 A spy is a real class in which only a subset of methods are fake. The rest are the real methods.

8.3   Creating partial mocks with spies

In this section you'll see how to create partial mocks.[8] Chapter 6 explained how Spock can create fake objects that are useful for testing and showed you mocks and stubs. Spock supports a third type of "fake" object: spies.

Spies, shown in figure 8.5, work as partial mocks. They take over a Java object and mock only some of its methods. Method calls can either by stubbed (like mocks) or can pass through to the real object.

I purposely didn't show you spies in chapter 6 because they're a controversial technique that implies problematic Java code. They can be useful in a narrow set of cases. Their primary use is in creating unit tests for badly designed production code that can't be refactored (a common scenario with legacy code).

8.3.1   A sample application with special requirements

Let's see an example that's well-suited for writing a Spock test with spies instead of mocks/stubs. Say you're tasked with the development of unit tests for an existing Java application. The Java application in question is a security utility that gets video feed from an external camera, and upon detecting intruders, deletes all files of the hard drive (to hide incriminating evidence).

The application code is implemented by two Java classes. The first class is responsible for deleting the hard drive, and the second class implements the face-recognition algorithms that decide whether the person in front of the camera is a friend or enemy, as shown in the next listing.

Listing 8.23   Java code with questionable design

```
public class CameraFeed {                          ◄─── Gets frames from
                                                         video camera
    [...code redacted for brevity...]

    public void setCurrentFrame(Image image){
        [...code redacted for brevity...]
    }
}
```

---

[8] And why you shouldn't use them!

```
public class HardDriveNuker {                           ◄─┐  Responsible for
                                                            hard disk deletion
        public void deleteHardDriveNow(){
                [...code redacted for brevity...]
        }
}                                                       ◄─┐  Contains complex image-
public class SmartHardDriveNuker extends HardDriveNuker{    recognition logic

        public void activate(CameraFeed cameraFeed){    ◄─┐  Calls deleteHardDriveNow()
                [...code redacted for brevity...]          behind the scenes
        }
}
```

Immediately deletes the hard drive (annotation pointing to `deleteHardDriveNow()`)

You should instantly see the flawed design of this Java code. Figure 8.6 provides an overview.

The application doesn't use dependency injection. Instead of splitting responsibilities into separate entities, the application contains both the logic of deletion and the face recognition in a single "object."

You see this design flaw and start refactoring the application in order to write your unit tests. Unfortunately, your boss says that the binary application is digitally signed, and changing even the slightest thing in the source code will create an invalid signature.[9] Your boss adds that even if you successfully refactor the code, your department

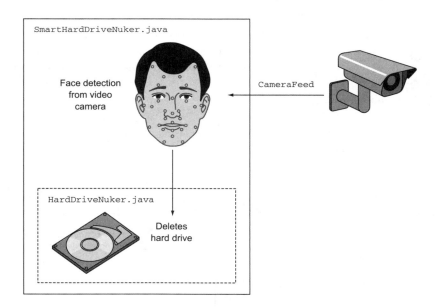

Figure 8.6   Hard drive deletion logic is hidden inside the face-recognition logic

---

[9]   My example is a bit extreme. Usually code can't be changed for political reasons.

doesn't have access to the digital certificate, so you couldn't re-sign the binary after your change.

You need to write a unit test with the source code as is. You're asked to examine the effectiveness of the face-recognition software by using images of both kinds (those that have a threat and those that don't). This is one of the rare occasions that spies can be employed for unit testing.

8.3.2 Spies with Spock

You need to write a unit test that examines the `activate()` method of the `SmartHardDriveNuker` class. You know that behind the scenes it calls the `deleteHardDriveNow()` method. It wouldn't be realistic to delete your hard drive each time you write a unit test that triggers the face-recognition logic. You need to find a way to mock the dangerous method while the real method of the face-recognition logic is kept as is.

Spock supports the creation of spies, as shown in the next listing. A spy is a fake object that automatically calls the real methods of a class unless they're explicitly mocked.

Listing 8.24 Creating a spy with Spock

```
def "automatic deletion of hard disk when agents are here"() {
    given: "a camera feed"
    CameraFeed cameraFeed = new CameraFeed()

    and: "the auto-nuker program"
    SmartHardDriveNuker nuker = Spy(SmartHardDriveNuker)
    nuker.deleteHardDriveNow() >> {println "Hard disk is cleared"}

    when:"agents are knocking the door"
    cameraFeed.setCurrentFrame(ImageIO.read(getClass().getResourceAsStream(
                "agents.jpg")))
    nuker.activate(cameraFeed);

    then: "all files of hard drive should be deleted"
    1 * nuker.deleteHardDriveNow()
}
```

Creates a spy for the SmartHardDriveNuker class

Mocks the dangerous method—all other methods are real

Real face-recognition code runs

Examines the mocked method

Here you create a spy of your class under test. By default, after creation, all methods are real and pass through to the real object.[10] Then you specifically mock the method that deletes the hard drive. But the method that employs the face-recognition logic is still the real one.

When the `activate()` method is called, it runs its real code (so you can pass it different images and test the effectiveness of the face-recognition code). In the case of an image that represents a "threat" and so triggers the hard drive deletion process, you know that the mocked method will be called (and thus your hard drive is safe).

---

[10] Creating a spy without mocking any method is the same as using the object itself—not very exciting.

This listing shows only one test, but in reality you'd need to write a parameterized test with multiple images that examines the behavior of the face-recognition code.

8.3.3 *The need for spies shows a problematic code base*

Spies are used for legacy code primarily because of the bad quality of legacy code.[11] Well-designed code doesn't ever need spies in the first place. Figure 8.7 shows a flow diagram of using spies that you should keep in your head at all times. The diagram isn't specific to Spock. It applies to all testing frameworks (including Mockito).

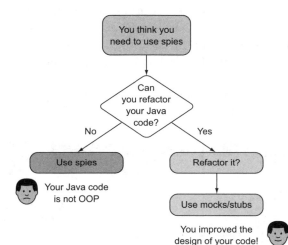

Figure 8.7   **Spies can always be replaced with mocks in well-designed code.**

In the example of the security utility, a spy is essential because the Java code doesn't use dependency injection. This is just one of the code smells of badly designed code. Java code that comes as a big ball of mud,[12] breaks the SOLID principles,[13] contains God[14] objects, and generally suffers from big design flaws isn't directly testable with mocks/stubs, and spies are needed.

In those cases, you should resist the temptation to write a Spock test with spies and instead refactor the code before writing your unit tests. You'll find that in most cases (if not all), spies aren't needed after the refactoring is complete.

8.3.4 *Replacement of spies with mock*

You use spies with the security utility because you can't refactor the Java code first, as this would invalidate the digital signature of the binary. If that constraint didn't hold,

---

[11] A universal fact: legacy code is always badly designed code.
[12] https://en.wikipedia.org/wiki/Big_ball_of_mud
[13] https://en.wikipedia.org/wiki/SOLID_(object-oriented_design)
[14] https://en.wikipedia.org/wiki/God_object

you'd instead modify the Java code to properly use dependency injection. An obvious decoupling of dependencies is shown in the following listing.

Listing 8.25   Refactoring Java code to avoid spies

```
public class SmartHardDriveNuker{                          ◄──── No inheritance is used.

    private final HardDriveNuker hardDriveNuker;

    public SmartHardDriveNuker(final HardDriveNuker hardDriveNuker)
    {
            this.hardDriveNuker = hardDriveNuker;          ◄──── Gets hard drive nuker via
    }                                                            constructor injection

    public void activate(CameraFeed cameraFeed)
    {
            [...code redacted for brevity..]
            hardDriveNuker.deleteHardDriveNow();           ◄──── Calls the dangerous method
            [...code redacted for brevity..]                     of the external dependency
    }

}
```

Code reuse via composition → `private final HardDriveNuker hardDriveNuker;`

Here you refactor your Java code to use composition instead of inheritance. You also introduce the "dangerous" hard drive deletion code as an external dependency. After this refactoring, you can rewrite your unit test by using a normal mock, as shown in the next listing.

Listing 8.26   Using a mock instead of a spy

```
def "automatic deletion of hard disk when agents are here"() {
    given: "a camera feed and a fake nuker"
    CameraFeed cameraFeed = new CameraFeed()
    HardDriveNuker nuker = Mock(HardDriveNuker)            ◄──── Uses a mock
                                                                 instead of a spy
    and: "the auto-nuker program"
    SmartHardDriveNuker smartNuker = new SmartHardDriveNuker(nuker)

    when:"agents are knocking the door"
    cameraFeed.setCurrentFrame(ImageIO.read(getClass().getResourceAsStream(
            "agents.jpg")))
     smartNuker.activate(cameraFeed);                      ◄──── Calls the mocked nuker
                                                                 class behind the scenes
    then: "all files of hard drive should be deleted"
    1 * nuker.deleteHardDriveNow()                         ◄──── Examines the interaction
}                                                                of the mock
```

Mock is passed as a dependency → `SmartHardDriveNuker smartNuker = new SmartHardDriveNuker(nuker)`

If you've read chapter 6, the code in listing 8.26 should be easy to understand. Because you've refactored the Java code and hard drive deletion is now an external dependency, you can mock that class and pass it the face-recognition code. This way, your class under test—SmartHardDriveNuker—is a real one, and a mock is used for the collaborator class: HardDriveNuker.

The end result is that no spies are used. What you need to take away from this section of the book is that despite Spock support for spies, you should avoid using them, and instead spend time improving the design of your code so that spies aren't needed.

And with that knowledge about spies, we conclude this book! You can now put it down and go write your own Spock tests!

8.4   Summary

- You can create Spock tests that will pass if a certain exception is thrown.
- You can explicitly define the type of exception and perform assertions on it to refine the conditions for passing a test when an exception is thrown.
- The @Issue annotation can be used for documentation (and possibly reporting) purposes on a Spock test. Use it to show which issue is verified by a Spock test.
- Spock supports the @Timeout annotation that will forcibly fail a test if it takes too long.
- You can ignore specific Spock tests. They will be skipped by the Spock runner.
- You can automatically skip Spock tests according to the running environment. Tests can be skipped under specific operating systems, JVM configuration, system properties, environment variables, and any other custom code you can implement yourself.
- The @AutoCleanup annotation automatically releases resources at the end of a Spock test, even if the test has failed. This is an alternative to the cleanup: block and/or the cleanup()/cleanupSpec() methods.
- All Spock blocks (the when: block in particular) should be short and concise. Large code segments should be extracted into helper methods.
- Helper methods for assertions need to use the assert keyword or the with() method (otherwise, Spock can't understand that the code is Groovy assertions).
- Helper methods for interactions should be wrapped in an interaction block (otherwise, Spock can't understand the special syntax used for interaction verification).
- Spies in Spock offer the possibility of partial mocking. A spy can mock some methods of an object while leaving the rest of the methods in the original implementation.
- Spies are an advanced feature that should be used mostly in legacy code that can't be refactored. Spy usage inside Spock tests should be minimal.
- The presence of Spock spies usually indicates badly designed production code. Refactoring the code should make spies redundant.

appendix A
Installing Spock

This appendix explains how to install and begin using Spock in your Java project (even when you already have existing JUnit tests). It also covers installation of Groovy support in popular development environments and how to best use the source code for the book.

I assume you already have a Java project (that you want to write Spock tests for) and so have the following available:

- Java development Kit (www.oracle.com/technetwork/java/javase/downloads /index.html)
- Maven build system (http://maven.apache.org/) *or* Gradle build system (https://gradle.org/)
- Your favorite Integrated Development Environment (for example, Eclipse)

A.1 Optional Groovy installation

First, let's get a big misunderstanding out of the way. It's perfectly possible to use Spock in your Java project without installing Groovy itself. It's nice to have the Groovy tools available for quick tests and small scripts, but they're by no means necessary.

To install Groovy, go to http://groovy-lang.org/download.html and follow the instructions for your operating system. The easiest way is to download the zip file, extract it in a directory of your choice, and set your PATH variable accordingly.

After installing Groovy, you should have the following commands available:

- groovyc—Groovy compiler. Apart from simple tests, you typically don't use this directly.
- groovy—Groovy runner. You can use this to run individual Groovy scripts.
- groovysh—Groovy shell. This is an interactive way to run Groovy statements.
- groovyconsole—Graphical Groovy console. This is the recommended way to start your Groovy journey because it provides a friendly GUI application you can use to evaluate Groovy statements.

A.2   *Choosing a Spock version*

At the time of this writing, Spock has the following versions:

- Spock 1.0-groovy2.4
- Spock 1.0-groovy2.3
- Spock 1.0-groovy2.0

All versions are available in Maven Central (http://search.maven.org/) and are production-ready. The Groovy versions have little effect on Java projects. If you want to add Spock to a Groovy project, choose the matching Groovy version. In the sample code of this book, I chose the Spock version for Groovy 2.4 because it's the latest at the time of writing.

A.3   *Master example for Maven, Ant, and Gradle*

Your first stop regarding Spock installation should be the Spock-example GitHub repository (https://github.com/spockframework/spock-example). This full project with Spock tests contains build files for Gradle, Maven, and Ant (depending on your build system, you may not need all of them). All my instructions for the next sections are extracted from this project.

All code listings in this appendix are segments of the pom.xml file located in that repository. I summarize the instructions for Maven and Gradle.[1] I assume that you already have a Java project up and running and you want to add Spock tests.

A.3.1   *Spock with Maven*

If you use Maven, add the code in the following listing to your pom.xml file in the Build > Plugins section.

Listing A.1   Adding Groovy support in Maven

```
<plugin>
        <groupId>org.codehaus.gmavenplus</groupId>
        <artifactId>gmavenplus-plugin</artifactId>
    <version>1.4</version>
    <executions>
    <execution>
      <goals>
                <goal>compile</goal>
                <goal>testCompile</goal>
      </goals>
    </execution>
    </executions>
</plugin>
<plugin>
        <artifactId>maven-surefire-plugin</artifactId>
```

---

[1] Ant isn't a build system. It's a relic of the past and should die in flames. If you're starting a new Java project with Ant, please bang your head against the wall now.

```
      <version>2.6</version>
      <configuration>
        <useFile>false</useFile>
        <includes>
                <include>**/*Spec.java</include>
                <include>**/*Test.java</include>
        </includes>
      </configuration>
</plugin>
```

This sets up Groovy support in Maven and Surefire. In pom.xml, in the `dependency` section, add the code shown in the next listing.

Listing A.2   Adding Spock dependencies in Maven

```
<dependency>
    <groupId>org.spockframework</groupId>
    <artifactId>spock-core</artifactId>
    <version>1.0-groovy-2.4</version>
    <scope>test</scope>
</dependency>
<dependency> <!-- enables mocking of classes
                      (in addition to interfaces) -->
    <groupId>cglib</groupId>
    <artifactId>cglib-nodep</artifactId>
    <version>3.1</version>
    <scope>test</scope>
</dependency>
<dependency> <!-- enables mocking of classes without default
            constructor (together with CGLIB) -->
    <groupId>org.objenesis</groupId>
    <artifactId>objenesis</artifactId>
    <version>2.1</version>
    <scope>test</scope>
</dependency>
```

That's it. Now you can build Spock tests via Maven. Running `mvn test` from the same directory where the pom file exists should correctly detect and run your Spock tests (assuming they all have names that end in *Spec, as I show in the book).

A.3.2   *Spock with Gradle*

If you use Gradle in your Java project, things are even simpler. Groovy compilation is already taken care of, and you only need the Spock dependencies in your build.gradle file, as shown in the next listing.

Listing A.3   Gradle settings for Spock

```
dependencies {

    [....other dependencies here...]
// mandatory dependencies for using Spock
```

```
  compile "org.codehaus.groovy:groovy-all:2.4.1"
  testCompile "org.spockframework:spock-core:1.0-groovy-2.4"

// optional dependencies for using Spock
  testRuntime "cglib:cglib-nodep:3.1"            // allows mocking of classes
  (in addition to interfaces)
  testRuntime "org.objenesis:objenesis:2.1"     // allows mocking of classes
          without default constructor (together with CGLIB)
}
```

In addition, make sure that you already use Maven Central, as the following listing shows.

Listing A.4   Gradle settings for Spock repository

```
repositories {
  // Spock releases are available from Maven Central
  mavenCentral()
}
```

Now you're ready to use Spock from the command line. Running `gradle test` from the same directory that holds the build.gradle file will run all Spock tests.

A.3.3   *Spock in an enterprise environment*

If you want to use Spock inside a company that has a binary repository like Nexus (www.sonatype.org/nexus/) or Artifactory (www.jfrog.com/open-source/), you should consult their documentation on how to use them as a proxy for Maven Central. Talk with the administrator of these repositories for guidance on company policies regarding external library usage.

Let's see how IDEs handle Spock support.

A.4   *Spock tests in your IDE*

Because Spock tests are in Groovy, the support of Spock in your IDE will be as good as the existing support for Groovy. As explained previously, you don't need to install Groovy support in your IDE in order to run Spock tests. It's a nice-to-have feature because of its syntax highlighting and autocomplete facilities. The only thing specific to Spock is the test output result that should be set up to use a fixed-width font so that failure messages show up properly. For more information, see http://www.groovy-lang.org/ides.html. I use Eclipse, but Groovy is supported on most major environments.

A.4.1   *Spock in Eclipse*

To gain Groovy support in Eclipse, install either the vanilla Groovy plugin or the full-featured Groovy/Grails plugin. Both can be found in the Eclipse marketplace, as shown in figure A.1. The Eclipse marketplace is accessible from the Help > Marketplace menu.

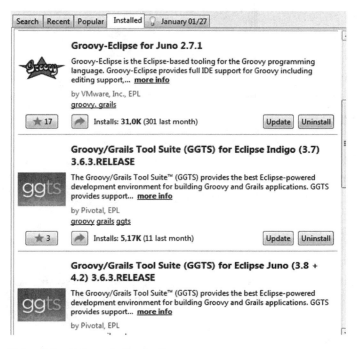

Figure A.1   Eclipse plugins for Groovy

Once you do that, Groovy/Spock files will gain syntax highlighting and autocomplete support, as shown in figure A.2.

You can still use the Maven/Gradle commands to compile and run Spock tests.

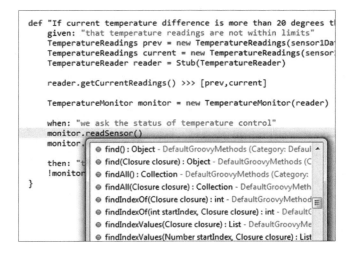

Figure A.2   Groovy support in Eclipse

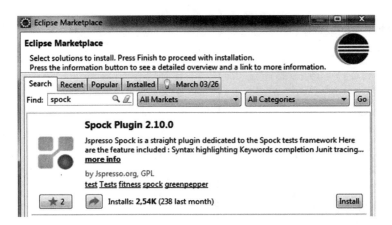

Figure A.3   Jspresso Spock plugin (optional)

There's also a plugin dedicated to Spock, but upon installing it, I haven't noticed any additional functionality (it also depends on the Groovy plugin, so it isn't a true alternative). You can find it in the Eclipse marketplace, as shown in figure A.3.

A.4.2 Spock in the IntelliJ IDE

Groovy support in IntelliJ IDEA is built in, so there's no need to download an external plugin. You need only to enable it, as shown in figure A.4.

When the Groovy plugin is enabled, you gain syntax highlighting and autocomplete in Groovy files, as shown in figure A.5.

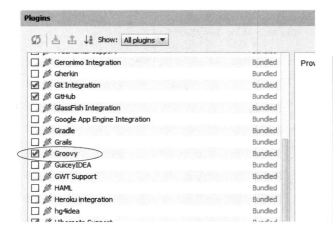

Figure A.4   Enabling Groovy support in IntelliJ

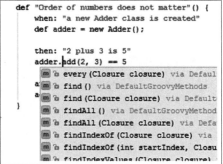

Figure A.5   Groovy support in IntelliJ IDEA

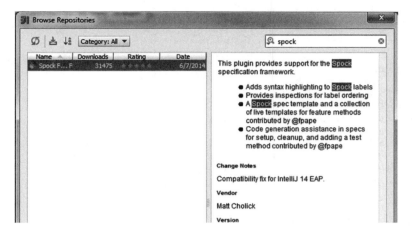

Figure A.6   IntelliJ plugin for Spock

Again, as with Eclipse, you can still use the command-line Maven/Gradle commands to compile and run Spock tests. A dedicated Spock plugin for IntelliJ IDEA adds extra optional goodies, such as syntax highlighting for Spock labels (see figure A.6).

Again, this is something that's nice to have, but is not otherwise essential for running Spock tests.

A.4.3   Spock in NetBeans

I haven't tried NetBeans with Groovy, but it also supports Groovy. See https://netbeans.org/features/groovy/ for more details.

A.5   How to use the source code of this book

All the source code is located at https://github.com/kkapelon/java-testing-with-spock. Each chapter is an independent Maven project. You can check out any chapter by itself and run the command mvn test (or mvn verify) to run all Spock/JUnit tests. You need an active internet connection so that all dependencies are downloaded. You can obtain the code in multiple ways:

- If you're not familiar with Git and/or GitHub, you can download all the code as a zip file from https://github.com/kkapelon/java-testing-with-spock/archive/master.zip.
- If you're familiar with Git, you can also clone the https://github.com/kkapelon/java-testing-with-spock.git repository by using your favorite Git client.
- If you already have a GitHub account and know how GitHub works, you can directly fork the repository or download it locally with the GitHub client.

Feel free to import any chapter into your favorite IDE (as a Maven project) to examine the code more thoroughly. All code listings of the book are shown in the GitHub

- Listing 1.7 A JUnit test where method names are unrelated to business value
- Listing 1.8 A Spock test where methods explain the business requirements

Chapter 2

- Listing 2.1 Groovy class conventions
- Listing 2.1 Groovy class conventions
- Listing 2.2 Groovy field conventions
- Listing 2.3 A complete Groovy script
- Listing 2.4 A Spock test using concise Groovy code
- Listing 2.5 Creating and using a Java class from Groovy
- Listing 2.5 Creating and using a Java class from Groovy
- Listing 2.6 Groovy optional typing in variables
- Listing 2.7 Groovy optional typing in methods

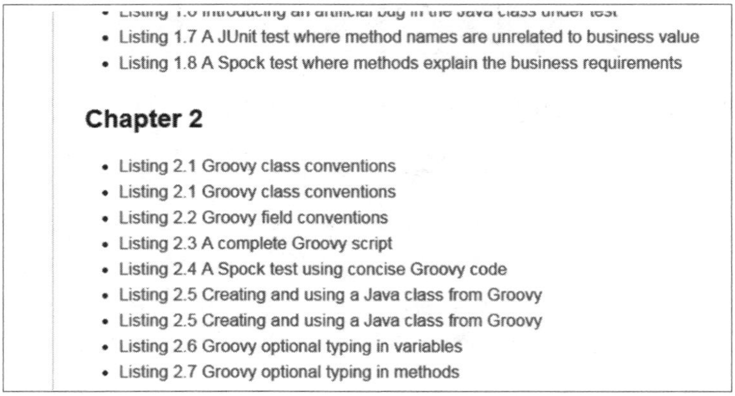

Figure A.7 Code listings with links in the home page of the GitHub repository

repository; figure A.7 shows an example. You can click any of them, and you'll be transferred directly to the respective source file.

I've set up continuous integration on the GitHub page. Seeing the current status of the code at the front page is easy.

A.6 How to use the chapter code in Eclipse

Here I provide step-by-step instructions on how to import a chapter in Eclipse and run a Spock test. This section refers to chapter 1, but all chapters work in the same way.

Check out the source code and place it somewhere on your local filesystem.[2] Then, from Eclipse, choose File > Import and select a Maven project, as shown in figure A.8.

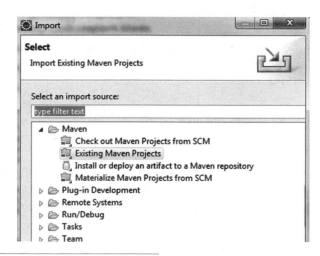

Figure A.8 Importing as a Maven project

[2] Your Eclipse workspace is a good place as it will make things easier.

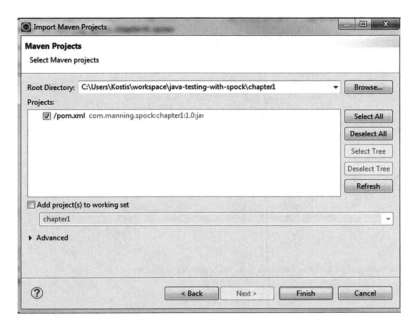

Figure A.9   Locating the pom file

Navigate to the folder that contains the chapter code and click the Finish button in the dialog box that appears, as shown in figure A.9.

Eclipse will attempt to find connectors for the Gmaven-plus plugin and will fail because this plugin is fairly new (see figure A.10). Choose to ignore this (it won't affect your build in any way). When you work with cutting-edge technology like Spock, your IDE can't keep up with you!

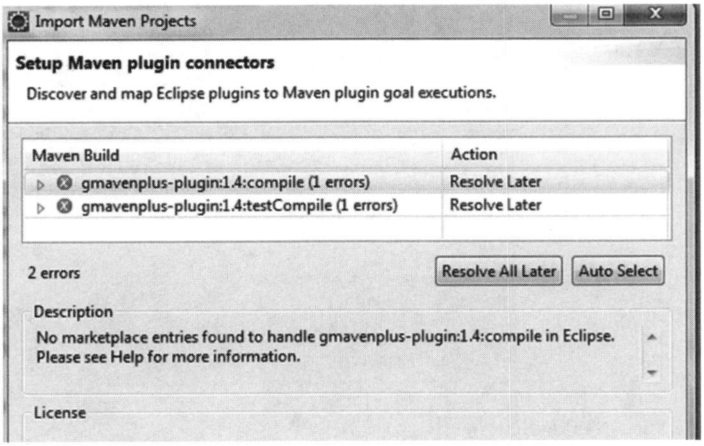

Figure A.10   Ignoring Eclipse warnings

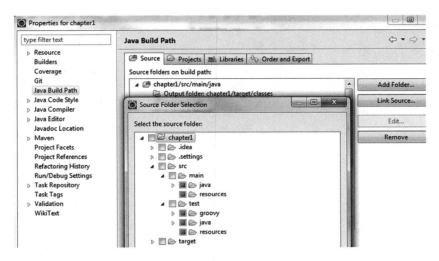

Figure A.11   Ensuring that Eclipse handles src/test/groovy correctly

Next, make sure that the src/test/groovy directory is handled as a source directory, as shown in figure A.11:

- Right-click the project in Eclipse and select Properties (the last item on the menu). In the dialog box that appears, click Java Build Path.
- Click the Add Folder button.
- If the test/groovy directory isn't already included, check it yourself.

To build the project, you can run `mvn test` from the command line. Alternatively, in Eclipse, you can choose "Maven test" from the project right-click menu, as shown in figure A.12.

Then you can individually run any Spock test exactly as you would run a JUnit test (by right-clicking it), as shown in figure A.13.

Figure A.12   Running the Maven build

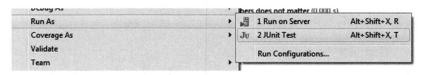

Figure A.13   Running a Spock test in Eclipse

The results of the test appear in the JUnit console, as shown in figure A.14.

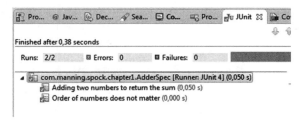

A.7 How to use the chapter code in IntelliJ IDEA

As with Eclipse, this section provides instructions on how to use chapter 1 in IntelliJ IDEA. Repeat the process for each chapter. In the opening screen of IntelliJ IDEA, choose to import a new project and navigate to the source code in your filesystem, as shown in figure A.15.

You're presented with a series of wizard screens. Accept the defaults. Make sure the project is imported as a Maven project, as shown in figure A.16.

Figure A.14   Results of a Spock test

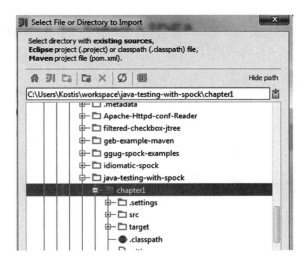

Figure A.15   Importing a project in IntelliJ IDEA

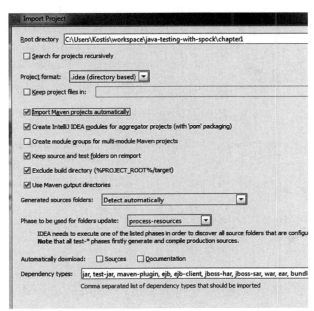

Figure A.16   Importing as a Maven project

After the import is finished, find the Maven Goals window (located at the top right) and double-click the "test" goal as shown in figure A.17. This builds the whole project. As an alternative, you can run the command `mvn test` from the same folder that contains the pom.xml file of the chapter.

As with Eclipse, you need to mark the src/test/groovy folder as a source folder. Right-click the folder and choose Mark Directory As > Test Sources Root, as shown in figure A.18.

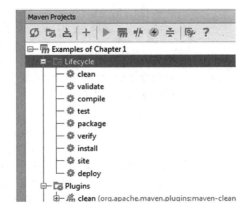

Figure A.17   Maven goals inside IntelliJ IDEA

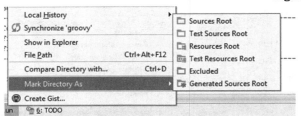

Figure A.18   Instructing IntelliJ to handle Spock folders

Finally, you can run any Spock test as you run JUnit (via the right-click menu), as shown in figure A.19.

The results appear in the JUnit console. See figure A.20.

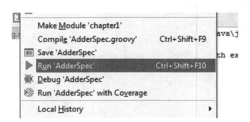

Figure A.19   Running a Spock test inside IntelliJ

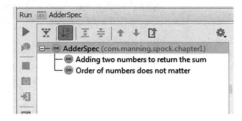

Figure A.20   Results of a Spock test

A.8   Other resources

Many other resources are available:

- Spock web page: http://spockframework.org/
- Spock mailing list: https://groups.google.com/forum/#!forum/spockframework
- Spock documentation:http://docs.spockframework.org
- Spock at Stack Overflow: http://stackoverflow.com/questions/tagged/spock
- Spock at GitHub: https://github.com/spockframework

appendix B
External Spock extensions and related tools

The official Spock source code found at https://github.com/spockframework/spock contains the core framework, along with extensions for Spring, Guice, Tapestry, and Unitils. Because of the extensible nature of Spock, several other extensions are available outside this repository created by the community.

This appendix presents several Spock extensions created by external contributors that may help your unit tests. Additionally, it covers several other unit-testing projects that play well with Spock or even have explicit support for it.

It's your responsibility to examine each of these projects and evaluate them for your needs. With the recent release of version 1.0 of Spock, more people will be writing extensions. The number of available Spock extensions will have grown by the time you're reading this book.

B.1 Detailed Spock reporting

As already mentioned, the Spock test runner is compatible with the JUnit runner, so all JUnit reporting tools will work normally for Spock tests as well.

To fully exploit Spock capabilities, you can also use Spock Reports (https://github.com/renatoathaydes/spock-reports). This project can create test reports with all the finer details of Spock tests. It renders the text of block descriptions and supports the documentation annotations (such as @Title), as shown in figure B.1.

The project can be run either with Maven or Gradle, so regardless of your build system, you can easily create these reports with minimal effort. At the time of writing, the binaries are not yet released to Maven central, so you need to add an external repository to your pom file.

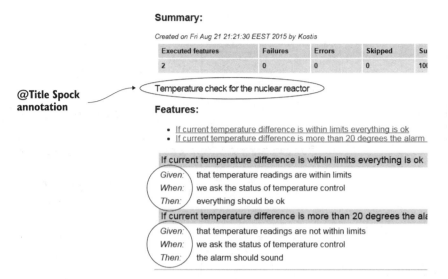

Summary:

Created on Fri Aug 21 21:21:30 EEST 2015 by Kostis

Executed features	Failures	Errors	Skipped	Su
2	0	0	0	100

@Title Spock
annotation

Temperature check for the nuclear reactor

Features:

- If current temperature difference is within limits everything is ok
- If current temperature difference is more than 20 degrees the alarm

If current temperature difference is within limits everything is ok

Given: that temperature readings are within limits
When: we ask the status of temperature control
Then: everything should be ok

If current temperature difference is more than 20 degrees the ala

Given: that temperature readings are not within limits
When: we ask the status of temperature control
Then: the alarm should sound

Figure B.1   Spock reports that show given-when-then labels and Spock annotations

B.2   *Gradle-style Spock reports*

Another project dedicated to Spock reporting is Damage Control, found at https://
github.com/damage-control/report. Again, it focuses on creating detailed Spock
reports. The output is similar to the Gradle style for test reports, shown in figure B.2.

You can use damage-control reports either with Maven or Gradle. The library is
already in Maven Central, so using it in your own projects is easy.

Damage Control Report

14	6	3	0.34999996s	57%
features	failures	skipped	duration	successful

Specifications

Specification	Features	Failures	Skipped	Duration	Result
AllGreenFeaturesTest	2	0	0	0.507s	passed
errors.CleanupErrorTest	2	2	0	0.024s	failed
errors.SetupFailureTest	2	2	0	0.023s	failed
failed.MultipleFeaturesTest	2	1	0	0.135s	failed
junit.SampleJUnitTest	2	1	0	0.02s	failed
skipped.ClassLevelIgnoreTest	1	0	1	0.005s	skipped
skipped.MethodLevelIgnoreTest	1	0	1	0.009s	skipped
skipped.OnlyOneFeatureIgnoredTest	2	0	1	0.017s	passed

Generated by Damage Control Report 1.1.0 at 2013-09-10 19:04:45 -0300.

Figure B.2   Damage-control example report

B.3 Spock Genesis

Spock Genesis (https://github.com/Bijnagte/spock-genesis) is a meta data-generator library for parameterized Spock tests. I briefly mentioned it at the end of chapter 5. At its core, Spock Genesis can be used as a data source for Spock tests. The following listing is an example directly from Spock Genesis' own samples.

Listing B.1 Creating test data with Spock Genesis

```
static class Person {                          ◄─── A Person class that
    int id                                          will be tested
    String name
    String title
    Date birthDate
    char gender
}

def 'complex pogo'() {
    expect:
        person instanceof Person
        person.gender in ['M', 'F', 'T', 'U'].collect { it as char }
        person.id > 199
        person.id < 10001
        person.birthDate >= Date.parse('MM/dd/yyyy', '01/01/1940')
        person.birthDate <= new Date()
    where:
        person << Gen.type(Person,
            id: Gen.integer(200..10000),
            name: Gen.string(~/[A-Z][a-z]+( [A-Z][a-z]+)?/),
            birthDate: Gen.date(Date.parse('MM/dd/yyyy',
                '01/01/1940'), new Date()),
            title: Gen.these('', null).then(Gen.any('Dr.', 'Mr.',
                'Ms.', 'Mrs.')),
            gender: Gen.character('MFTU')
        ).take(3)
}
```

Mass creation of Person objects with all parameters of each domain

Parameters for created objects

Spock Genesis can work as an abstraction over existing data generators, as it can also do the following:

- Compose existing generators into new ones
- Filter existing generators using predicates/closures
- Randomize or order the output for other generators

You'll find Spock Genesis particularly useful if you're creating a scientific application in Java and want to cover a large amount of data variations in your unit tests.

B.4 Spock-Arquillian test runner

As mentioned in chapter 7, Spock only includes support for Spring and Guice in its core distribution, as far as containers are concerned. Spock-Arquillian (https://github.com/arquillian/arquillian-testrunner-spock) is a community extension that allows Spock tests to bootstrap the Arquillian (http://arquillian.org/) test container. Arquillian is commonly used for integration testing of Java EE applications. The next listing is an example from the Spock-Arquillian website.

Listing B.2   Using Spock and Arquillian together

```
@Deployment
def static JavaArchive "create deployment"() {                          ◀── Annotations
    return ShrinkWrap.create(JavaArchive.class)                         ◀── from Arquillian
            .addClasses(AccountService.class, Account.class,
            SecureAccountService.class)
            .addAsManifestResource(EmptyAsset.INSTANCE, "beans.xml");
}

@Inject
AccountService service                                    ◀── Standard CDI injection

def "transferring between accounts should result in account withdrawal and
            deposit"() {
    when:                        ◀ Spock parameterized test
    service.transfer(from, to, amount)

    then:
    from.balance == fromBalance
    to.balance == toBalance

    where:
    from <<         [new Account(100),   new Account(10)]
    to <<           [new Account(50),    new Account(90)]
    amount <<       [50,                 10]
    fromBalance <<  [50,                 0]
    toBalance <<    [100,                100]
}
```

Notice that the class containing the Arquillian code must be annotated with the `@Run-With(ArquillianSputnik)` annotation in order to successfully run the code shown in the listing.

B.5   *Using PowerMock with Spock*

Chapter 6 briefly discusses PowerMock (https://github.com/jayway/powermock) as a way to mock static/private methods, a capability that Spock doesn't have on its own.

I consider the use of PowerMock an antipattern. You should use it only as a last resort in your unit tests and only when it's impossible to refactor the Java code under tests. If you end up using PowerMock with Spock, you should look at the Spock-PowerMock project (https://github.com/kriegaex/Spock_PowerMock) that combines the two. The following listing shows an example taken from the project web page.

Listing B.3   Using Spock and PowerMock together

```
@PrepareForTest([Person.class])                          ◀── PowerMock annotation
class PersonTest extends Specification {      ◀ PowerMock JUnit rule
    @Rule PowerMockRule rule = new PowerMockRule();
```

```
private static Person person = new Person("Kriegisch", "Alexander", new
        Date(1971 - 1900, 5 - 1, 8))                        ◄

def "Person properties"() {
    expect:
    person.getLastName() == "Kriegisch"
    person.getFirstName() == "Alexander"
    person.getDateOfBirth().getYear() == 71
}
}
```

**Class under test that's
both private and static**

**Spock assertions
on the private/stat**

Spock is backward-compatible with JUnit rules and therefore gets its PowerMock support indirectly by the PowerMock JUnit rule (which allows PowerMock usage inside the code of a unit test).

B.6   *Spock InjectMocks extension*

In a complex unit test in which the class under test is using many other mocks (imagine an EJB class that uses other EJBs), it might be tedious to inject all mocks one by one using the respective setters.

The Spock Collaborators extension (https://github.com/marcingrzejszczak/spock-subjects-collaborators-extension) can be used to automatically inject these dependencies (in a similar manner to Spring automatic injection[1]) by type. Both constructor and setter injection are supported.

Using the extension is as simple as annotating the class under test with @Subject (which is different from the annotation already supported by Spock), and the mocks to be injected with the @Collaborator annotation. After the Spock test runs, you'll know that all classes marked with the latter annotation will be injected into the class marked with the former. You should have exactly one class marked with @Subject, and one or more classes marked with @Collaborator in each Spock specification.

Here's the example shown on its web page.

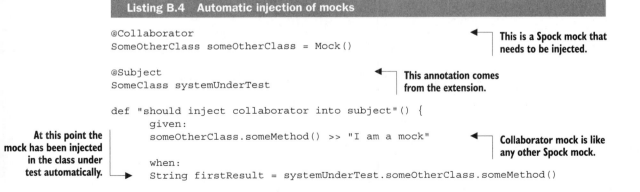

Listing B.4   Automatic injection of mocks

```
@Collaborator                                        ◄─┐  This is a Spock mock that
SomeOtherClass someOtherClass = Mock()                 │  needs to be injected.

@Subject                              ◄─┐  This annotation comes
SomeClass systemUnderTest               │  from the extension.

def "should inject collaborator into subject"() {
    given:
    someOtherClass.someMethod() >> "I am a mock"      ◄─┐  Collaborator mock is like
                                                        │  any other Spock mock.
    when:
    String firstResult = systemUnderTest.someOtherClass.someMethod()
```

**At this point the
mock has been injected
in the class under
test automatically.**

---

[1]   The Spock extension is inspired by the Mockito @InjectMocks annotation.

```
    then:
        firstResult == "I am a mock"
        systemUnderTest.someOtherClass == someOtherClass
}
```

If you want to use this extension, make sure that the @Subject annotation is imported with com.blogspot.toomuchcoding.spock.subjcollabs.Subject instead of the standard spock.lang.Subject that's used by core Spock for documentation purposes, as described in chapter 4.

The code can be found in Maven central and is therefore easy to use in your own Java project.

B.7　*Spock Retry extension*

In an ideal world, all your integration/functional tests would run in a deterministic way. In reality, this isn't always possible. Slow external systems, database bottlenecks, network load, and other undesirable factors can sometimes affect the result of a test (especially if you've marked it with the @Timeout annotation) in a semirandom manner.

I've worked on projects where a failed build doesn't mean that the code is broken, but that the network is congested (and rebuilding the code will make all tests pass). For those cases, you can save yourself some time by using the Spock Retry extension (https://github.com/anotherchrisberry/spock-retry). It offers you a special annotation that gives a second chance to your Spock test if it fails, as shown in the next listing.

Listing B.5　Fail a test only if it fails twice

```
class ExampleSpec extends Specification {

    @RetryOnFailure                                    ◄─┐ Will try to run twice
    def "a brittle Spock test"() {                       │ before failing
        [...implementation of Spock test here...]
    }
}
```

The annotation can also be used on the class level so that all feature methods gain this capability. By default, the test will be retried twice. You can change this value in the annotation itself, as the following listing shows.

Listing B.6　Fail all tests after three tries

```
@RetryOnFailure(times=3)                               ◄─┐ Gives three chances
class ExampleSpec extends Specification {                 │ to a failed test

    def "a brittle Spock test"() {
        [...implementation of Spock test here...]
    }
    def "another brittle Spock test"() {
        [...implementation of Spock test here...]
    }
}
```

At the time of writing, this Spock extension isn't yet in Maven Central, so you must either build it yourself or find another repository that contains it.

B.8 Spock dbUnit extension

Chapter 7 shows how to use the Groovy SQL package to preload your database with test data needed for the Spock test. If you like this approach, you can take it a step further with the Spock dbUnit extension (https://github.com/janbols/spock-dbunit).

The extension is based on the well-known DbUnit library (http://dbunit.source forge.net/), initially developed for JUnit, that can initialize a database to a known state, reading data from XML files. The Spock dbUnit extension allows you to use Groovy code instead of XML files, as shown in the following listing.

Listing B.7 Fail all tests after three tries

```
class MyDbUnitTest extends Specification{          ◄─── This data source is
                                                        used for data writing.
DataSource dataSource

    @DbUnit                                        ◄─── This method runs
    def content = {                                     before the Spock test.
        User(id: 1, name: 'John', createdOn: '[NOW]')
    }
```

Insert data on the USER table. ──► (points to `def content`)

Data on the DB is saved via a data source, which can be created by hand, or—even better—injected by Spring test, as shown in the next listing.

Listing B.8 Using dbUnit Spock with Spring

```
@ContextConfiguration(locations='classpath:/spring/context.xml')   ◄─
class DatasourceFromSpringTest extends Specification{

    @Autowired
    DataSource dataSource

    @DbUnit                                    ◄─── This method will run
    def content = {                                 before the test.
        User(id: 1, name: 'John')
    }

    def setup(){
        new Sql(dataSource).execute("CREATE TABLE User(id
            INT PRIMARY KEY, name VARCHAR(255))")
    }

    def cleanup() {
        new Sql(dataSource).execute("drop table User")
    }

    def "test"() {
        when:
        def result = new Sql(dataSource).firstRow("select * from User
                    where name = 'John'")
```

Injected by Spring ──► (points to `DataSource dataSource`)

Inserts data into the User table ──► (points to `def content`)

A Spring context that contains a data source ◄─ (points to @ContextConfiguration)

Creates the initial schema ◄─── (points to setup)

DB is preloaded with data at this point. ◄─── (points to `def "test"`)

```
        then:
        result.id == 1
    }
}
```

At the time of writing, this Spock extension is only in JCenter (https://bintray.com/bintray/jcenter), not Maven Central, so you must either build it yourself or configure JCenter in your pom.xml.

B.9   Spock Android extension

Android Java is not 100% compatible with desktop Java. Vanilla Spock can't run unmodified on Android because the mocking libraries it uses don't work on Android.

The Spock Android extension (https://github.com/pieces029/android-spock) not only fixes this problem but also allows you to inject Android objects (such as activities) in your Spock tests. Here's an example taken from the extension website.

Listing B.9   Using Spock with Android

```
class MainActivitySpec extends Specification {

    @UseActivity(MainActivity)              ◄─── Injects an Android screen
    def activity                                 that contains a button

    def "test activity setup"() {
        expect:
        activity != null
        activity instanceof MainActivity
    }

    def "test layout"() {
        given:
        def button = activity.findViewById(R.id.main_button) as Button
                                                    ◄── Locates the button on the screen
        when:
        def buttonText = button.getText()

        then:                                       Verifies the text
        buttonText == "Test"                    ◄── of the button
    }
}
```

The code can be found in Maven Central and is easy to use in your own Java project.

B.10   Spock Gherkin extension

If you're already familiar with BDD,[2] you should have noticed by now that Spock isn't a full BDD tool, as it caters mostly to developers. To allow business analysts and testers to

---

[2] Consult *BDD in Action* by John Ferguson Smart (Manning, 2014) for more information (www.manning.com/books/bdd-in-action).

create Spock tests, it's easier to use the Gherkin[3] language (https://github.com/cucumber/cucumber/wiki/Gherkin) as an intermediate format for describing what needs to be tested.

The Spock Pease extension (http://pease.github.io/) automatically converts Gherkin descriptions to Spock tests, making the cooperation between business analysts and developers much easier. Here's an example of Gherkin:

```
Feature: Addition
  Scenario: Add two numbers
    Given I have entered 50 into the calculator
    And I have entered 70 into the calculator
    When I press add
    Then the result should be 120 on the screen
```

This description can be converted automatically to the Spock test shown in the following listing.

Listing B.10   Generated Spock test from Gherkin

```
class Addition extends spock.lang.Specification {
    void "add two numbers"() {
    def calc = new Calculator()

    given: "I have entered 50 into the calculator"
    calc.push("50" as double)

    and: "I have entered 70 into the calculator"
    calc.push("70" as double)

    when: "I press add"
    calc.add()

    then: "the result should be 120 on the screen"
    calc.result == "120" as double
  }
}
```

Unfortunately, the project has been dormant since 2011, so it might need updating for the Spock 1.0 release.

B.11   *Spock support in Serenity*

Serenity (https://github.com/serenity-bdd) is a BDD tool that, among other things, provides a dashboard with test results. Unlike other reporting tools that focus on unit tests, Serenity focuses on features, making the dashboard readable even to nontechnical people (see figure B.3).

---

[3]   Used by cucumber (https://github.com/cucumber/cucumber-jvm).

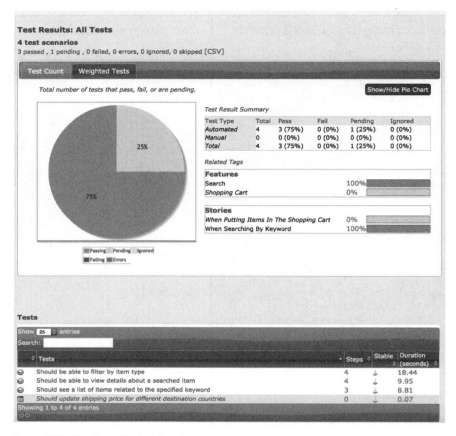

Figure B.3   The Serenity dashboard

The combination of Spock tests and Serenity is a perfect match, as Spock describes its tests in full English text and complements Serenity well.

Originally, Serenity supported JUnit, but Spock support was added as well. For more information on Serenity, you should read *BDD in Action* by John Ferguson Smart (Manning, 2014).

B.12   *Spock support in Allure*

Allure (http://allure.qatools.ru/) is another test dashboard for a different programming language. It's created by the testing team of Yandex.[4] Allure isn't constrained to Java, but instead supports several test frameworks for PHP, C#, JavaScript, Python, Ruby, and so on. Figure B.4 shows the Allure dashboard.

---

[4] Yandex is the largest search engine in Russia (www.yandex.com).

Figure B.4   Allure dashboard

Allure now contains support for Spock (https://github.com/allure-framework/allure-spock-adaptor), so you can think of it as an additional reporting tool for your Spock tests.

index

RELATED MANNING TITLES

Gradle in Action
by Benjamin Muschko

    ISBN: 9781617291302
    480 pages, $44.99
    February 2014

Java 8 in Action
*Lambdas, streams, and functional-style
programming*
by Raoul-Gabriel Urma, Mario Fusco,
   and Alan Mycroft

    ISBN: 9781617291999
    424 pages, $49.99
    August 2014

The Art of Unit Testing, Second Edition
with examples in C#
by Roy Osherove

    ISBN: 9781617290893
    296 pages, $44.99
    November 2013

Groovy in Action, Second Edition

by Dierk König, Paul King, Guillaume
   Laforge, Hamlet D'Arcy, Cédric
   Champeau, Erik Pragt, and Jon Skeet

    ISBN: 9781935182443
    912 pages, $59.99
    June 2015

For ordering information go to www.manning.com